IMAGES
of America

KINGSVILLE

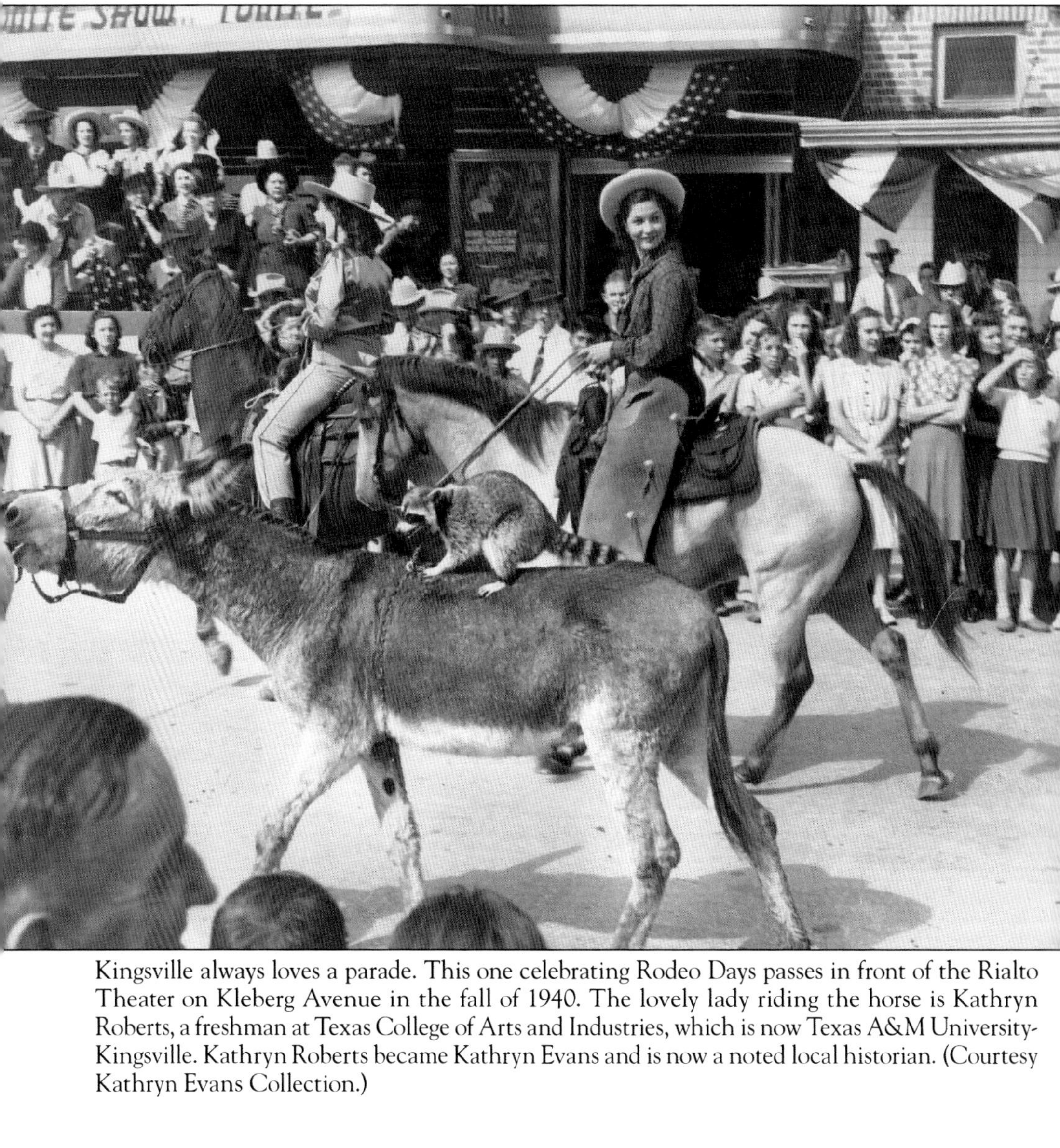

Kingsville always loves a parade. This one celebrating Rodeo Days passes in front of the Rialto Theater on Kleberg Avenue in the fall of 1940. The lovely lady riding the horse is Kathryn Roberts, a freshman at Texas College of Arts and Industries, which is now Texas A&M University-Kingsville. Kathryn Roberts became Kathryn Evans and is now a noted local historian. (Courtesy Kathryn Evans Collection.)

On the Cover: Looking east on Kleberg Avenue about 1915 shows the Kleberg Bank on the left and the John B. Ragland Mercantile Company building on the right. Horse-drawn buggies and wagons mingle with a few early automobiles. Local folklore says there was a secret tunnel constructed underneath the Kleberg Bank that led to the basement of the Flato Building. (Courtesy South Texas Archives, Texas A&M University-Kingsville.)

IMAGES
of America

KINGSVILLE

Pat Allison

ARCADIA
PUBLISHING

ISBN 978-0-7385-8482-9

Published by Arcadia Publishing
Charleston, South Carolina

Printed in the United States of America

Library of Congress Control Number: 2011925432

For all general information, please contact Arcadia Publishing:
Telephone 843-853-2070
Fax 843-853-0044
E-mail sales@arcadiapublishing.com
For customer service and orders:
Toll-Free 1-888-313-2665

Visit us on the Internet at www.arcadiapublishing.com

This book is dedicated to my husband, Charles, who brought me to Kingsville; to my best friend, Mony Lach, who insisted that I compile this book; to my grammatically correct cousin, Caitlin Young, who kept me on the right track; and to Kathryn Evans, keeper of Kingsville's memories.

Contents

Acknowledgments

Even in ancient times, there were those people and groups dedicated to preserving the bits and pieces of history so that our human memory would not forget where we came from and who we are. Kingsville is blessed with many such people. The most helpful folks are the kind keepers of history and Kingsville's coolest people at the South Texas Archives in the James C. Jernigan Library of Texas A&M University-Kingsville. I give special thanks for the patience and helpfulness of Sandra Rexroat, Brian Bingham, Carmen Martinez, Ramiro Hernandez, and Alan Lowe, who have helped me collect these pictures to share. All photographs from the South Texas Archives and Special Collections, James C. Jernigan Library, Texas A&M University-Kingsville are used with permission. The courtesy lines for South Texas Archives and Special Collections, James C. Jernigan Library, Texas A&M University-Kingsville will be abbreviated as South Texas Archives, Texas A&M University-Kingsville.

I offer a special thank-you to Carol Ann Anderson and the Kingsville Convention and Visitors Bureau for the support and encouragement to complete this project.

Thanks go to the King Ranch Archives and Lisa Neely for providing several key pictures. Lisa is the archivist for King Ranch, and her help in checking for accurate historical facts is greatly appreciated.

Thank you, to Marchia Hutchinson for proofreading and making needed suggestions. Thanks also go to the Kleberg County Historical Commission for their encouragement.

I must also thank the many community storytellers who have kept the secrets of Kingsville in their memories. At the top of that list is Kathryn Evans. Kathryn is a local author, retired teacher, curator of the 1904 Kingsville Train Depot Museum, and an inspiration for creating this publication.

Thanks also goes to Mony Lach, my best friend, who published her personal story and inspired me to believe that nothing is truly impossible. We can endure much more than we realize and triumph over everything that seeks to hold us back in life.

Introduction

South Texas was once a pretty wild part of the country. Shades of that wildness persist even today. It was home to many indigenous peoples. When the Spanish arrived on the shores of the New World, they began a struggle to conquer the region. Descendants of the Spanish who intermarried with the indigenous people became the first Texans, the Tejano people. They were Texans before Texas was ever born, before it became part of the United States. They were here before the great ranches, before the railroads, and before Kingsville. Tejanos live today in the communities of South Texas. They are among our leaders, teachers, and neighbors.

Many books have been written about King Ranch and the other giant ranches of the region, the cattle drives, and the struggles between the different groups of people who call South Texas home. There are many stories of heroes and villains. Often, the nature of the hero or villain changes depending on whom a person is talking with: one man's hero is another man's villain—which helps to illustrate the intensity of the struggle of the region to come into modern times. There are tales of cattle rustlers, Texas Rangers, bandits, bootleggers, and horse thieves. There are land-grant settlers, land thieves, immigrants, soldiers, ranchers, farmers, and railroad builders. It is an exciting place to study history. The pictures in this book are only part of the story that Kingsville has to tell.

Kingsville was carved out of the King Ranch in 1904 and was originally called "Townsite on the Santa Gertrudis Ranch." It was the dream of Capt. Richard King to have a railroad through South Texas to conveniently ship cattle to market. He would not live to see the settlement of Kingsville. His widow, Henrietta King, wanted to bring civilization to this region, and it is her personality that is indelibly stamped on the community.

The town of Kingsville started as 853 acres divided into 226 blocks and surrounded by a smooth wire fence that kept King Ranch cattle out of the settlement. The town's reason for existing was a handshake deal between Robert Kleberg and B.F. Yoakum. Kleberg was the manager of King Ranch and the son-in-law of Henrietta King. Yoakum dreamed of building a railroad from New Orleans to Panama. A handshake—a gentleman's agreement—determined that the headquarters for the new railroad would be in Kingsville. There would have been no reason to have a town here without the employment generated by the railroad headquarters.

Uriah Lott was responsible for the construction of the railroad, but the creation of Kingsville fell to a number of other interesting characters. Many of its founders were longtime friends of Robert Kleberg. He actually invited them to come and build a town. Several were already men of means, including Marcus Phillips, Charles Flato Jr., John B. Ragland, and many more—some of whom are introduced in this book's pictures. Other founders were railroaders and newcomers to the region. They were pioneers in the old-fashioned sense of the word.

A moving tent city followed the construction of the railroad. The first buildings were little more than shacks. Soon, the tents would give way to permanent homes. The first church services were held under mesquite trees or in the lumberyard. When the King's Inn Hotel was built, the first Catholic services were conducted in the hotel lobby. Schools and churches were constructed. Kingsville developed quickly and within five years the town looked quite inviting.

There were some hard times. As early as 1906, Houston had its eye on the railroad general offices. For more than a decade, a battle raged over the decision about which community would possess the railroad's general office and its corresponding employment. When the handshake contract went to court, a legal compromise had to be made to satisfy both Kingsville and the railroad.

At the time of these legal battles, the revolution in Mexico spilled over into South Texas. Trains were derailed and ranches attacked. In the decade before World War I, Kingsville struggled to entice settlers to the region, at least in part because of the underlying worry that the newcomers would fall victim to the anarchy. Kingsville was spared any direct attacks during this time, but there was a distinct level of concern among community leaders.

In 1916, a ferocious hurricane nearly washed Kingsville away. Harrowing stories emerged of people whose homes had been blown down and who had to take refuge in the mesquite brush until the hurricane was over. In dry times, fires ravaged the town. Whole blocks of businesses burned to the ground as volunteer firefighters vainly put water on the tinder-dry buildings.

The St. Louis, Brownsville & Mexico Railway (StLB&M) was sold to the St. Louis-San Francisco Railway (SLSF, or Frisco) in 1909, yielding a 75% profit to the initial investors. Frisco went into receivership in 1913 and became part of Gulf Coast Lines. Gulf Coast Lines struggled along and was finally taken over by Missouri Pacific Lines in 1925. Missouri Pacific, often called MoPac, controlled the railroad through the end of the steam age and the advent of diesel-electric locomotives. MoPac ushered out passenger service in 1966. The world changed, but Kingsville managed to survive and adapt with the times.

The Commercial Club and boosters battled in Austin for a normal school, which would start out as a teachers' college, in the Kingsville area. South Texas was a growing area and desperately needed trained teachers to meet the demands of the new population. In 1917, Kingsville won approval to construct a normal school, but World War I put the plans on hold. Finally, in 1923, the Texas government gave the word (and the money) to build the South Texas State Teachers College at Kingsville. This eventually became the Texas College of Arts and Industries, Texas A&I University, and Texas A&M University–Kingsville.

The school was the first in a series of diversifications that kept Kingsville growing. Oil exploration brought Humble Oil Company—which later merged with Standard Oil of New Jersey (Esso) to become Exxon—to town. World War II brought the Naval Air Station Kingsville (NAS Kingsville). Advances in the chemical industry saw the Celanese Corporation come to the region. As the prominence of the railroad faded away, residents found employment within these other industries.

Ranching and railroading gave birth to Kingsville. Texas A&M University–Kingsville, NAS Kingsville, Celanese, the oil and gas industry, and agriculture kept Kingsville alive through the decades of change. Kingsville was battered by fires, hurricanes, political storms, and economic traumas, but the town held on and became a center for the study of natural history and human history and a focal point for birding enthusiasts and hunters. The community has changed and evolved to meet the needs of time. Here, we ponder our history as we take a look at the first 50 years of Kingsville in pictures.

One

Carved from the Brush

The settlement of South Texas—a wild and rugged land commonly called the Wild Horse Desert—was limited by a number of things. Spanish land grants gave huge tracks of property to Spanish settlers, who struggled with the indigenous peoples, the weather, and the lack of water. Wars swept over the region. Texas won independence from Mexico in 1836 and became the 28th state in the union when it joined the United States in 1845. Texas then seceded from the United States in 1861 to become part of the Confederate States of America. What began as a simple smugglers' trail became the infamous Cotton Road. Confederate cotton was smuggled south to the Rio Bravo (Rio Grande River), where it was stamped with Mexican credentials and shipped down the Rio Grande for sale to waiting European ships. The profits helped fuel the Confederacy. The region was populated with large and small ranches but held no real towns. The area between Brownsville and Corpus Christi consisted of a lot of mesquite brush and cacti punctuated by a few large cattle ranches. Drought, bandits, and cattle rustlers often made the region nearly unlivable for ranchers. Long cattle drives proved unworkable for getting the product, beef on the hoof, to market. A railroad was needed.

One particular element was needed to make a railroad workable: water. Robert Justus Kleberg, manager of King Ranch and son-in-law of Henrietta King, wanted to solve this critical problem so the region could be opened to settlement. Using new drilling techniques and going down some 532 feet, Kleberg pierced a huge underground lake and was able to drill a successful artesian well. The bubbling well would signal the beginning of Kingsville, the railroad, and migration to this region for farming.

Four hundred men were brought to the area to prepare the right-of-way and lay down the railroad tracks. Construction began in Robert Driscoll's pasture on July 28, 1903. On Tuesday, June 7, 1904, the St. Louis, Brownsville & Mexico Railway made it to the city limits of Brownsville.

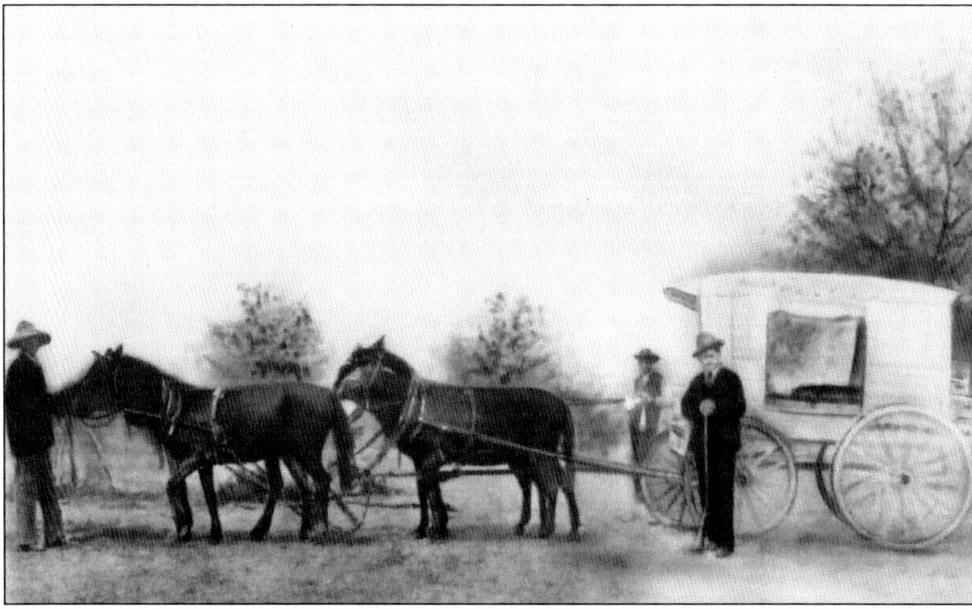

Travel through South Texas was a challenge before 1904. The stagecoach ride from Corpus Christi to Brownsville was a painful, bone-jarring, three-day ordeal. There were relay stations all along the way to change out the horses so that the actual stagecoach and passengers would be in constant motion. (Courtesy South Texas Archives, Texas A&M University-Kingsville.)

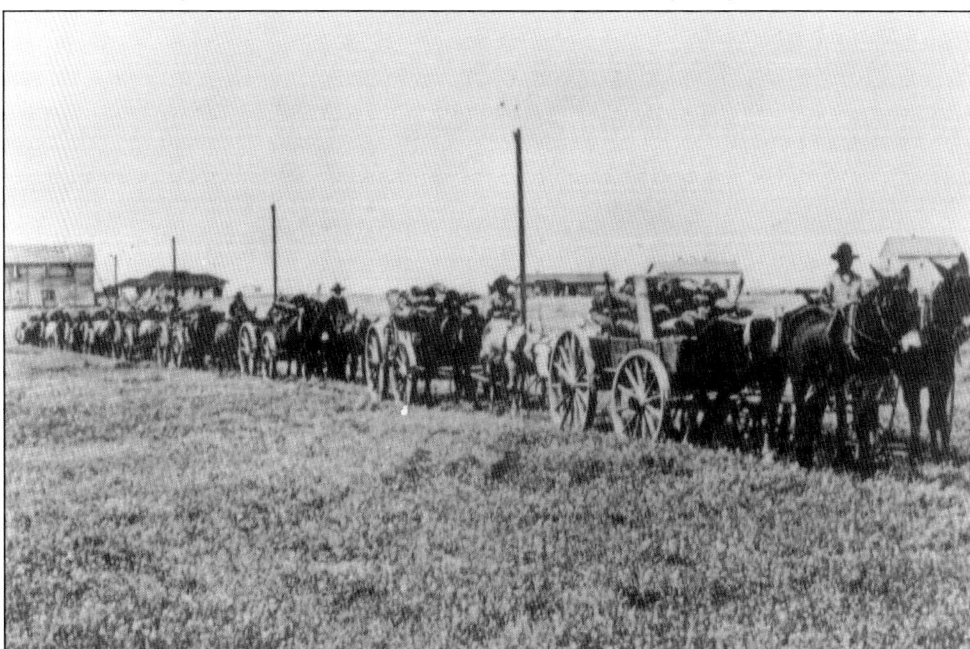

Transportation of goods was even more difficult than moving passengers. Northern Mexico was hungry for goods, tools, and supplies. Traditionally, the Spanish and Mexican governments wanted to tax incoming goods. People in northern Mexico looked to New Orleans for importation of valued products and a bypass of taxation. By the mid-1800s, a mule caravan was a common sight in the Wild Horse Desert. (Courtesy King Ranch, Inc., Kingsville, Texas.)

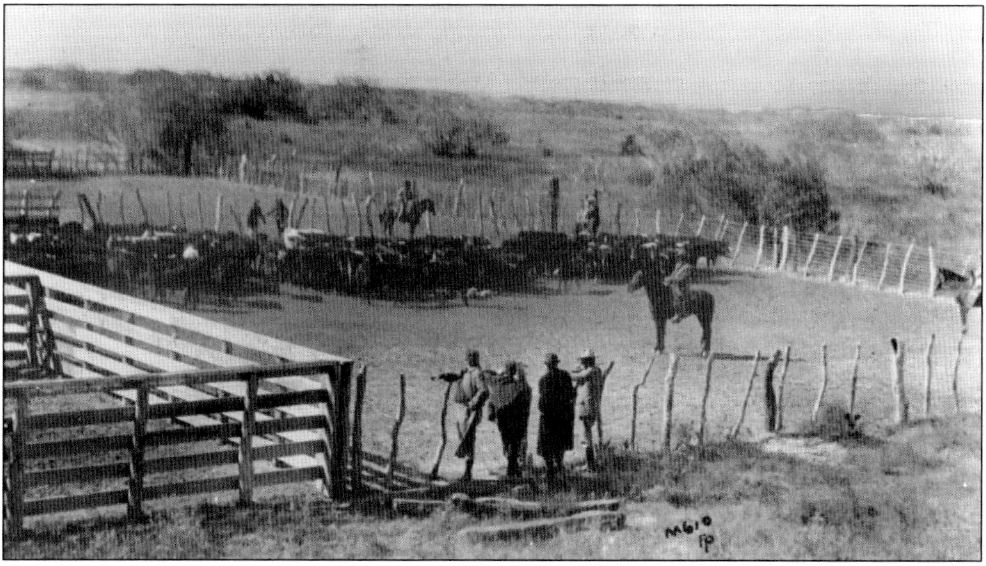

As the ranches grew and cattle became an important export for the region, ranchers needed to find a way to transport livestock to market that was more efficient than long and risky cattle drives. The ticks in South Texas sickened northern cattle. Shotgun quarantines were sometimes used to blockade the cattle drives. A railroad provided part of the solution for the pestilence problem. (Courtesy King Ranch, Inc., Kingsville, Texas.)

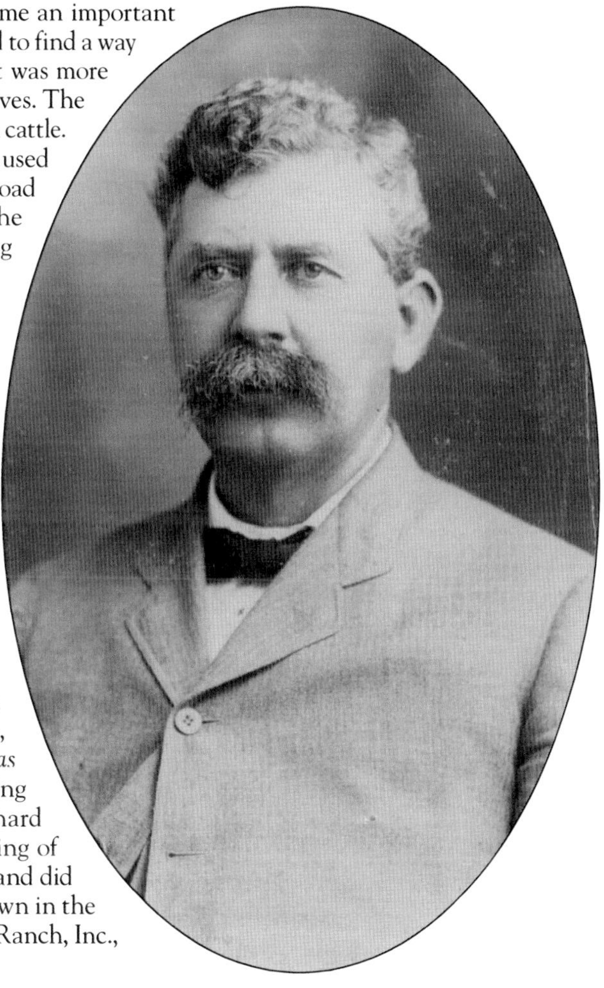

Robert Justus Kleberg was born in 1853 on a farm near Meyersville, Texas, according to the *Kleberg County Texas* history. He became the manager of King Ranch after the death of Capt. Richard King. Kleberg spearheaded the opening of the Kingsville region to the railroad and did everything he could to help build a town in the middle of ranch land. (Courtesy King Ranch, Inc., Kingsville, Texas.)

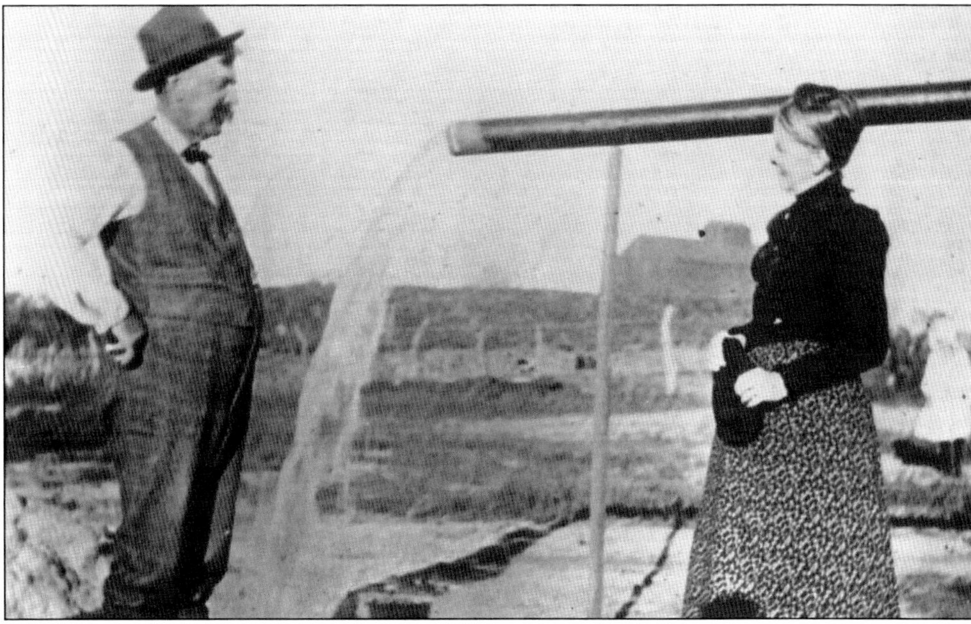

Robert Justus Kleberg and Henrietta King stand next to a gushing artesian well. The key to opening South Texas was water. Kleberg researched drilling methods and tried numerous times to drill wells to bring water to a parched land. Boring down 532 feet, he tapped into a huge underground lake on June 6, 1899. This signaled the opening of South Texas for settlement. (Courtesy King Ranch, Inc., Kingsville, Texas.)

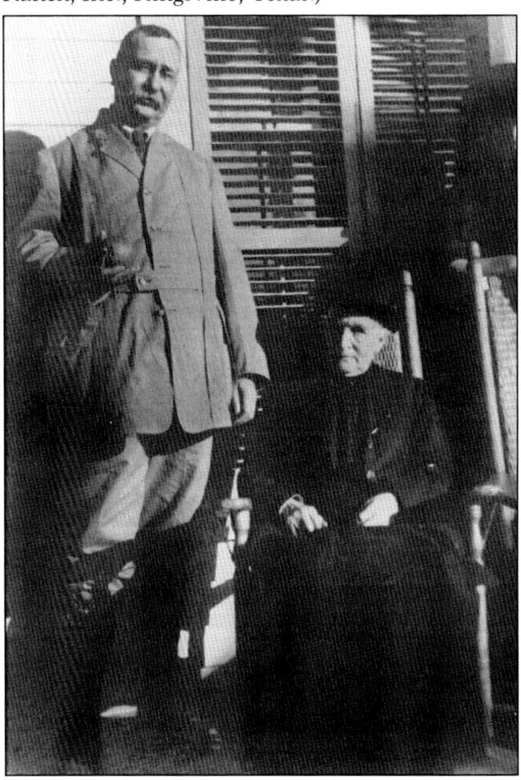

Born in 1859 near Tehuacana, Texas, Benjamin F. Yoakum would become key in the creation of Kingsville, Texas. A gentleman's handshake with Robert Kleberg secured the general office, roundhouse, and railroad shops for Kingsville. In 1902, Yoakum organized the syndicate that would finance the St. Louis, Brownsville & Mexico Railway. Pictured here are Benjamin Yoakum and Henrietta King. (Courtesy King Ranch, Inc., Kingsville, Texas.)

Uriah Lott is credited with building several railways in Texas, including the StLB&M that went through Kingsville. Lott was born in Albany, New York, in 1842, and made and lost his fortune building railroads. He lived out his last years at the Casa Ricardo Hotel, courtesy of Robert Kleberg, and died in 1915. (Courtesy King Ranch, Inc., Kingsville, Texas.)

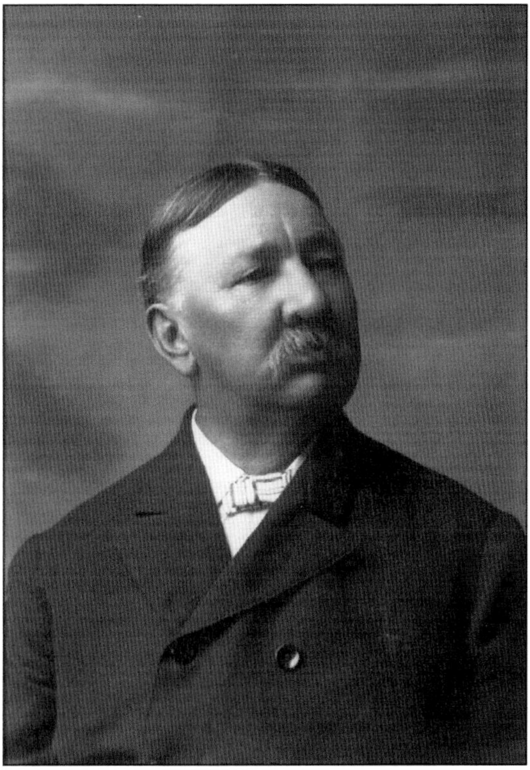

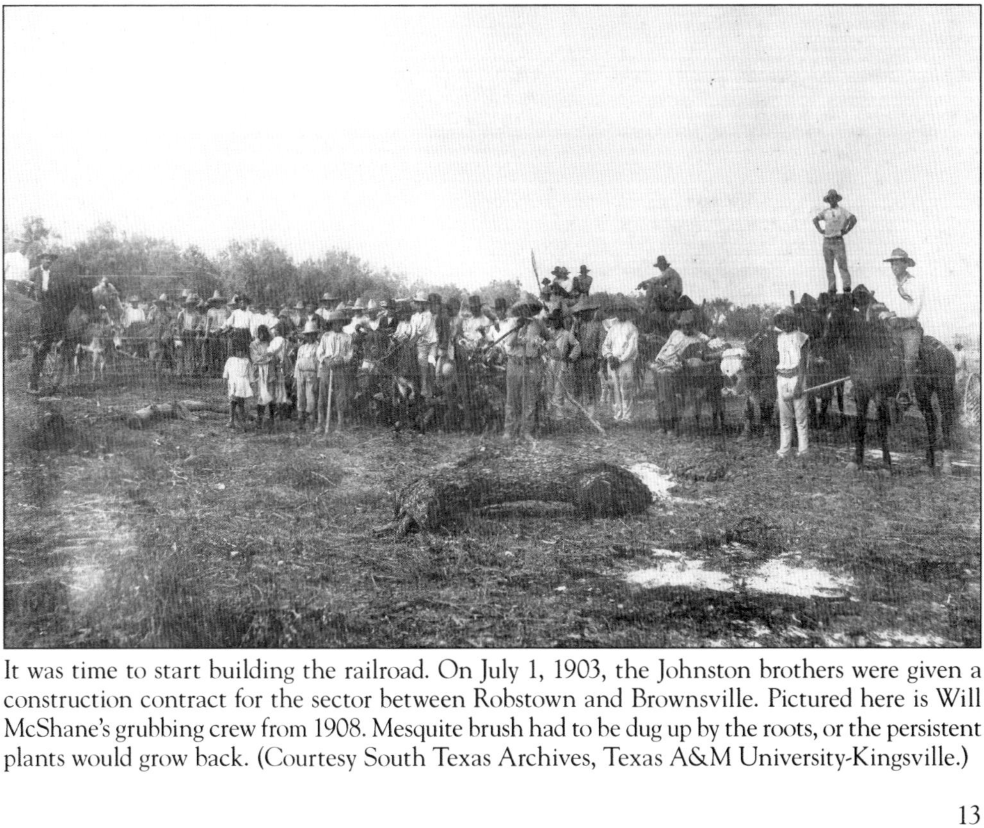

It was time to start building the railroad. On July 1, 1903, the Johnston brothers were given a construction contract for the sector between Robstown and Brownsville. Pictured here is Will McShane's grubbing crew from 1908. Mesquite brush had to be dug up by the roots, or the persistent plants would grow back. (Courtesy South Texas Archives, Texas A&M University-Kingsville.)

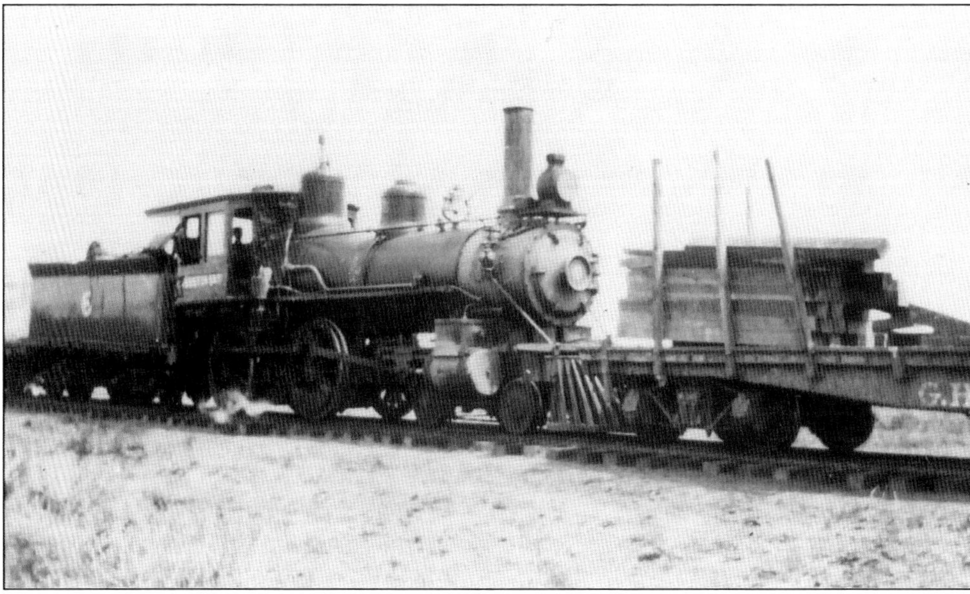

Construction of the new railroad began in Robert Driscoll's pasture at a junction of the Texas Mexican Railway (Tex-Mex) 15.9 miles outside of Corpus Christi. Billing for supplies went to "Mile Post 145, Texas Mexican Railway." All of the supplies to build the railroad came to this point and were pushed out to the construction site by steam locomotive. (Courtesy South Texas Archives, Texas A&M University-Kingsville.)

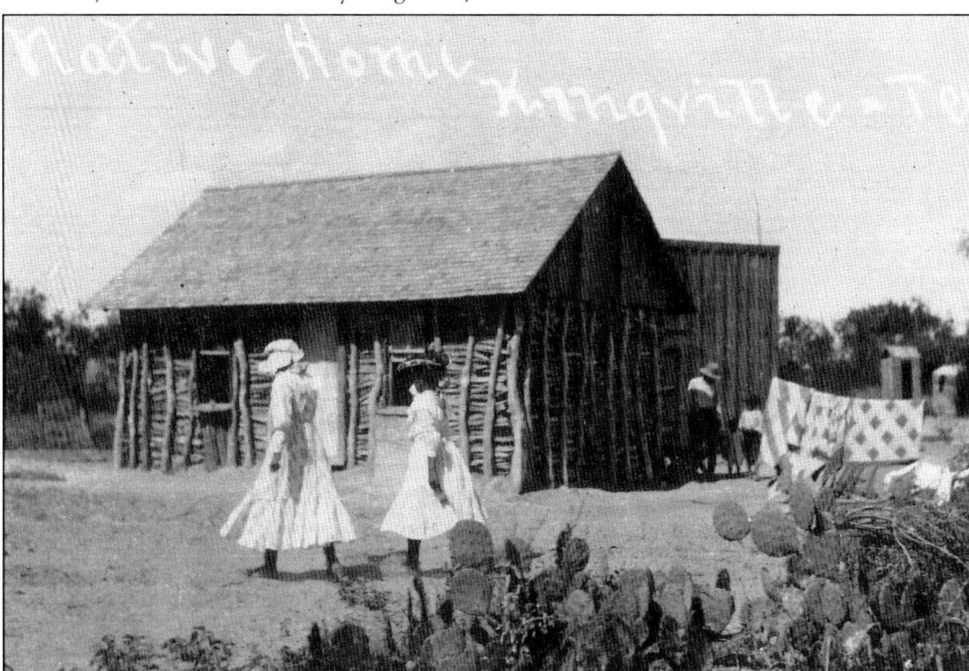

This photograph from 1904 is titled "Native Home Kingsville Tex" and shows a building called a jacal. In South Texas, this was a familiar construction method that used native wood, such as mesquite, to form the walls. Before the arrival of the railroad, there was no easy way to acquire building supplies. (Courtesy South Texas Archives, Texas A&M University-Kingsville.)

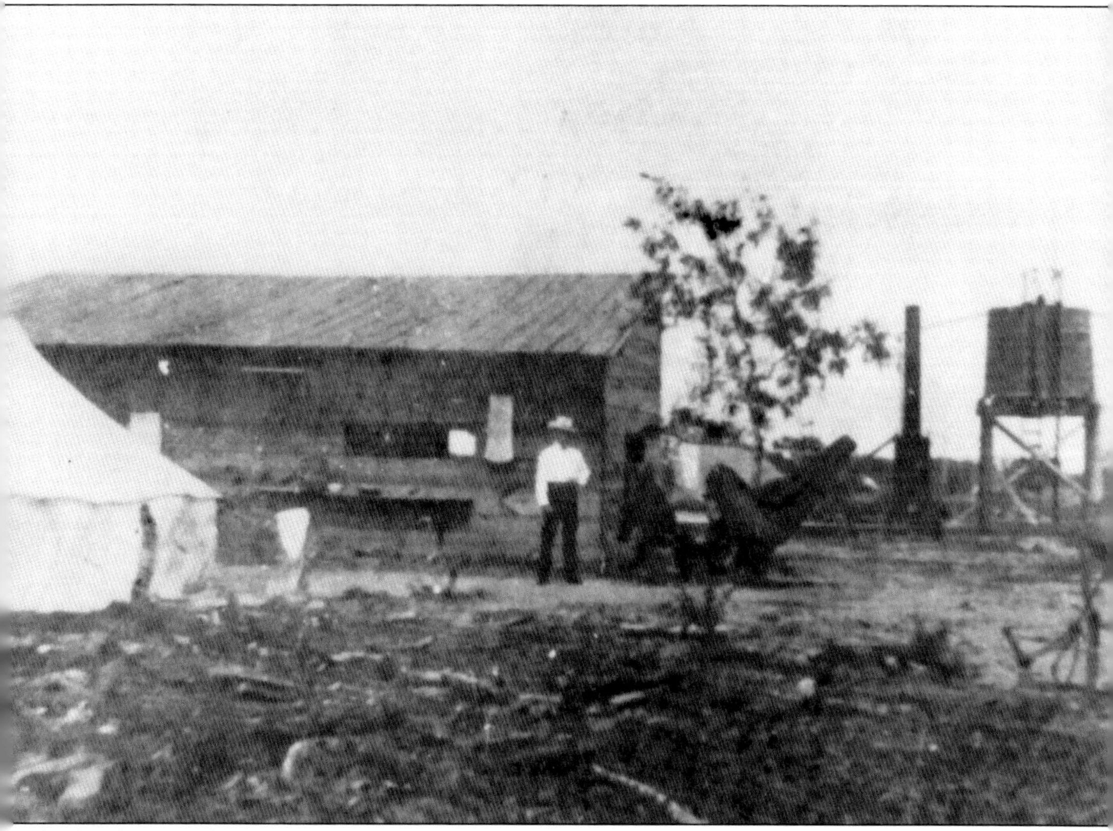

Charles Flato stands in front of a wooden shack. The tent is a primitive boardinghouse. Kingsville was a tent city while the railroad was being built. From sunup to sundown, 400 men worked clearing, leveling, and laying track. Tents were often pitched on flatcars to keep sleeping workers safe from the numerous rattlesnakes inhabiting the Wild Horse Desert. Henrietta King offered a bounty on rattlesnakes and within two weeks had collected more than 10,000 rattles. The original bounty was 5¢ per rattle. Even after lowering the bounty to 3¢ per rattle, she still collected 250,000 rattles during the months of railroad construction. This photograph shows the dinner shack by the boardinghouse tent at Kingsville. The water tower, which provided water for the train and the new citizens of Kingsville, is in the background. (Courtesy South Texas Archives, Texas A&M University-Kingsville.)

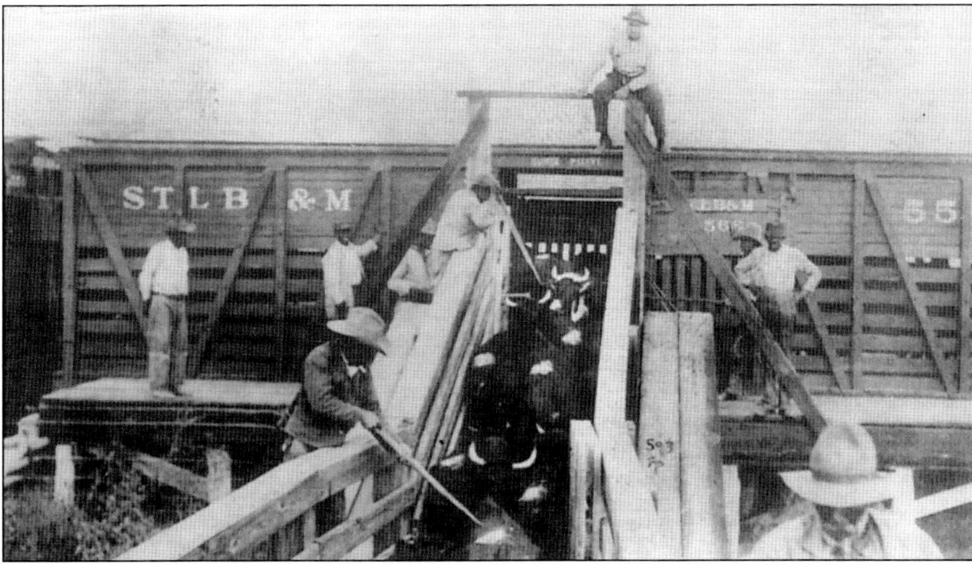

The StLB&M set up sidings in several places along the railroad line for local ranchers, who could move their cattle to the tracks for easy loading onto railcars for transport to market. (Courtesy King Ranch, Inc., Kingsville, Texas.)

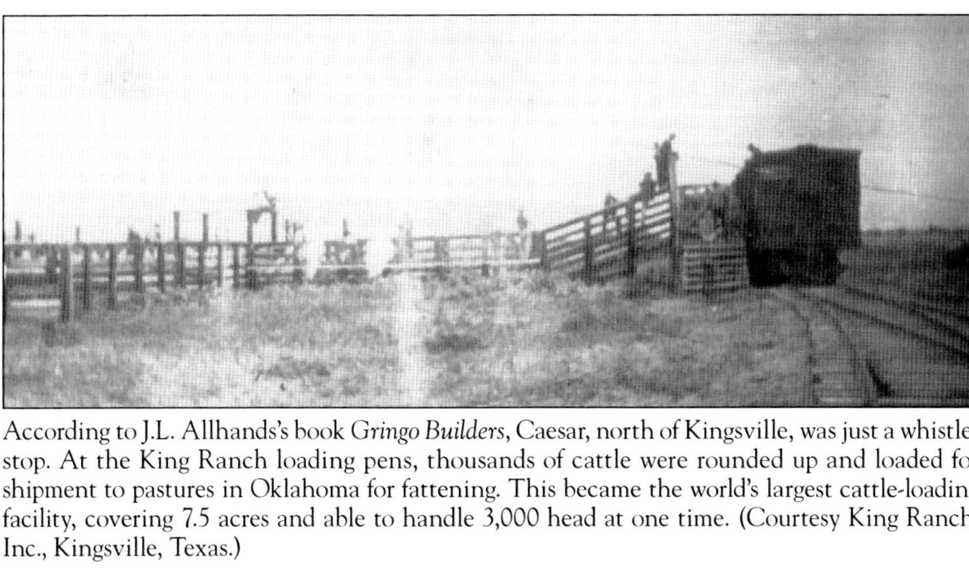

According to J.L. Allhands's book *Gringo Builders*, Caesar, north of Kingsville, was just a whistle-stop. At the King Ranch loading pens, thousands of cattle were rounded up and loaded for shipment to pastures in Oklahoma for fattening. This became the world's largest cattle-loading facility, covering 7.5 acres and able to handle 3,000 head at one time. (Courtesy King Ranch, Inc., Kingsville, Texas.)

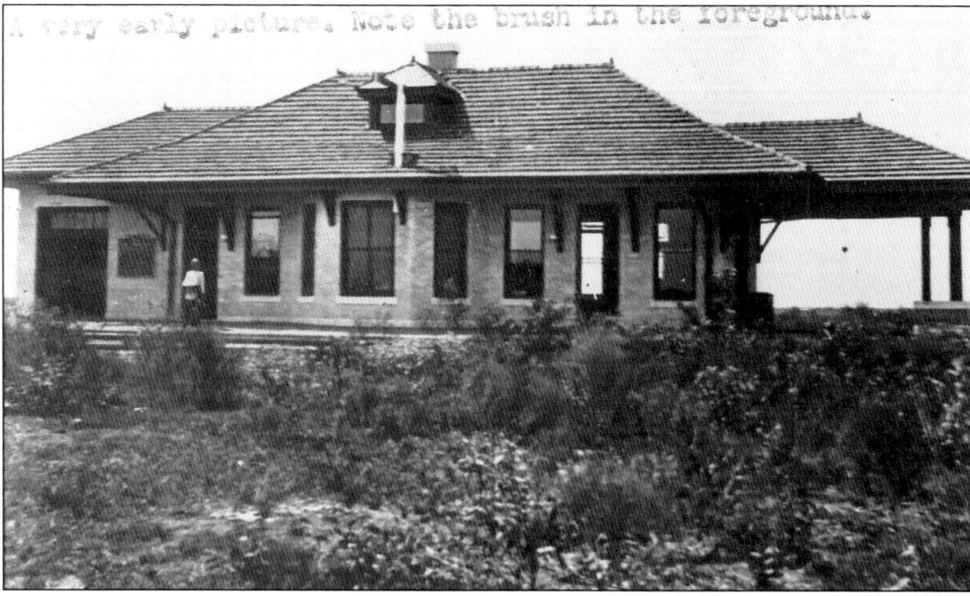

Construction of the Kingsville passenger depot got off to a late start. The first passenger trains officially passed through Kingsville on July 4, 1904, but the depot was not completed until September of that year. This is possibly the first picture of the structure. Bricks for the depot were locally manufactured. (Courtesy South Texas Archives, Texas A&M University-Kingsville.)

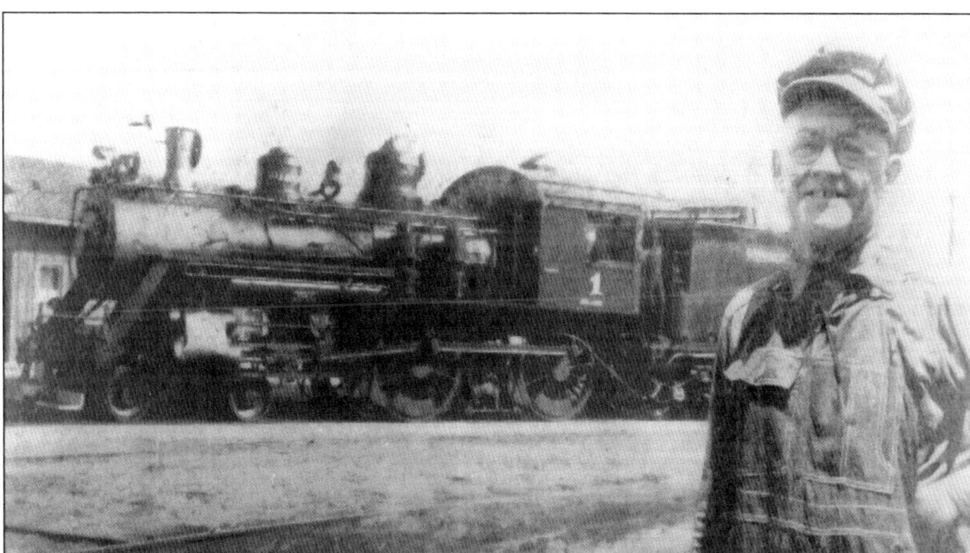

Three brand-new Baldwin 4-4-0 locomotives were purchased for passenger service on the new StLB&M railway. Will Jordan was the fireman on locomotive no. 1 for the first passenger run from Brownsville to Corpus Christi. Henrietta King provided two US flags to fly at the front of the locomotive. (Courtesy South Texas Archives, Texas A&M University-Kingsville.)

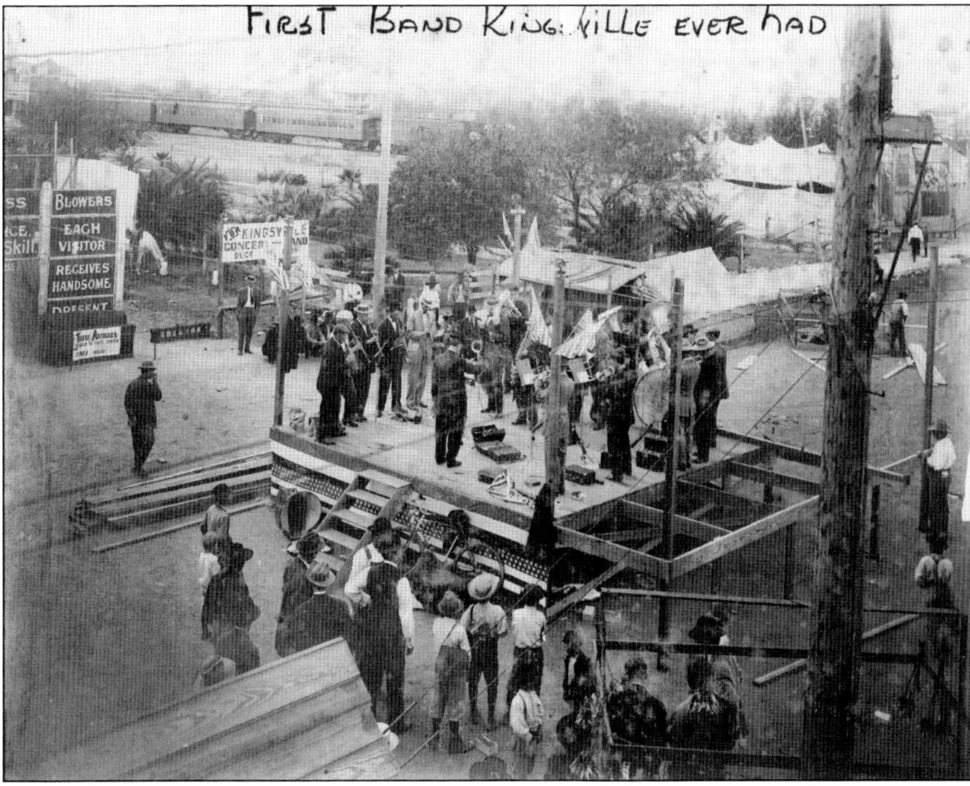

Even in Kingsville's infancy, entertainment was important. Pictured here is the town's first bandstand. The passing train and few frame buildings are visible in the background. Mostly railroad workers and merchants, the musicians were members of the community. (Courtesy King Ranch, Inc., Kingsville, Texas.)

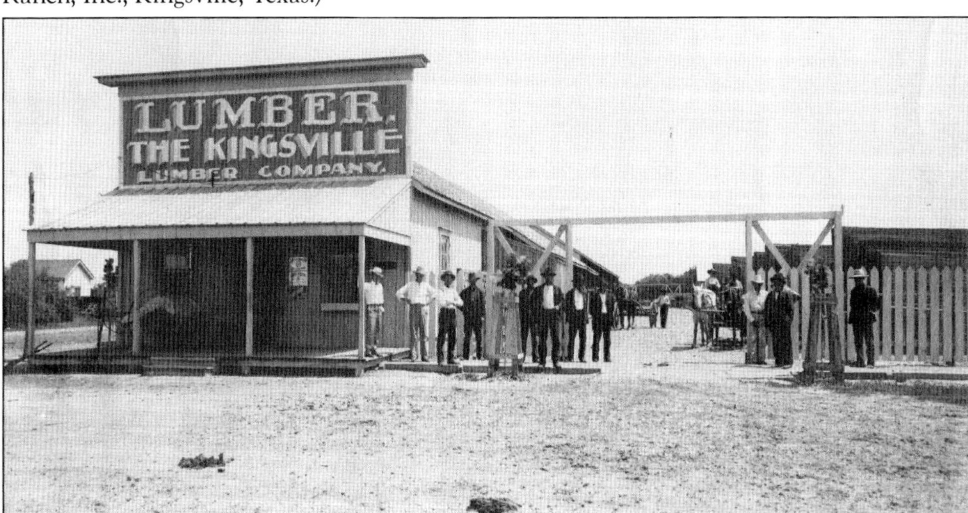

The Kingsville Lumber Company erected one of the first permanent buildings in the new town. A railroad spur ran into the lumberyard for easy off-loading of supplies. Kingsville's first motion picture was shown on a canvas tarp suspended at the lumberyard. Seating was devised from nail kegs and wooden planks. (Courtesy South Texas Archives, Texas A&M University-Kingsville.)

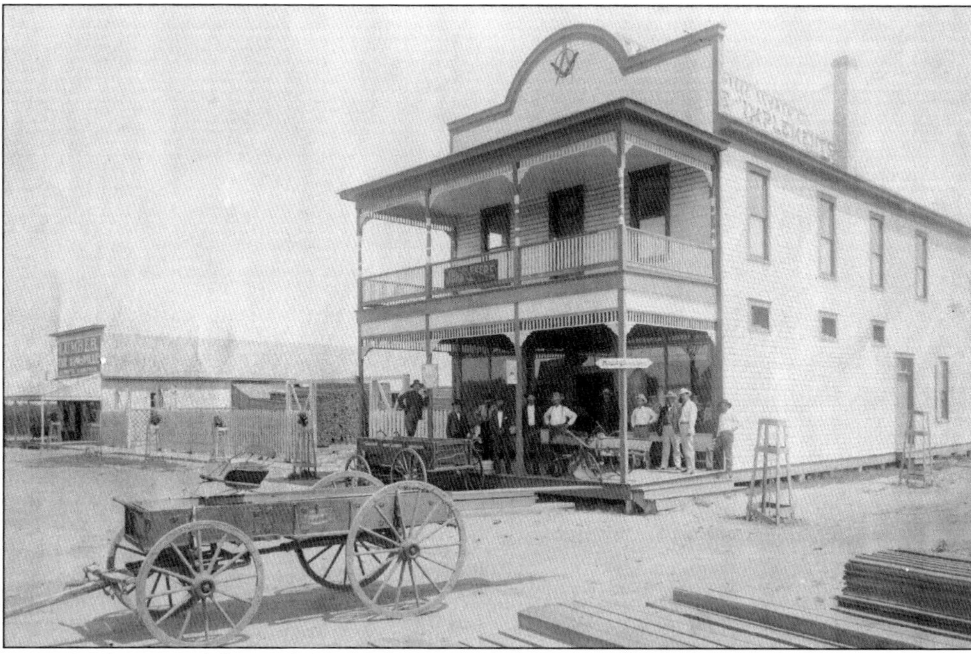

In 1907, the second floor of the Kingsville Lumber Company and Hardware Store served as a Masonic lodge. The hardware store was constructed just west of the lumberyard and railroad spur. Whatever was needed for building had to be fabricated from local materials or transported in on the new railroad. (Courtesy South Texas Archives, Texas A&M University-Kingsville.)

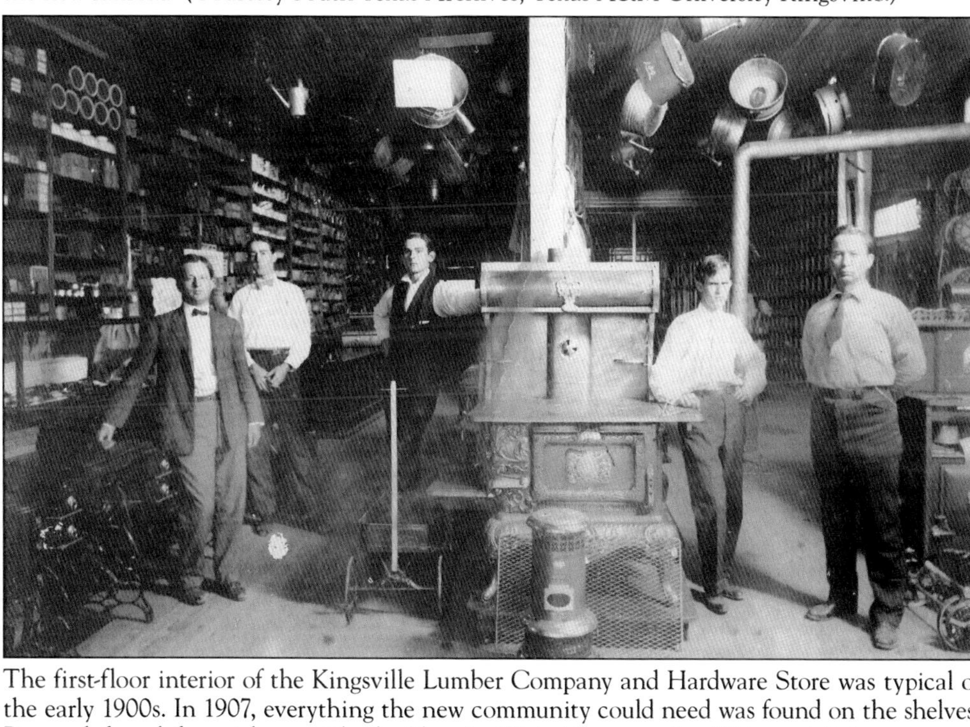

The first-floor interior of the Kingsville Lumber Company and Hardware Store was typical of the early 1900s. In 1907, everything the new community could need was found on the shelves. Pictured, from left to right, are Charles Flato Jr., W.A. Clampett, Jim Walton, A.B. Lawson, and T.A. Hill. (Courtesy South Texas Archives, Texas A&M University-Kingsville.)

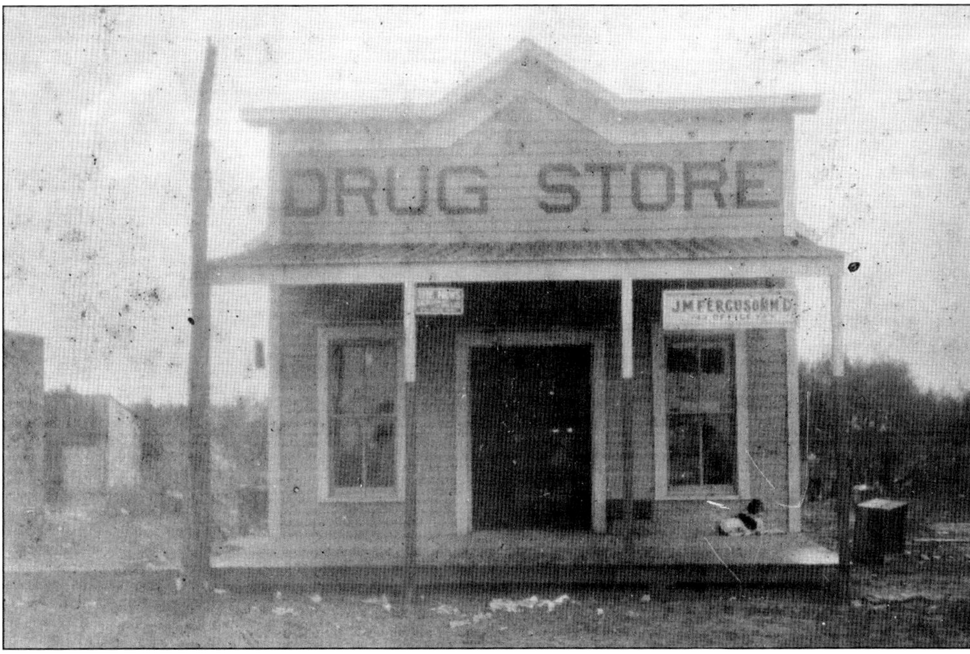

Marcus Phillips's Drug Store was among the first businesses to open in 1904. This little drugstore can be seen between other businesses in later photographs of Fifth Street. The building also housed the office of J.M. Ferguson, MD, and the post office for the new town. (Courtesy South Texas Archives, Texas A&M University-Kingsville.)

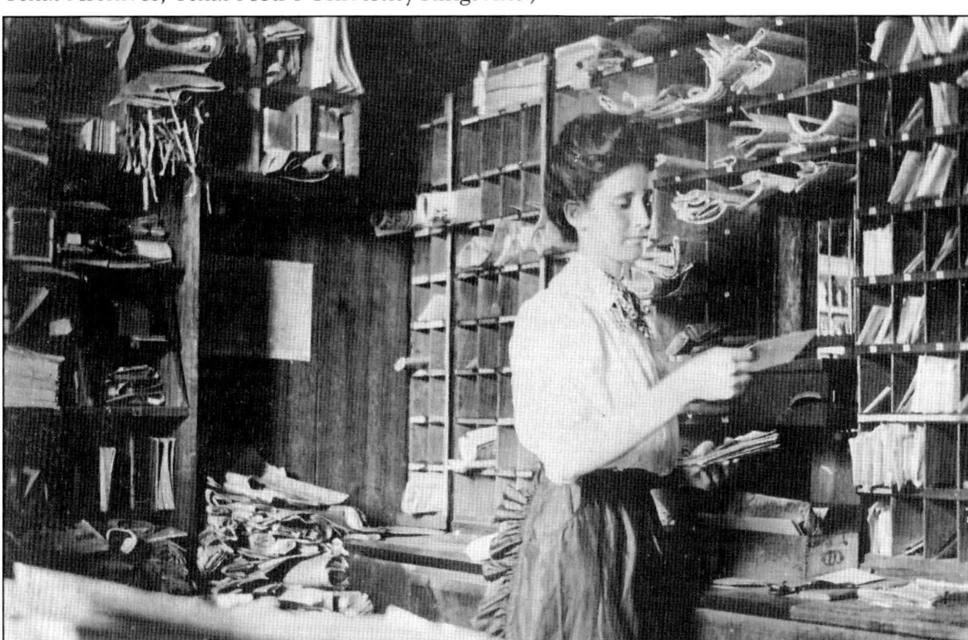

Mail delivery was often a challenge in the Wild Horse Desert. For Kingsville, delivery was initially made to King Ranch, forcing people to go out to the ranch to collect their mail. Following the advent of regular train service, mail arrived at Marcus Phillips's Drug Store. Here, Mary Nickels "delivers" mail in the store. (Courtesy South Texas Archives, Texas A&M University-Kingsville.)

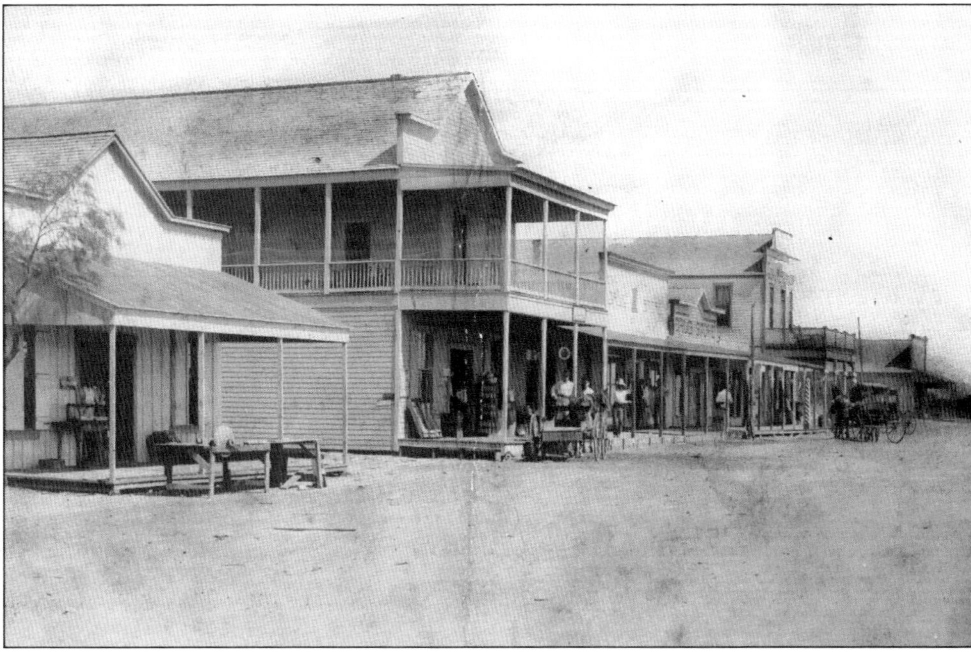

Fifth Street, west of the railroad tracks, became Kingsville's first business district. Boardinghouses and merchants lined the street. Marcus Phillips's Drug Store can be seen in the middle of this block of businesses. This area was often called "Main Street." (Courtesy South Texas Archives, Texas A&M University-Kingsville.)

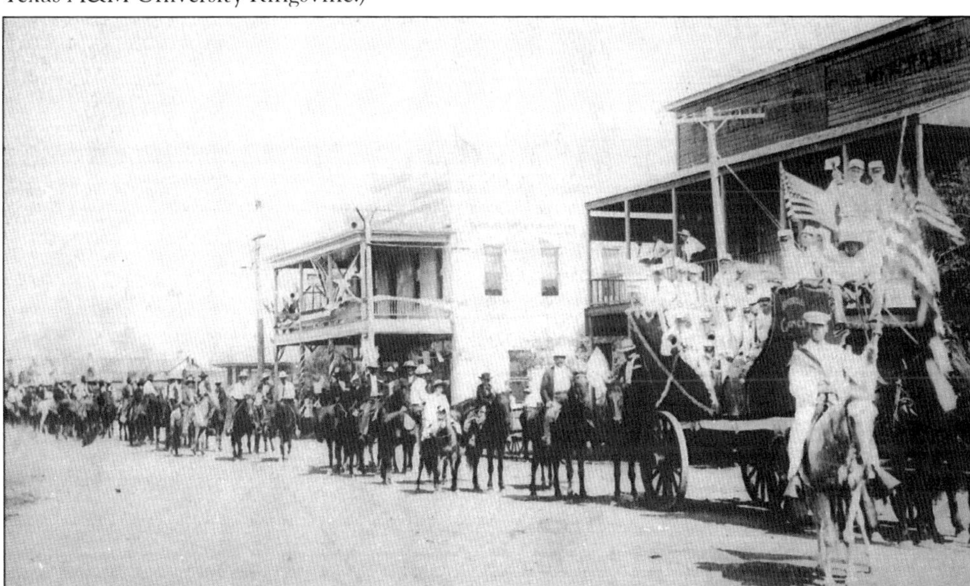

There is some dispute about the location in this picture. Page 208 of *Kleberg County Texas* reports it is the December 20, 1910, parade down Fifth Street. Close examination of the background buildings on the left of the picture reveals the passenger depot and the StLB&M general office, which makes it more probable that this is Kleberg Avenue and the 1908 parade proceeding east. The same leading wagon and rider are in another photograph identified as being from 1908. (Courtesy South Texas Archives, Texas A&M University-Kingsville.)

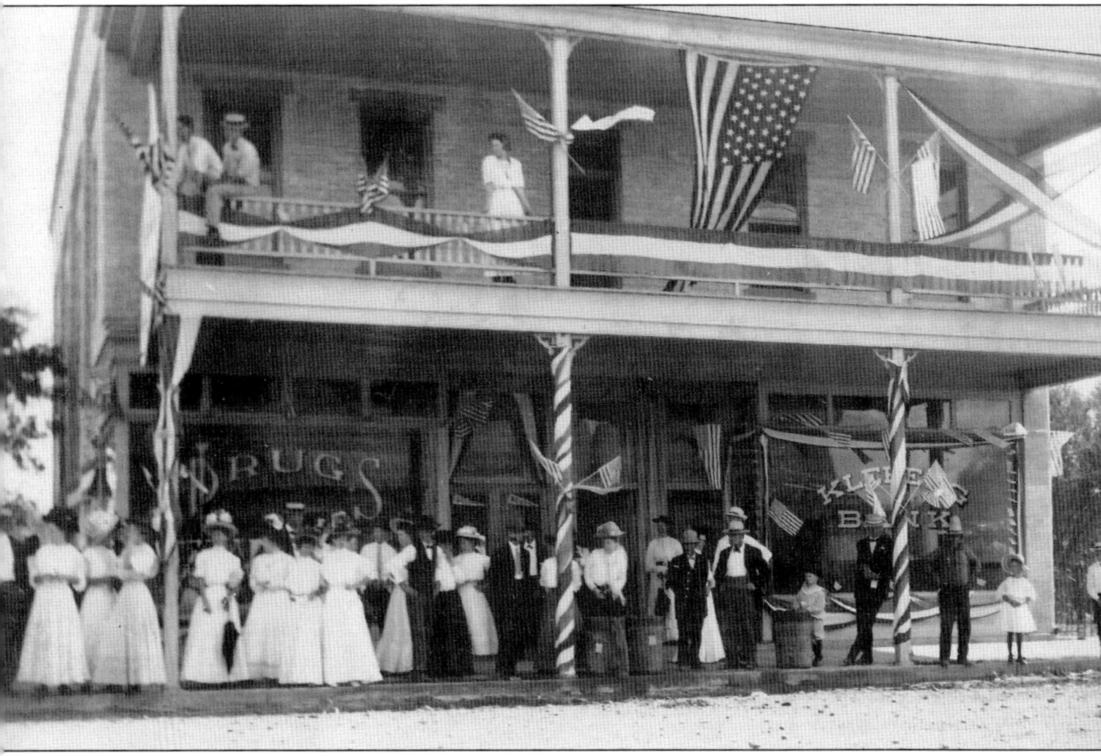

Kleberg Bank was organized as a private financial institution in 1905, and the first Kleberg Bank building was constructed in 1908 on Kleberg Avenue. It was temporarily housed in the Kingsville Lumber Company building because the lumber company had a huge safe able to accommodate both businesses. The pictured structure housed Dr. H. Allison's Drugstore on the first floor and the telephone exchange and apartments on the second floor. The crowd is waiting for the 1908 parade to pass. Flags, sashes, and ribbons decorate the building, which was destroyed in a dramatic fire on December 31, 1909. The volunteer fire department heroically managed to save the bank vault and its contents. Clyde Allen, owner of Allen Furniture Company and member of the newly organized volunteer fire department, manned a hose that sprayed water on the door of the bank's safe to save the town's records and cash. (Courtesy South Texas Archives, Texas A&M University-Kingsville.)

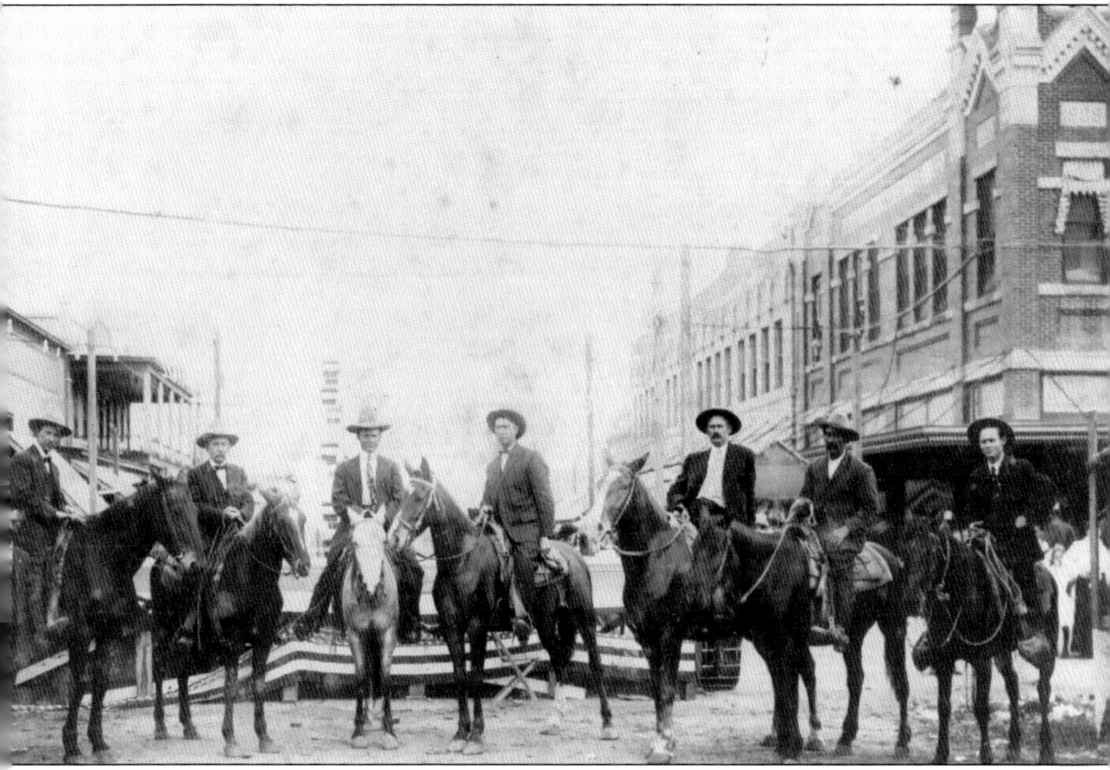

The Kingsville Mounted Police pause for a photograph at an early carnival on Kleberg Avenue. Kingsville was a fairly tame town for the western frontier. The main criminal activities included horse theft, cattle rustling, and bootlegging. Early newspapers record the activities of the police force and, later, the Kleberg County sheriff in somewhat dramatic prose. A 1911 report of a chase of an escaped bootlegger includes the term "hot pursuit." B.C. Baldwin, pictured here at far left on a horse, was Kingsville's first police chief. He was also involved in the 1911 effort to arrest the bootlegger. Baldwin was ambushed by four of the bootlegger's friends and shot in the struggle. The bootlegger was eventually captured and brought to trial. Baldwin survived his wounds. One can only imagine a frantic horseback chase through the dusty streets of tiny Kingsville. (Courtesy King Ranch, Inc., Kingsville, Texas.)

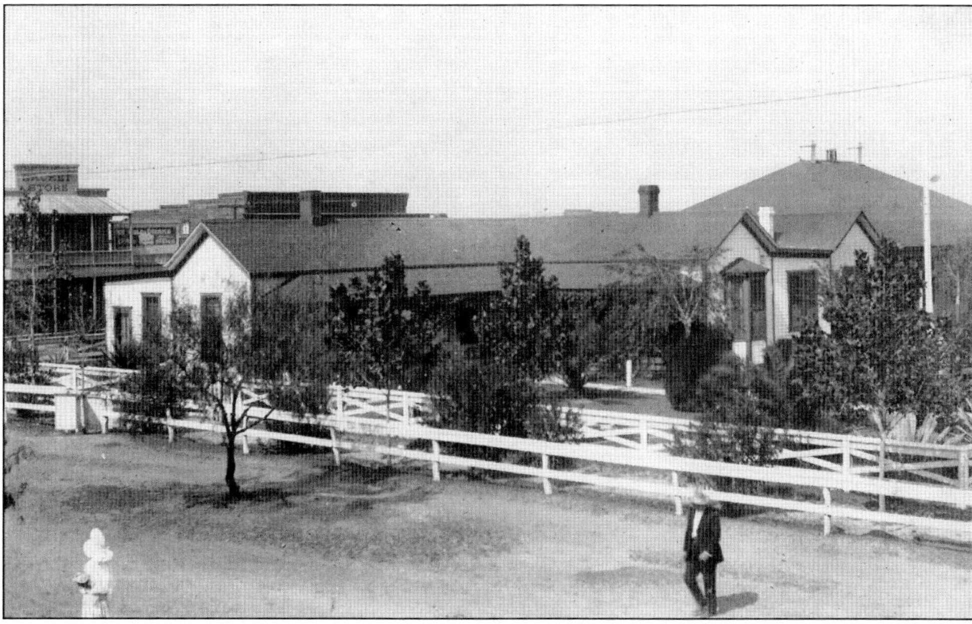

As promised, the general office building for the new St. Louis, Brownsville & Mexico Railway was located in Kingsville. This wood frame building served as the general office until the sale of the StLB&M in 1909. After construction of the new Frisco Lines general office building in 1911, this block was cleared and turned into Miller Park. (Courtesy South Texas Archives, Texas A&M University-Kingsville.)

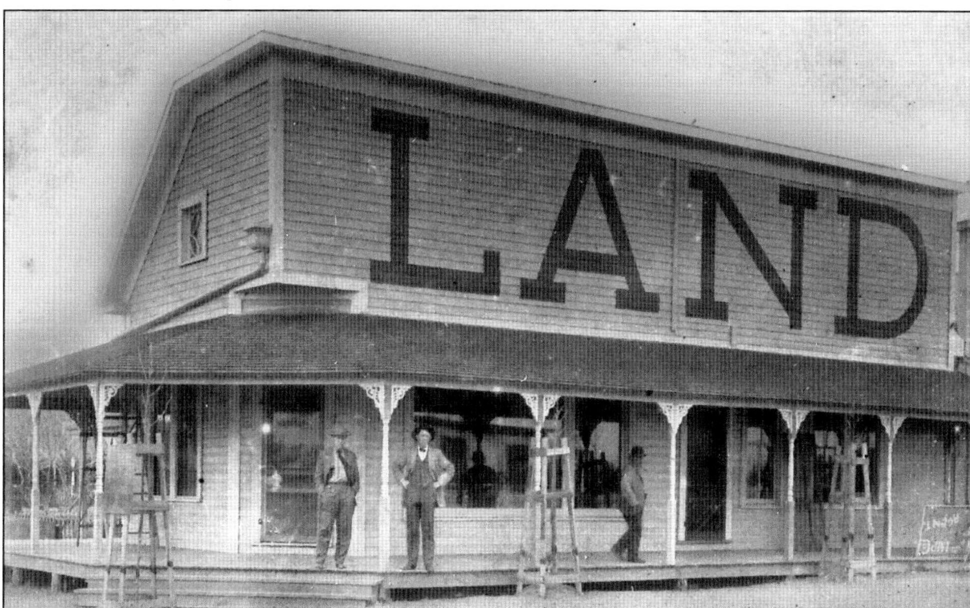

The Kleberg Town and Improvement Company was recognizable from a distance thanks to its distinctive signage—"LAND," spelled out in boxcar letters taller than a man. This building was on Fifth Street, directly across the street from the StLB&M general office. C.P. House (left) and B.O. Sims, two of the prominent developers of Kingsville, stand in front. (Courtesy South Texas Archives, Texas A&M University-Kingsville.)

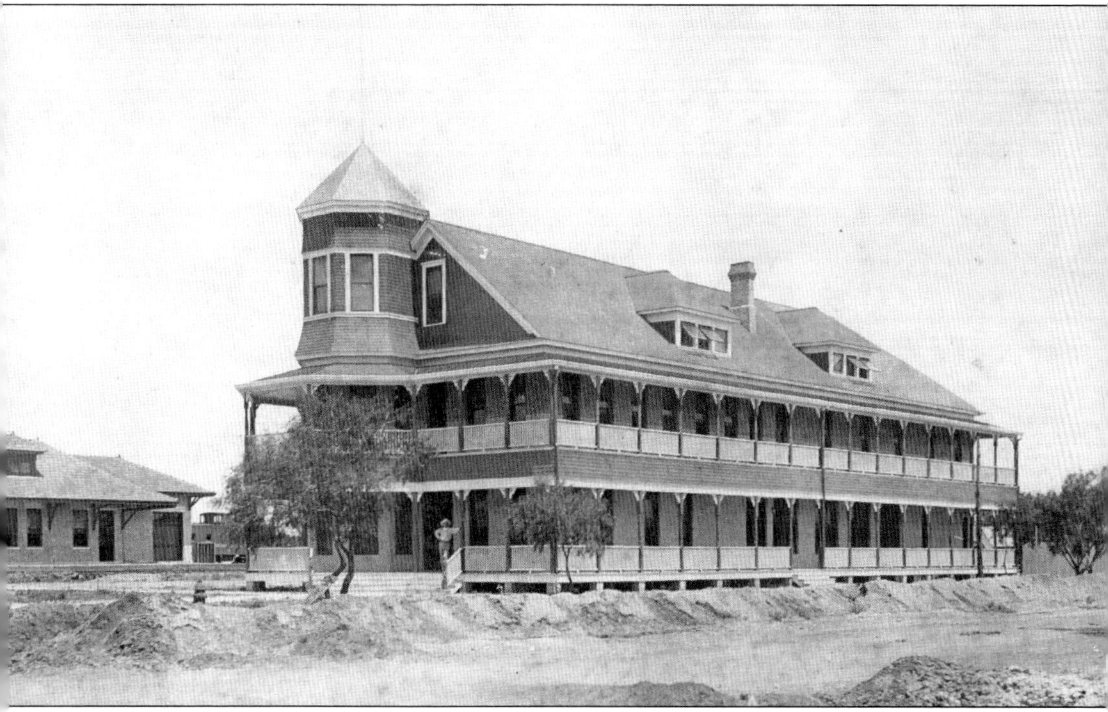

In 1905, not long after the first passenger trains passed through town, the beautiful Victorian-style King's Inn Hotel was built. A growing town needed a place for visitors to stay and a good restaurant to replace the makeshift one that served railroad construction workers. A spacious dining room provided home-cooked meals. A fine dinner of fillet of snapper or prime rib of beef with side dishes and a dessert cost 25¢. King's Inn was comfortable but not overly elegant. In 1905, it was the most modern hotel in Texas south of San Antonio. The second floor had 37 rooms and eight private baths available for guests. King's Inn had hot and cold running water, and it even had heating for the days when blue northers chilled the air. The steam heat was courtesy of the railroad boilers. (Courtesy King Ranch, Inc., Kingsville, Texas.)

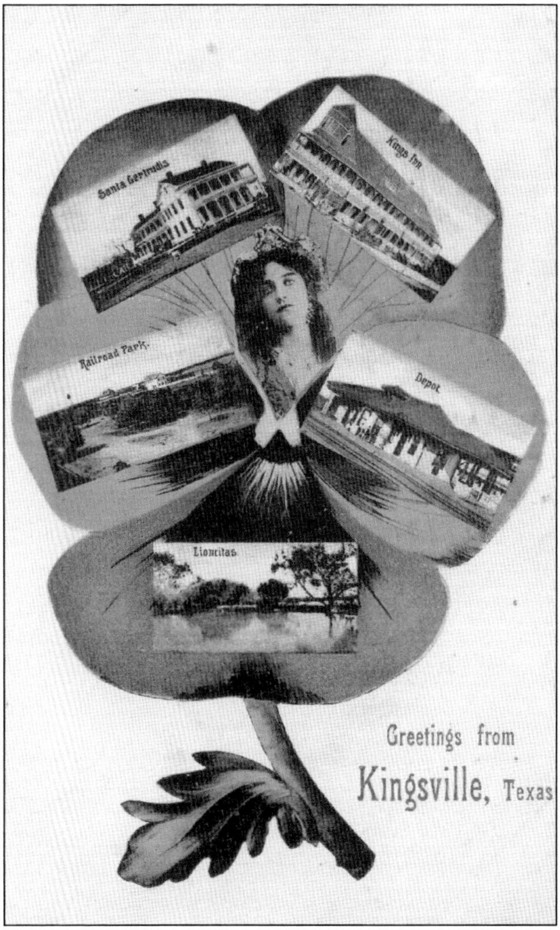

The railroad was established and running well. Homeseekers were being invited to settle in South Texas. New farms were being established. With irrigation from the artesian wells, the land seemed able to grow anything. This composite photograph is printed in a postcard format and reflects the optimism of the community with local images on each petal of a pansy. (Courtesy King Ranch, Inc., Kingsville, Texas.)

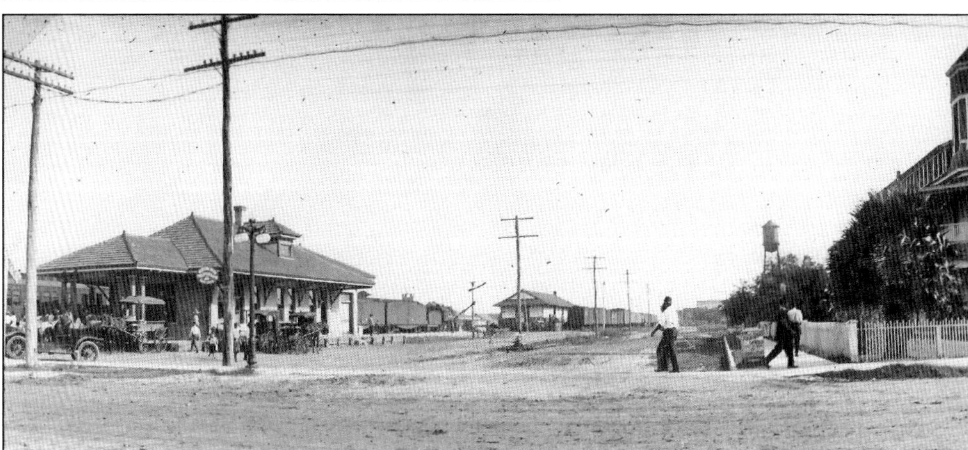

This photograph offers a northward view of the corner of Kleberg and Park Streets, between the passenger depot and the King's Inn Hotel. For visitors, it was a short walk from the depot to the hotel. Park Street has since been renamed PFC Daniel Alarcon Street, in honor of one of Kingsville's military heroes, who was killed in action in the Korean War on August 15, 1950. (Courtesy South Texas Archives, Texas A&M University-Kingsville.)

Two

Season of Problems

Kingsville existed because of the railroad and the large ranching concerns of the area. Survival depended on the railroad, but there were dark clouds on the horizon in more ways than one. As early as 1906, Houston city officials started eying Kingsville's general office and shops. In 1909, the St. Louis, Brownsville & Mexico Railway was sold to Frisco Lines, and the main question became whether the new parent company would honor the handshake agreement. Shortly after the sale, railroad officials wanted Frisco Lines to move the general office, shops, and roundhouse from Kingsville to Houston. Kingsvillians were in a panic, fearing they would lose the whole reason for having a town here. By 1913, the Frisco Lines was in receivership, making the future even less certain.

In 1915, bandits, anarchists, and other troublemakers roamed the Wild Horse Desert. There were intentional train derailments and attacks on ranches, and Kingsville braced for the worst. But nature hit Kingsville even harder with a 1916 hurricane. Hurricanes were not named back then, but this one almost washed Kingsville away into the brush of the desert. During World War I, the railroads were taken over by the federal government, and many of Kingsville's men headed off to war.

In 1920, a roundhouse fire nearly burned the railroad out of existence. Only an intense salvage effort and the involvement of the whole community put the railroad back in action. The trains were running on schedule within a couple of days, but rebuilding the roundhouse and shops took longer.

The town rallied and faced down each disaster. These were Texas pioneers, and they were not going to give up without a serious fight. A compromise was made with the railroad, and Missouri Pacific Lines ran a profitable division based in Kingsville. Those seeking a place to settle could flow into South Texas in safety. People rebuilt their homes and businesses after the hurricane and the fires. Kingsville survived.

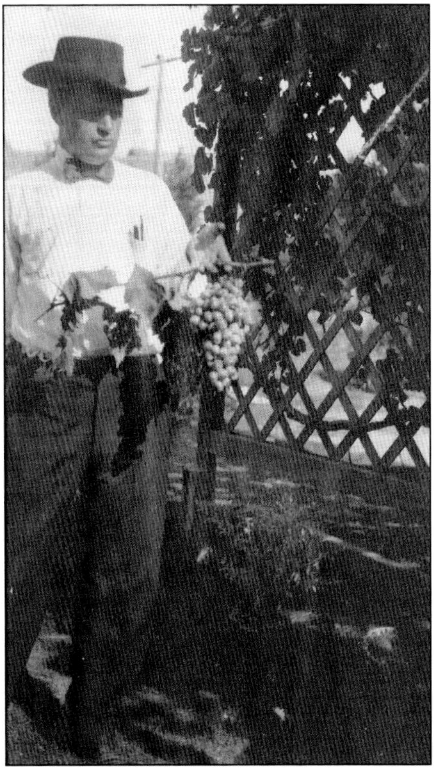

Charles Flato Jr. examines grapes in his back yard. Promoters put a lot of personal effort into experimental gardens to entice visitors to select Kingsville as their new home. Local mythology tells of early land promoters who would tie oranges to the mesquite trees and tell potential buyers they were orange groves. (Courtesy South Texas Archives, Texas A&M University-Kingsville.)

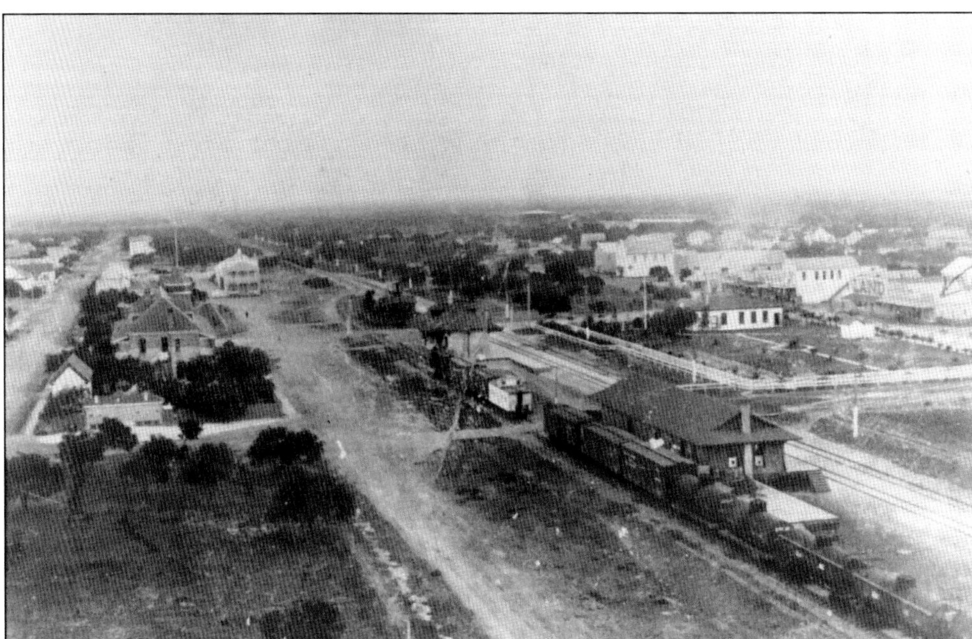

Around 1910, an intrepid early Kingsville photographer climbed up the water tower to take this picture looking south at the King's Inn Hotel, the passenger and freight depots, and the St. Louis, Brownsville & Mexico Railway general office. (Courtesy South Texas Archives, Texas A&M University-Kingsville.)

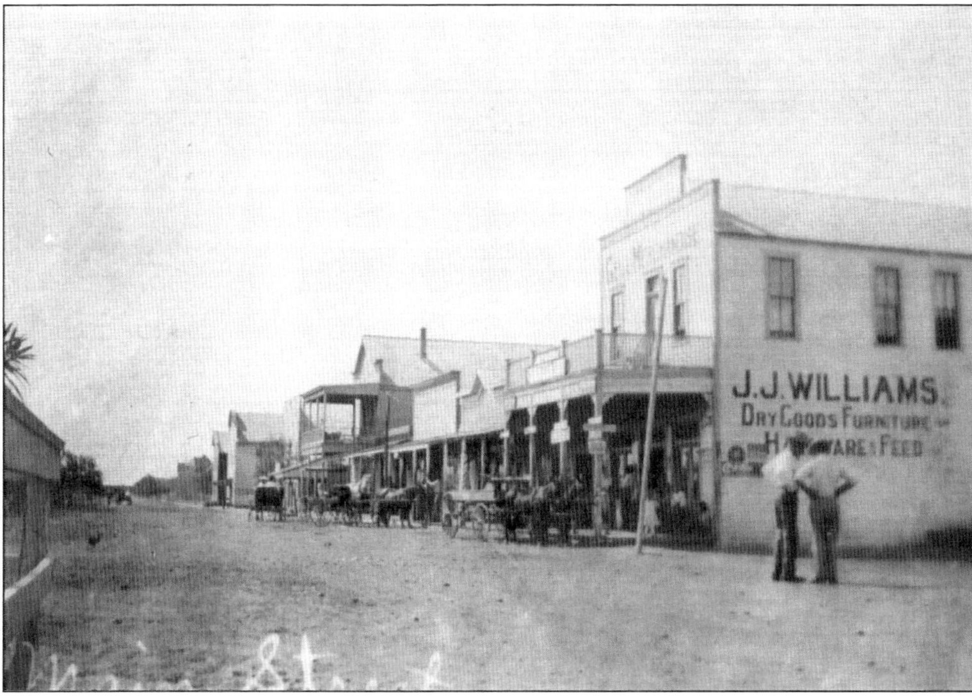

A southward view toward the railroad yards shows Fifth Street bustling and lined with businesses. No one expected that a 1908 fire would destroy half of the block. The Kingsville Volunteer Fire Department was organized in 1909, and nearly everyone in town was considered a volunteer firefighter. (Courtesy Kathryn Evans Collection.)

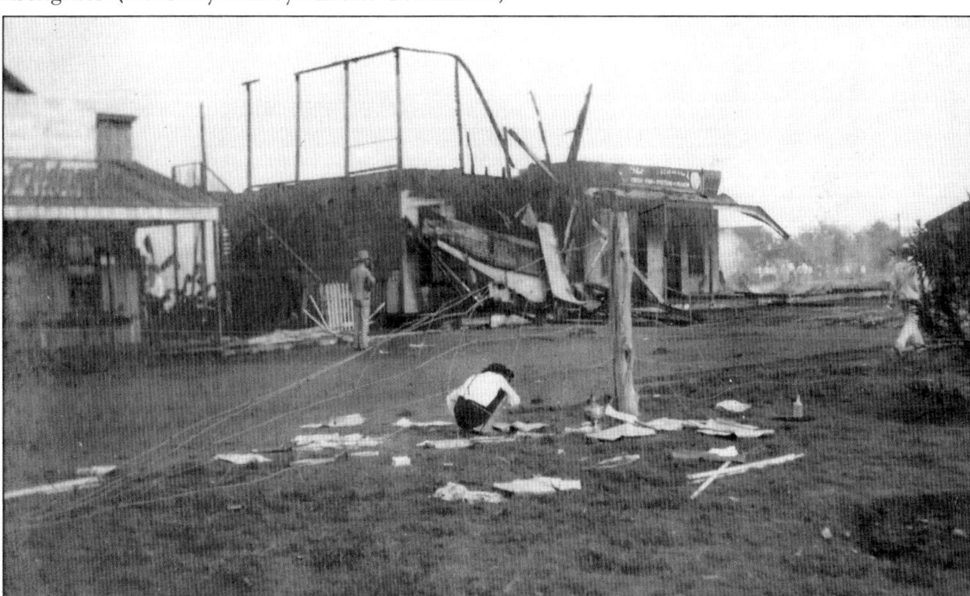

According to Kathryn Evans' book *Come Aboard*, the Fifth Street fire started in a pool hall and quickly spread to neighboring buildings. J.J. Williams Dry Goods store was a total loss. Pictures of the Fifth Street fire are in the John F. Goode Collection at the South Texas Archives. (Courtesy South Texas Archives, Texas A&M University-Kingsville.)

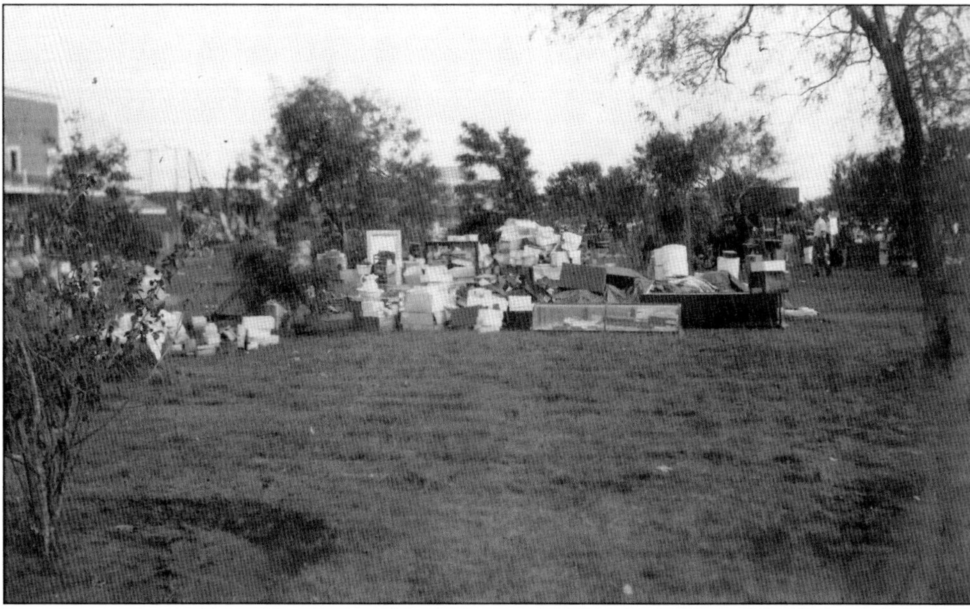

The switch engine in the railroad yard blew to sound the alarm. As people struggled to save whatever they could from the flames, items were simply stacked in the park across the street. (Courtesy South Texas Archives, Texas A&M University-Kingsville.)

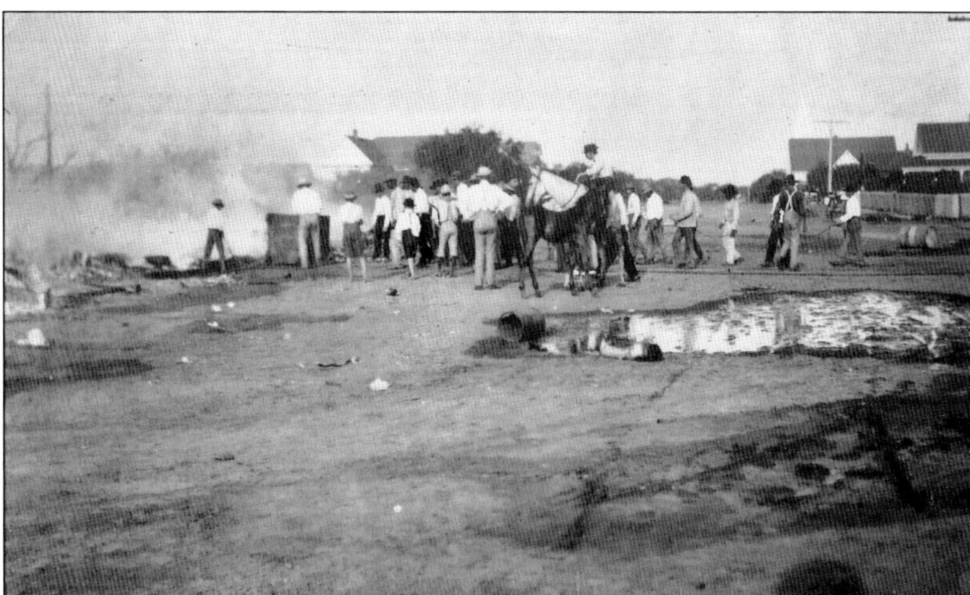

In this photograph, the ruins of the Fifth Street fire are still smoldering. The entire town rushed to help or watch. The 1908 fire gave businesses on the east side of the railroad tracks a temporary competitive edge, but the east side was not immune to fire, either. (Courtesy South Texas Archives, Texas A&M University-Kingsville.)

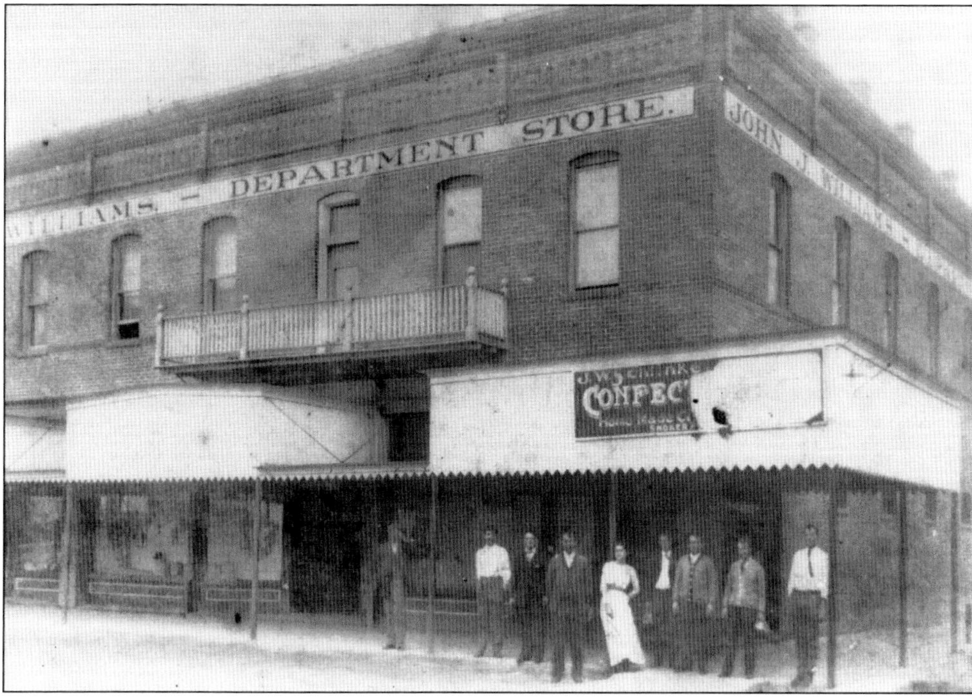

J.J. Williams rebuilt his business on four lots at the same location on Fifth Street. The new brick structure was home to the J.J. Williams Department Store for many years. The building also housed a barbershop and J.B. Otto's Jewelry, the official watch certification jeweler for the railroad. (Courtesy South Texas Archives, Texas A&M University-Kingsville.)

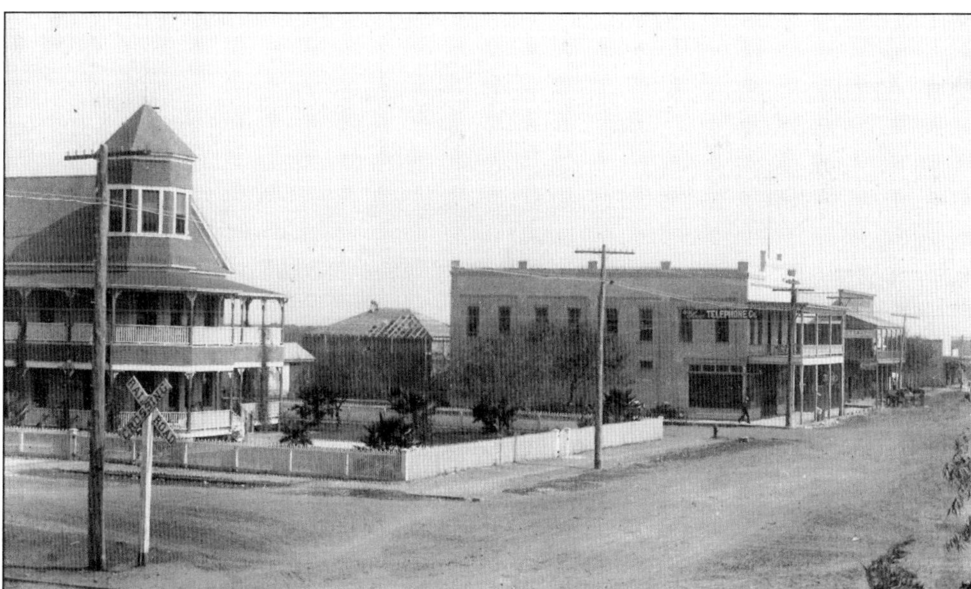

In the early years of Kingsville, there was a building effort underway at all times, as evidenced by the structure under construction behind the bank building. (Courtesy South Texas Archives, Texas A&M University-Kingsville.)

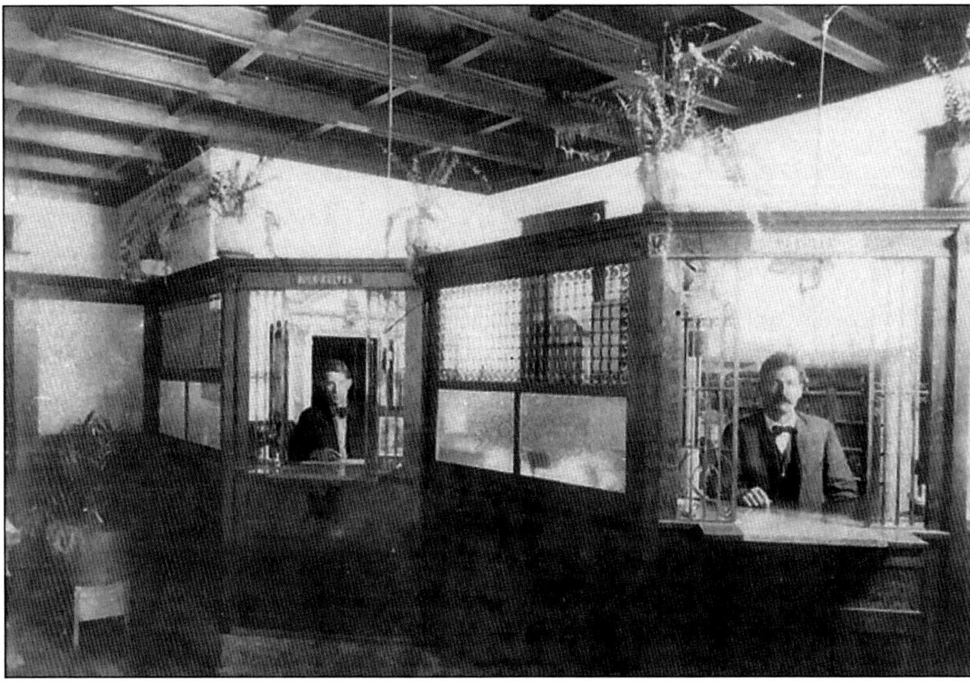

The first Kleberg Bank building also held a drugstore and offices on the second floor. This structure burned to the ground in a dramatic New Year's Eve fire in 1909. The volunteer fire department saved the vault, which contained the critical documents and money of the fledgling town. The Kleberg bank employees pictured here are cashier E.W. House (left) and vice president W.H. McCracken. (Courtesy South Texas Archives, Texas A&M University-Kingsville.)

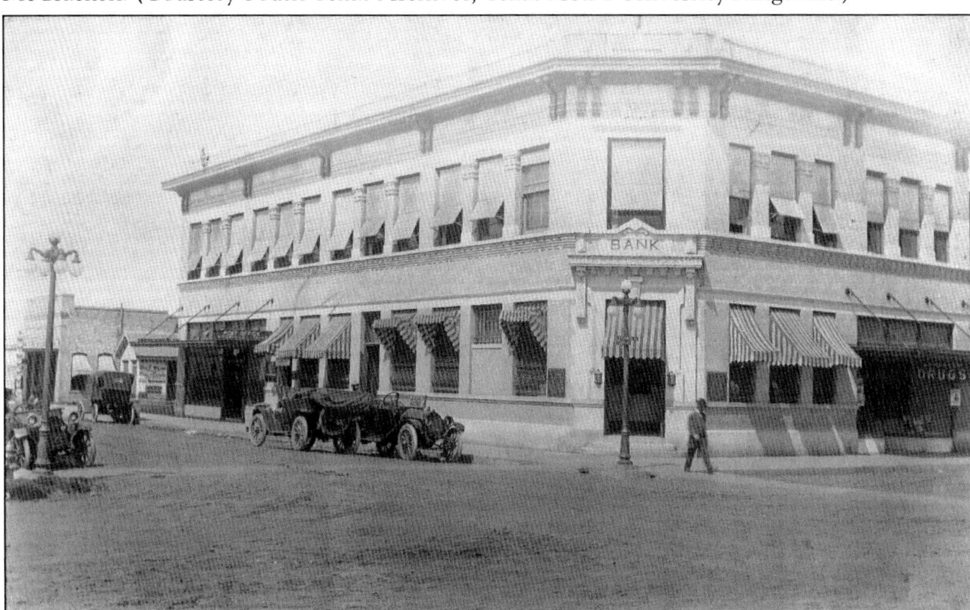

After the 1909 fire destroyed the bank building, this lovely structure was built on the site. It became home to Wakeman Drugs, the post office, and the Kingsville Telephone Company, as well as the R.J. Kleberg and Company Bank. (Courtesy King Ranch, Inc., Kingsville, Texas.)

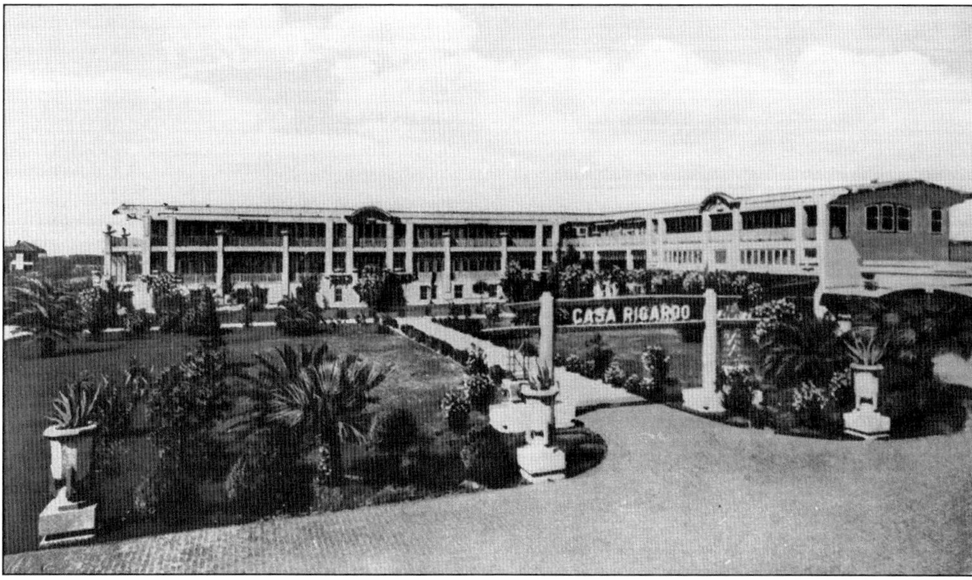

This picture of the elegant Casa Ricardo Hotel was taken in 1919. Frisco Lines built the railroad hotel under the direction of B.F. Yoakum. The building, designed by Louis Curtiss, used steel-reinforced concrete construction and was based on the Harvey House style of hotel. (Courtesy South Texas Archives, Texas A&M University-Kingsville.)

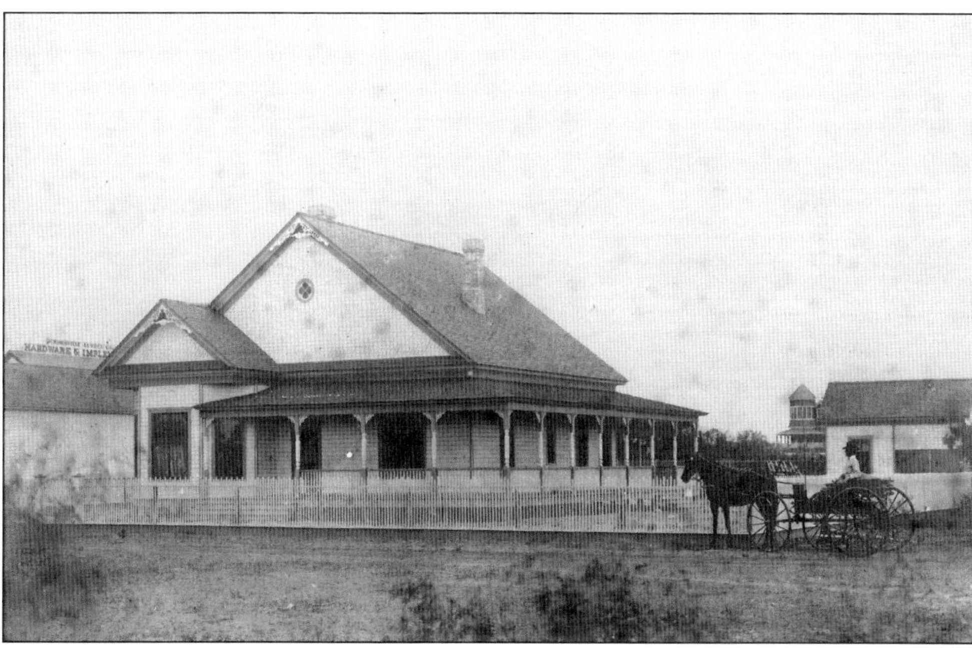

The Charles Henry Flato Jr. home was located on northeast corner of Sixth Street and Kenedy Avenue. This picture shows the Kingsville Lumber building peeking above the house on the left and the King's Inn Hotel in the background at right. (Courtesy South Texas Archives, Texas A&M University-Kingsville.)

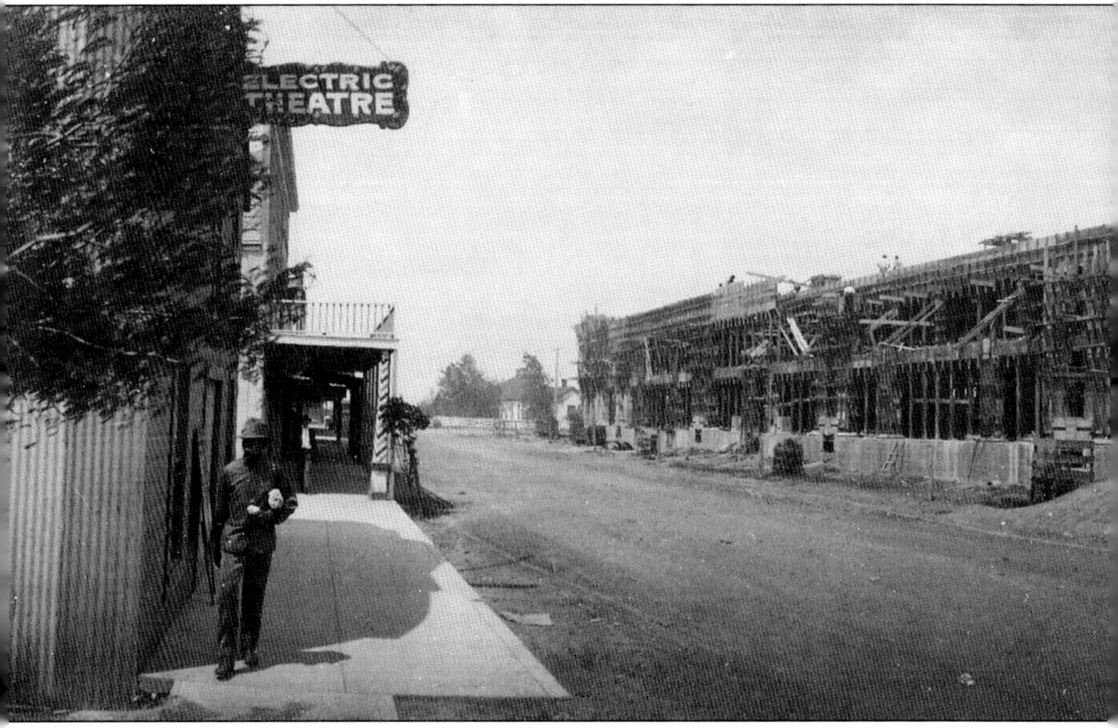

With the sale of the St. Louis, Brownsville & Mexico Railway to Frisco Lines, the battle to keep Houston from taking the general office, roundhouse, and shops out of Kingsville became urgent. In an effort to calm the nerves of locals, B.F. Yoakum built the new Frisco Lines general office building in Kingsville. This photograph, taken from the corner of Fifth Street and King Avenue

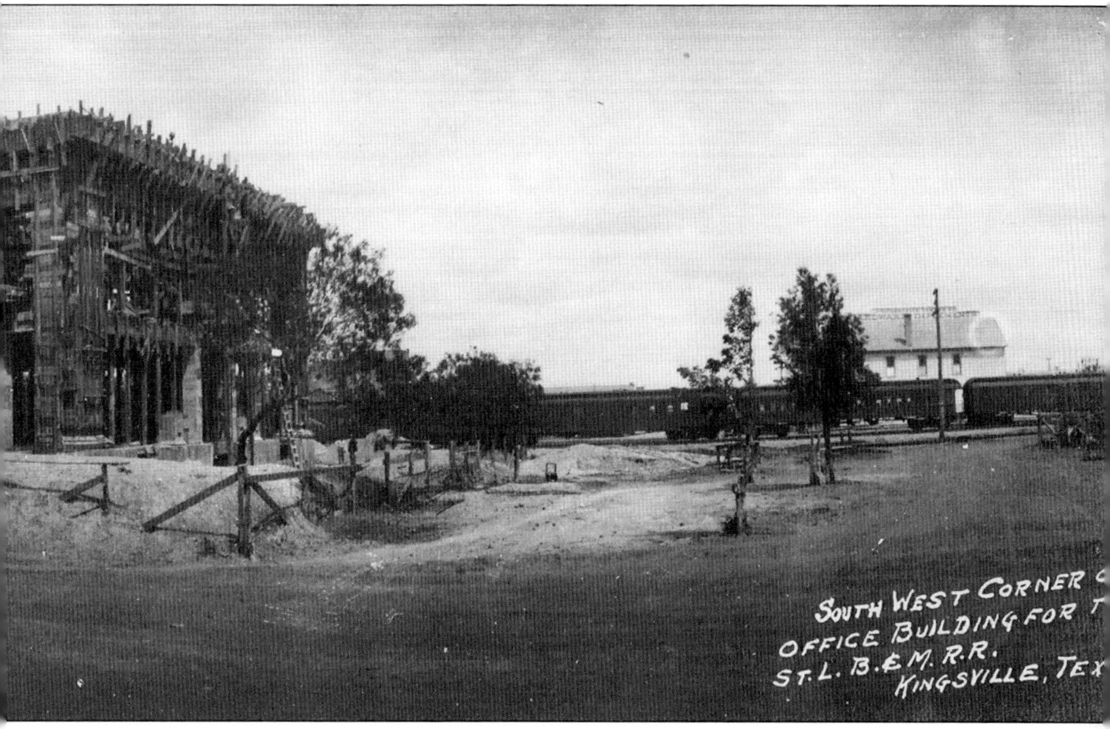

around 1911, shows the building under construction. Another point of interest is the Electric Theatre (at left), one of the first movie theaters in Kingsville. (Courtesy South Texas Archives, Texas A&M University-Kingsville.)

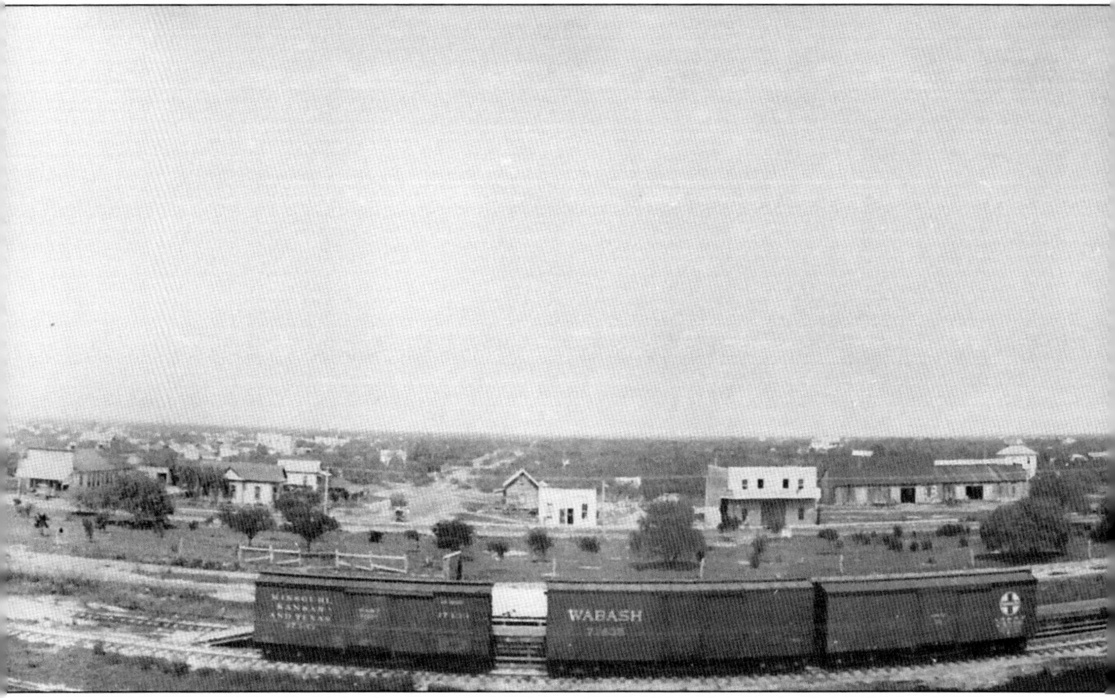

This c. 1912 panorama looking southeast from the roof (or chimney) of the then new Casa Ricardo Hotel shows the railroad spur off of the main line that brought construction supplies directly to the Casa Ricardo building site. The main line of the railroad crosses the length of the picture. The freight depot is prominent in the middle of the picture, and the old StLB&M general office

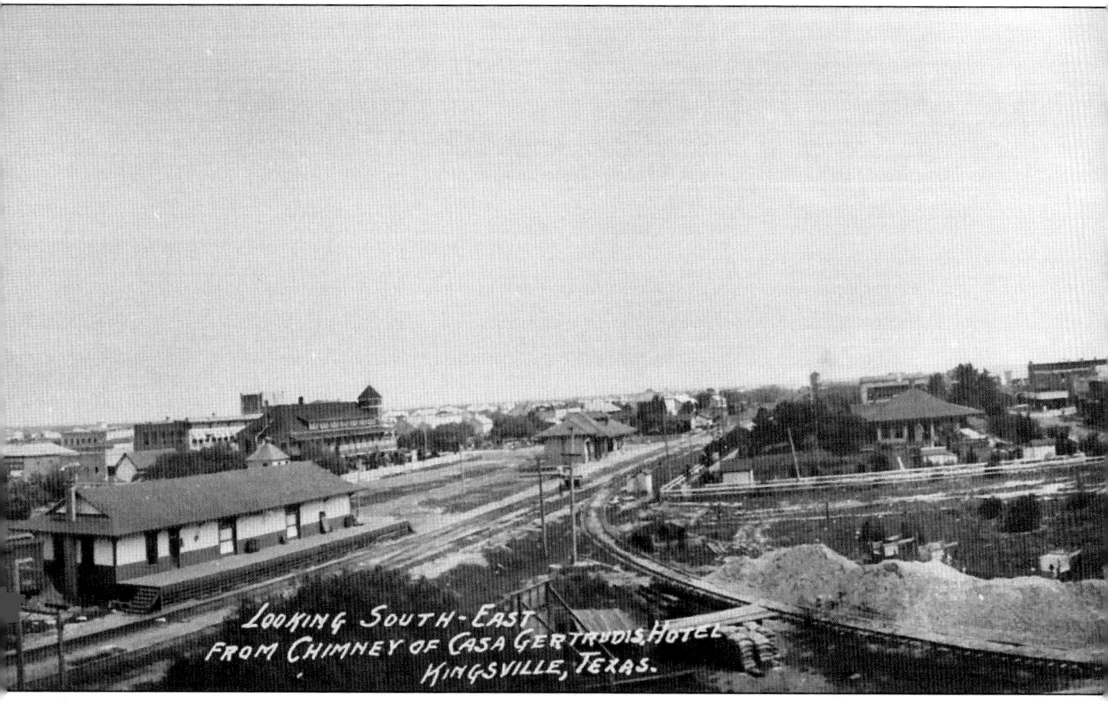

can be seen at right. At the time this photograph was taken, the Casa Ricardo was still being called the "Casa Gertrudis" in honor of the Santa Gertrudis land grant property of King Ranch. (Courtesy South Texas Archives, Texas A&M University-Kingsville.)

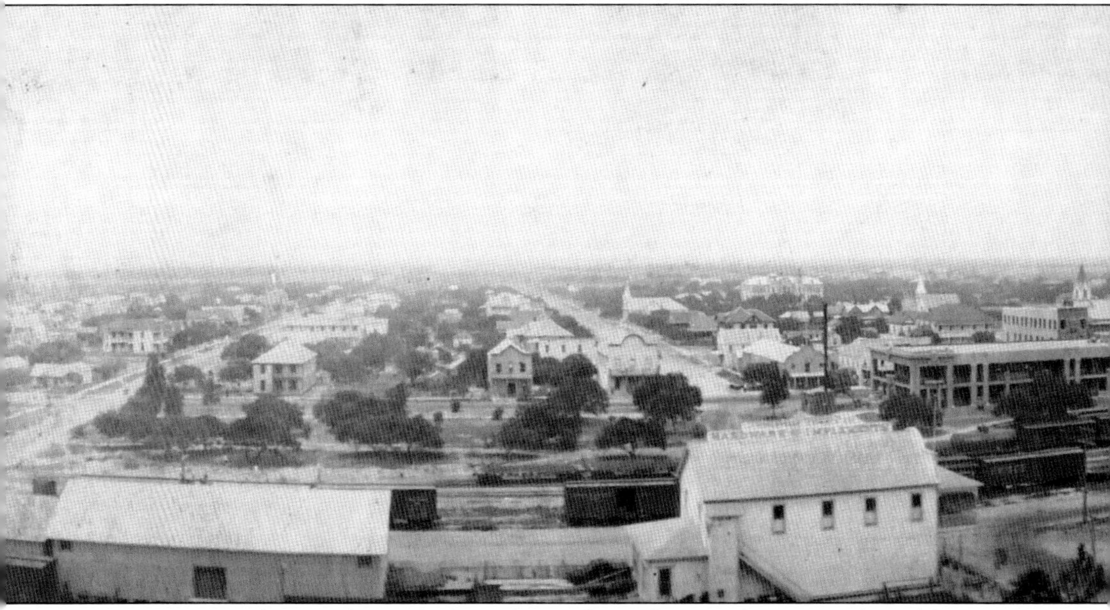

A panorama taken in July 1912 looks to the northwest from Sixth Street and possibly King Avenue. The new Frisco Lines general office is across the tracks. The tiny passenger depot is near the center of the picture. The stunning Casa Ricardo Hotel is behind the depot. The large structure at right is the Flato Building, which was constructed to house the Kingsville Lumber Company.

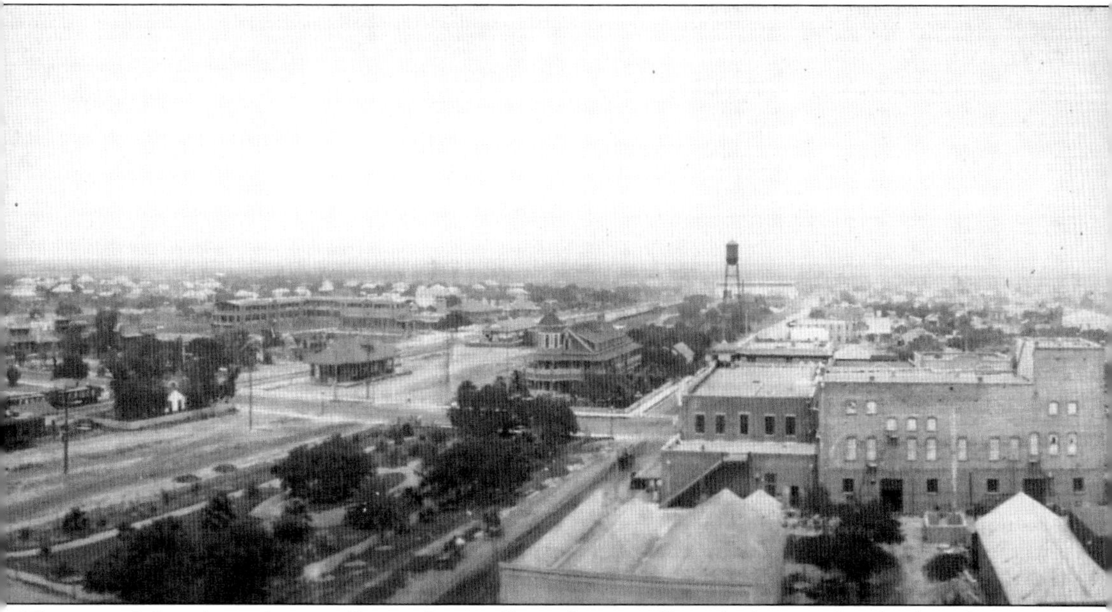

The ground floor has a large walk-in safe as well as a large, well-stocked gun safe. The fact that this area was nothing but brush, cactus, cattle, and rattlesnakes just eight years earlier testifies to the energy expended to build a modern city. (Courtesy King Ranch, Inc., Kingsville, Texas.)

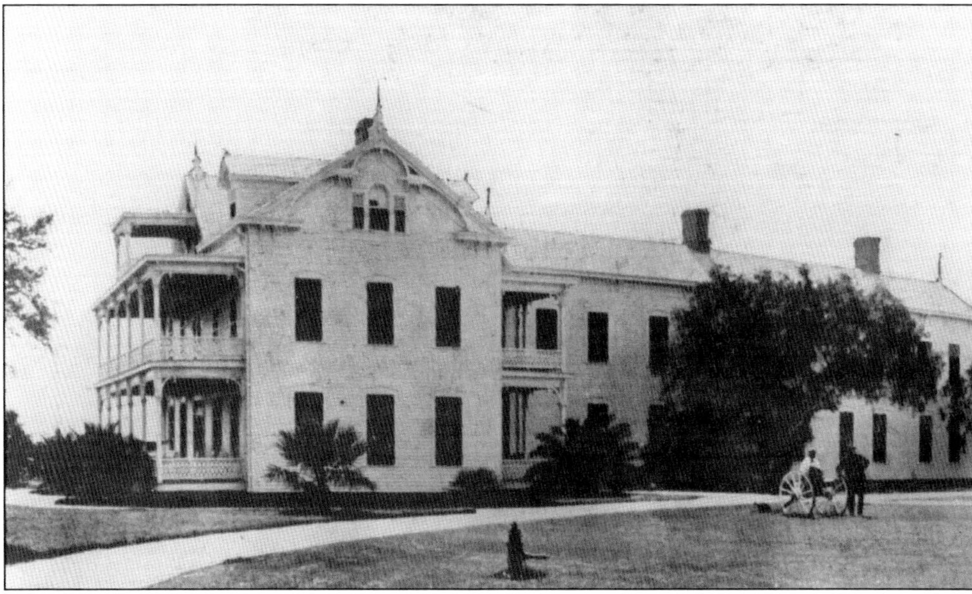

In 1912, fire destroyed the King Ranch main house. Henrietta King and all of her guests escaped safely. People wanted to rescue everything they could from the flames, but when an attempt was made to rescue the piano, King, fearing loss of lives more than the loss of things, ordered them to stop. (Courtesy King Ranch, Inc., Kingsville, Texas.)

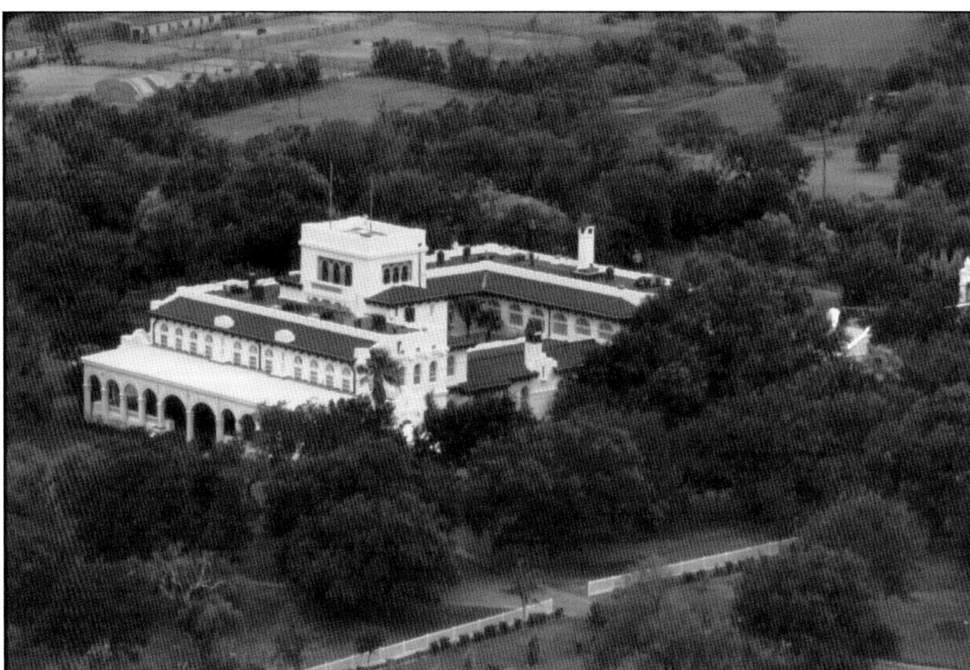

Plans were quickly made to rebuild the King Ranch main residence, and the results are pictured here. It is said that Henrietta King left the details of rebuilding to her son-in-law, Robert Kleberg, with only one stipulation: the house must be one where anybody could enter wearing boots. (Courtesy King Ranch, Inc., Kingsville, Texas.)

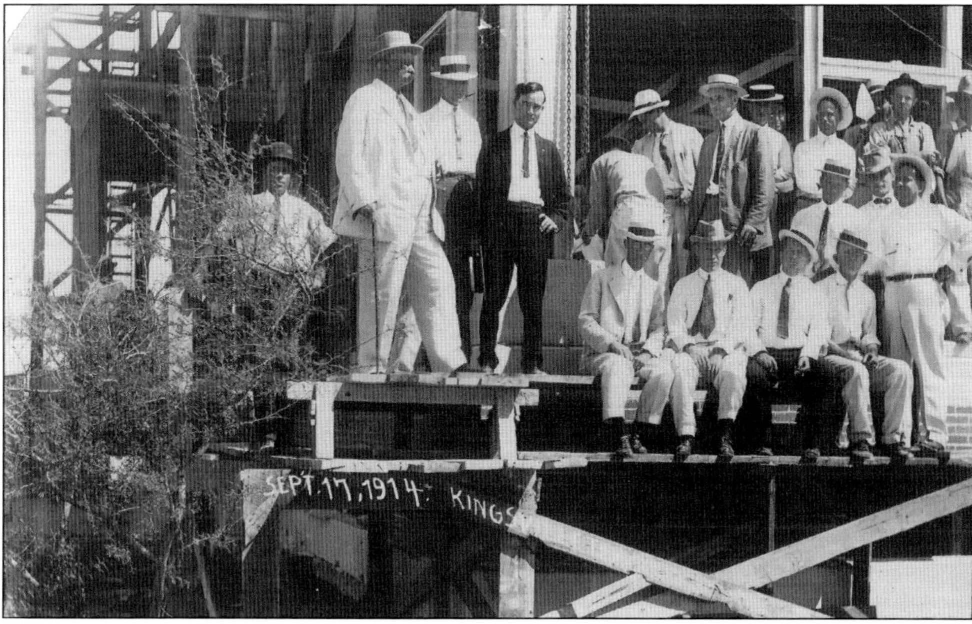

Kleberg County was created and organized in 1913. The 33rd state legislature carved the new county from 698 square miles of Nueces County. This September 1914 picture shows community leaders gathered on the scaffolding of the new courthouse. Construction of the Kleberg County Courthouse was completed in January 1915. (Courtesy South Texas Archives, Texas A&M University-Kingsville.)

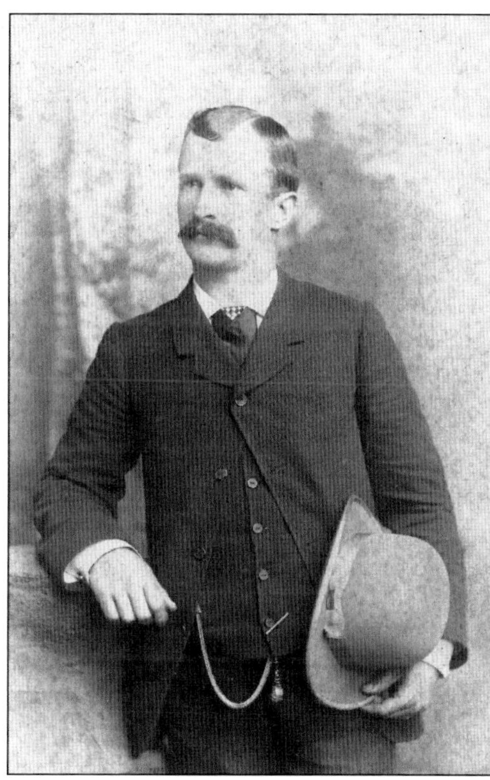

This photograph of M.O. Milliken was taken around 1920. Milliken was the first sheriff of Kleberg County, a position he held for about a year. Jim Scarborough and Tom Moseley, who each served longer terms in office, followed Milliken. Bootlegging, horse thieving, and cattle rustling were some of the criminal activities in early Kleberg County. (Courtesy South Texas Archives, Texas A&M University-Kingsville.)

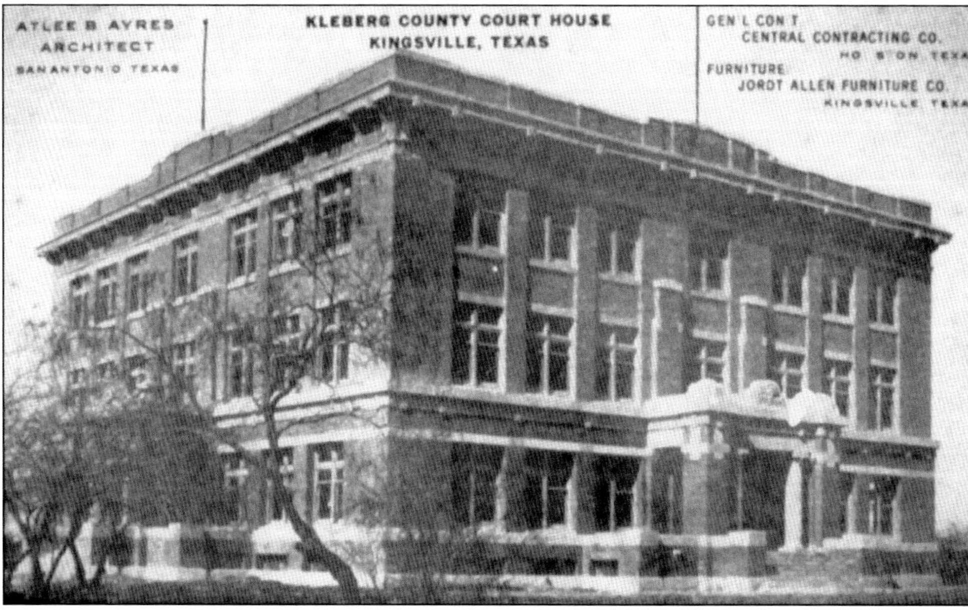

In 1914, the *Kingsville Record* kept track of the construction efforts for the new "Temple of Justice." Detailed descriptions were made of the marble wainscot that would be used throughout the Kleberg County Courthouse, and the beautiful gray marble was on display at the construction site for all of Kingsville to view. (Courtesy King Ranch, Inc., Kingsville, Texas.)

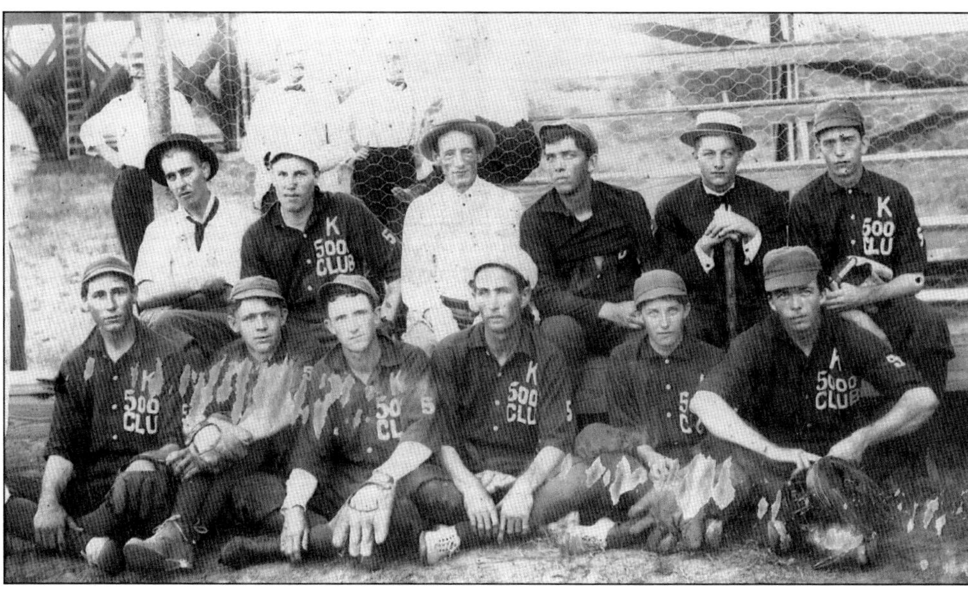

Pictured here is the baseball team for the 5000 Club of Kingsville. The purpose of the 5000 Club was to encourage people to take up residence in Kingsville. The goal was a population of 5,000 citizens. Numerous community organizations promoted settlement in Kingsville over the years. Railroad booster clubs also advocated for the development and improvement of the young populace. (Courtesy King Ranch, Inc., Kingsville, Texas.)

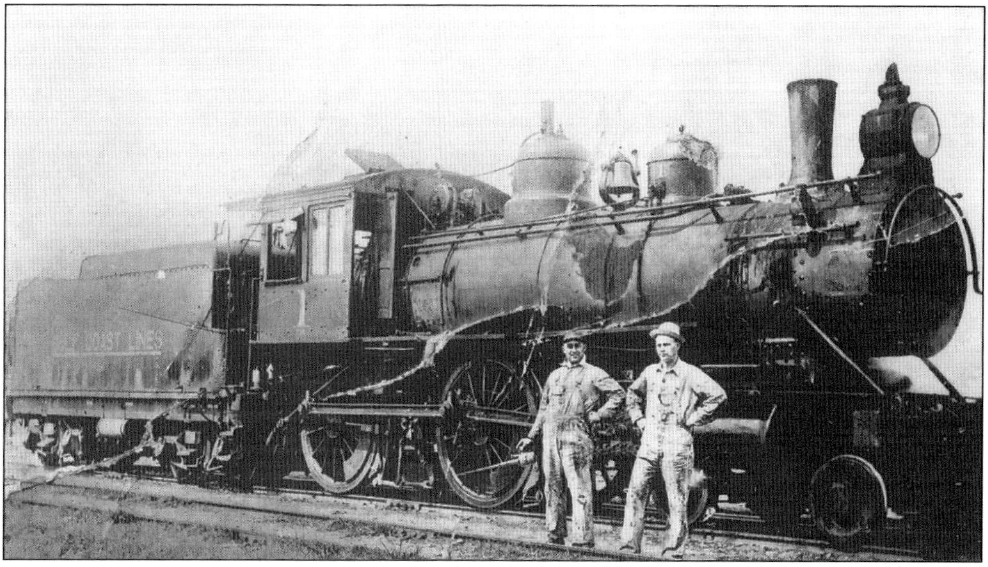

In the early 1900s, the railroad threw nothing away. The original locomotive no. 1 from the StLB&M railroad was repainted with the Gulf Coast Lines logo. This first locomotive was seen up and down the line for decades. Pictured here in front of the no. 1 are engineer Joe Bodin (left) and fireman R.F. Kirkpatrick. (Courtesy South Texas Archives, Texas A&M University-Kingsville.)

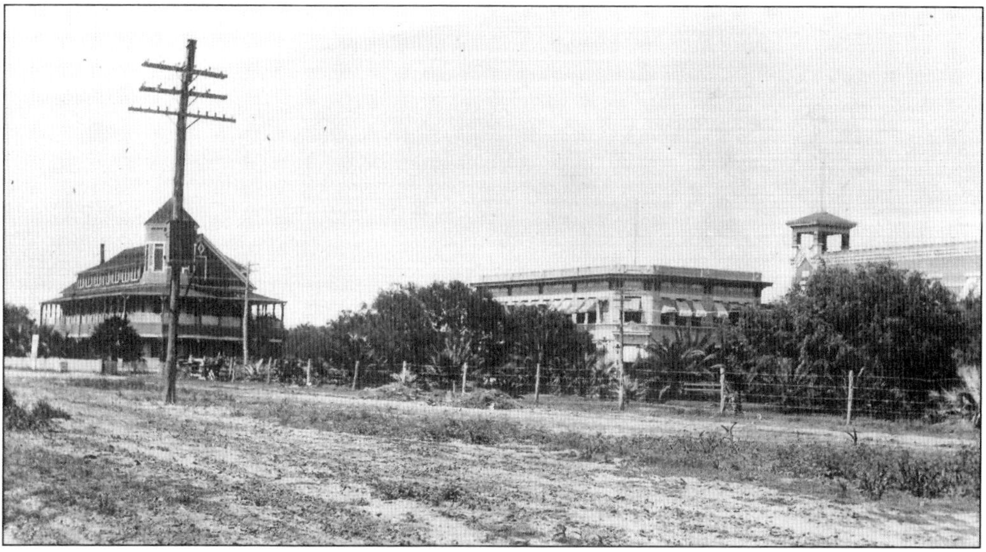

This image of the King's Inn Hotel (left), the Kleberg Bank (center), and John B. Ragland Mercantile Company was taken about 1910 or 1911. The view looks through Caesar Park, where Kingsville's first artesian well was located. (Courtesy South Texas Archives, Texas A&M University-Kingsville.)

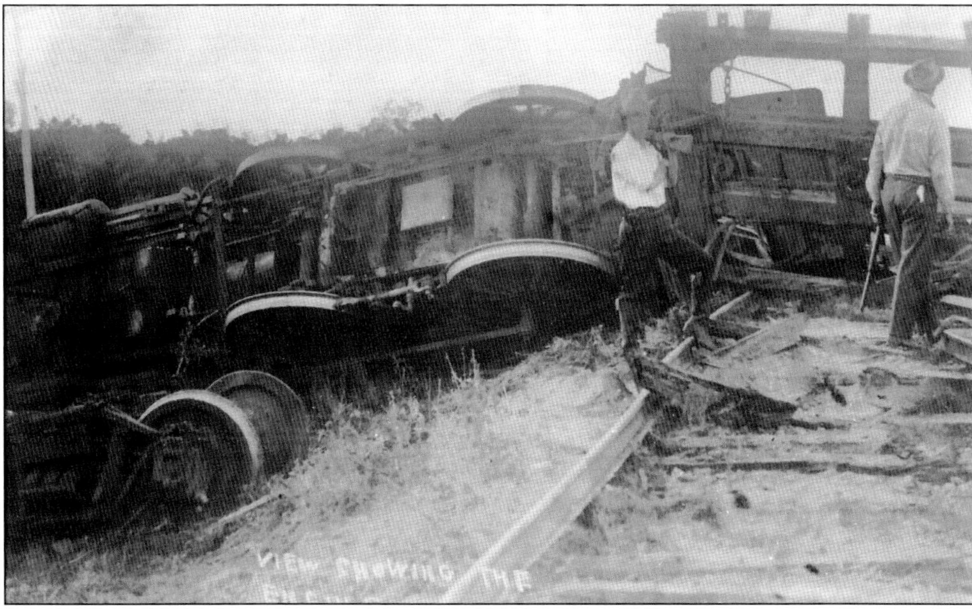

The scene from 1915 shows a StLB&M train wreck just north of Olmito, Texas, in which "Mexican bandits" wrecked the train. The railroad faced a serious crisis as the trains bringing new families into South Texas dwindled and ranching and agriculture were threatened on the Mexican border. Kingsville, though far north of the problematic region, felt the tension of the times. (Courtesy South Texas Archives, Texas A&M University-Kingsville.)

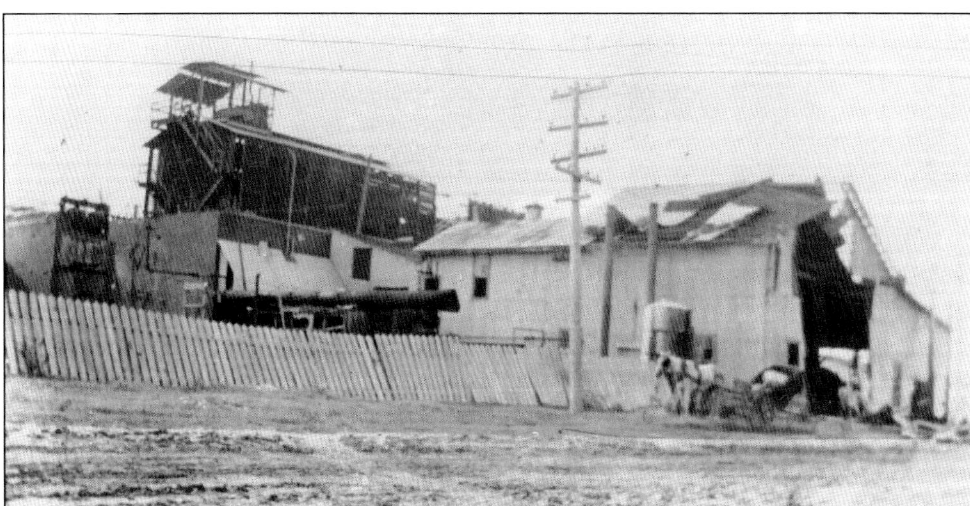

Weather was a constant issue in the Wild Horse Desert. Drought was a problem for agriculture, and Kingsville was not immune to hurricanes. On August 18, 1916, a storm nearly washed the town away. The damage to the Kingsville Power Company shown here was caused by the 1916 hurricane. (Courtesy South Texas Archives, Texas A&M University-Kingsville.)

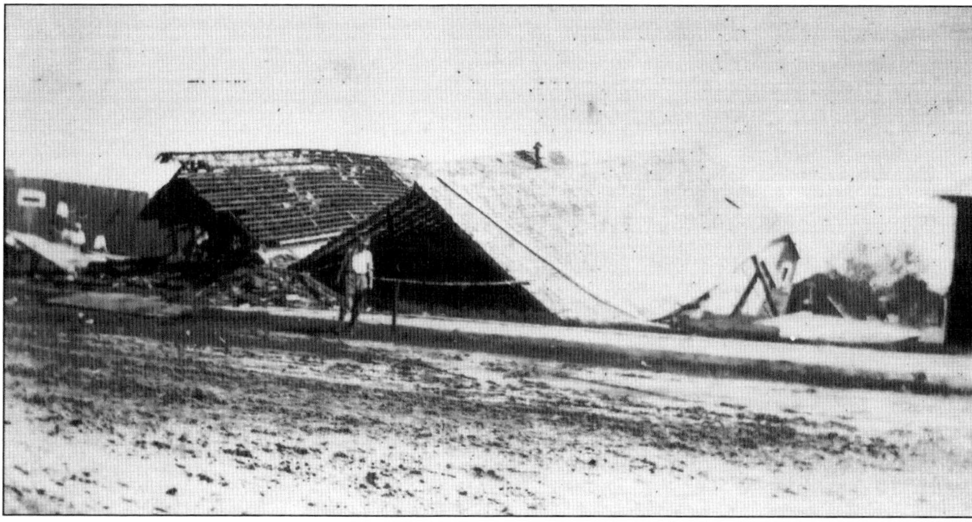

Many frame buildings collapsed during the hurricane. The building codes of the early 20th century were nothing compared to modern requirements. Several automobiles stored in the Ford Garage on Kleberg Avenue between Seventh and Eighth Streets were crushed under the collapsed roof in the 1916 hurricane. (Courtesy South Texas Archives, Texas A&M University-Kingsville.)

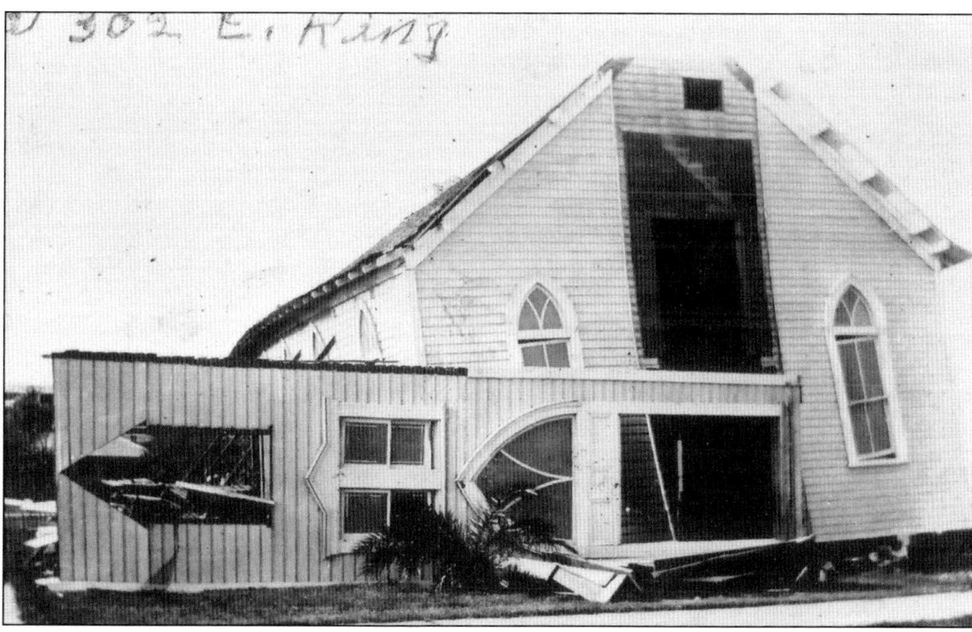

In 1916, hurricanes were not yet being named, but the one that struck Kingsville has been estimated to have been a Category 4 storm that made landfall on Padre Island. According to National Weather Service records, there were at least 20 fatalities. This picture shows hurricane damage to St. Gertrude's Catholic Church at 302 East King Avenue. (Courtesy South Texas Archives, Texas A&M University-Kingsville.)

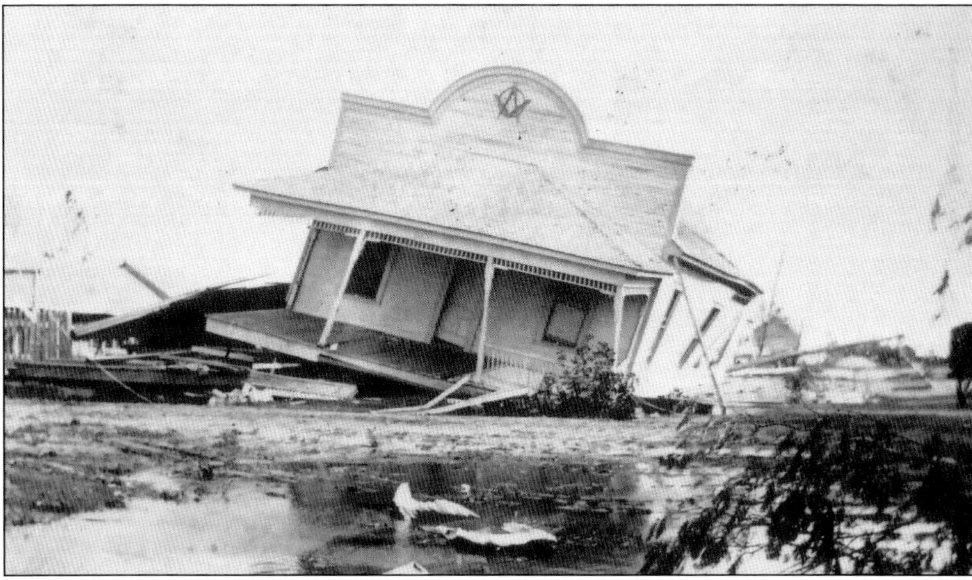

This photograph shows damage to the Kingsville Lumber and Hardware Company caused by the 1916 hurricane. The community had no warning that the terrible storm was coming. Citizens noted a very hot and sultry day before the storm hit. Some estimates placed the total cost of regional damage at $1,800,000. Another hurricane in 1919 also caused significant damage. (Courtesy South Texas Archives, Texas A&M University-Kingsville.)

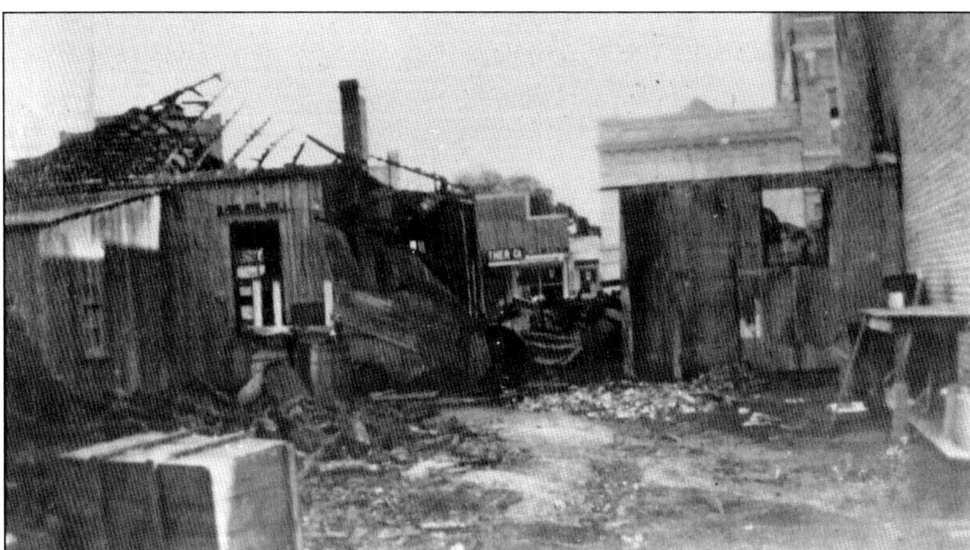

There was little left of the Busy Bee restaurant, viewed here from behind, after a huge fire in 1918. The blaze destroyed five frame businesses on the north side of Kleberg Avenue. The two-story brick structure at right was built in 1911 and survived the 1918 fire. (Courtesy South Texas Archives, Texas A&M University-Kingsville.)

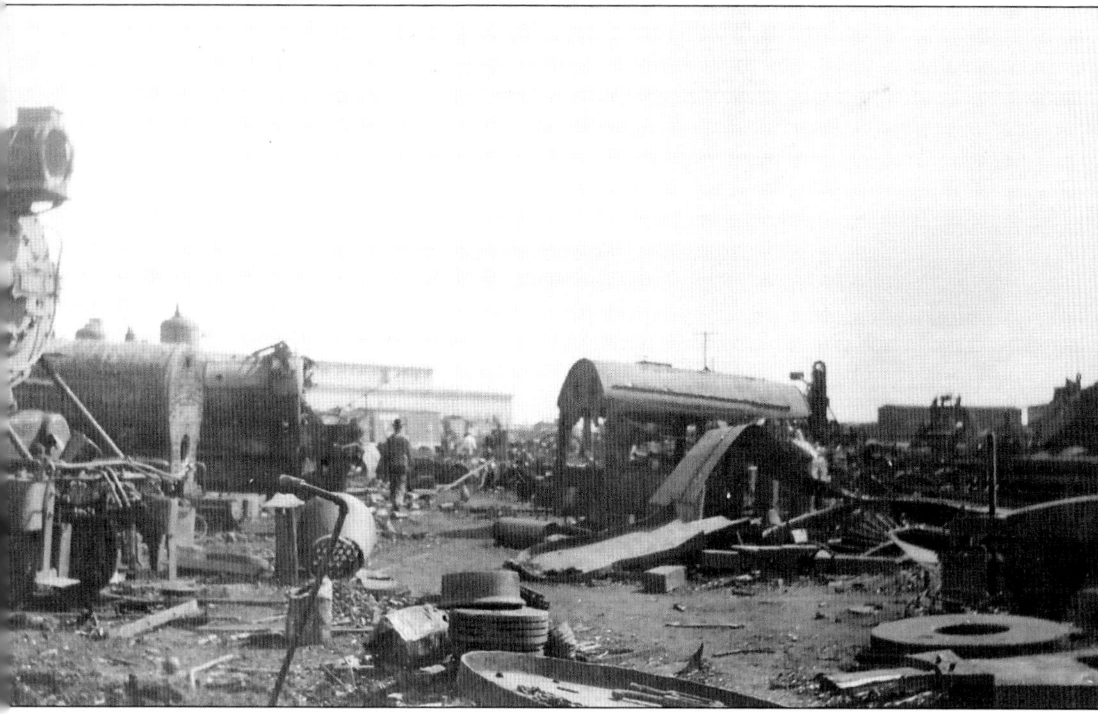

On October 1, 1920, a lit lantern carelessly left in a roundhouse locker started an epic blaze. The day after the Kingsville roundhouse fire, the front page of the *Corpus Christi Caller-Times* screamed, "$1,000,000 fire damage in Kingsville," and offered an apocalyptic account of the sky filled with firebrands and workers struggling to move the precious locomotives out of the burning buildings with their bare hands. That night, Kingsville's main industry, the railroad, almost died. By morning, railroad officials were able to make a better evaluation of the damage. There were 14 locomotives in and around the shop building, but only nine were in the roundhouse. The woodwork on the locomotives was burned, but the engines were salvageable. Estimates of the actual losses were reduced to $250,000. Work started immediately to repair the damage, and trains were running on schedule within a day of the disaster. (Courtesy South Texas Archives, Texas A&M University-Kingsville.)

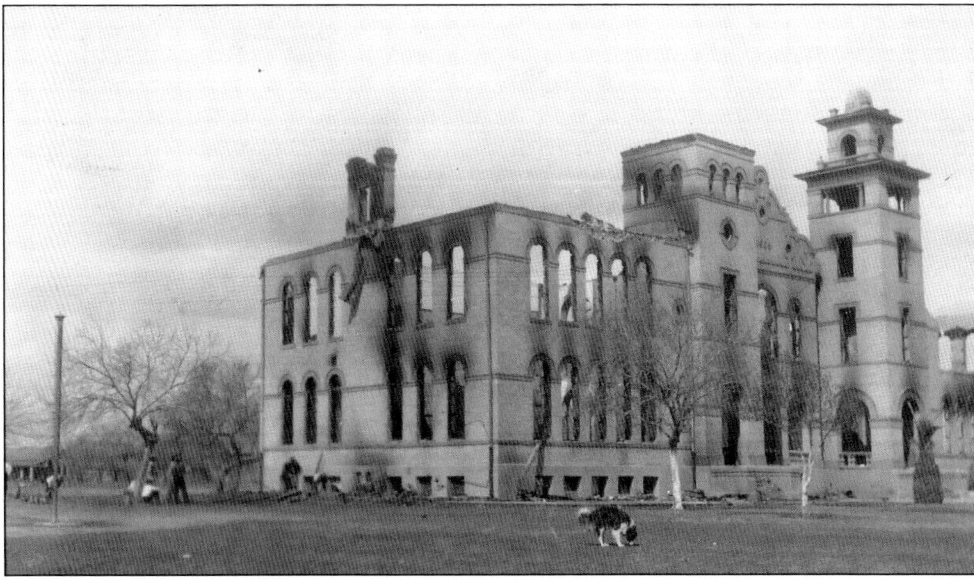

In February 1925, the *Kingsville Record* reported the saddest disaster of Kingsville's young life: when fire destroyed the beautiful Henrietta M. King High School. The fire started in the northwest corner of the building. The fire alarm was sounded at 1:00 a.m., and the building was still burning at 8:00 a.m. The town's water supply was totally exhausted in fighting the blaze. (Courtesy South Texas Archives, Texas A&M University-Kingsville.)

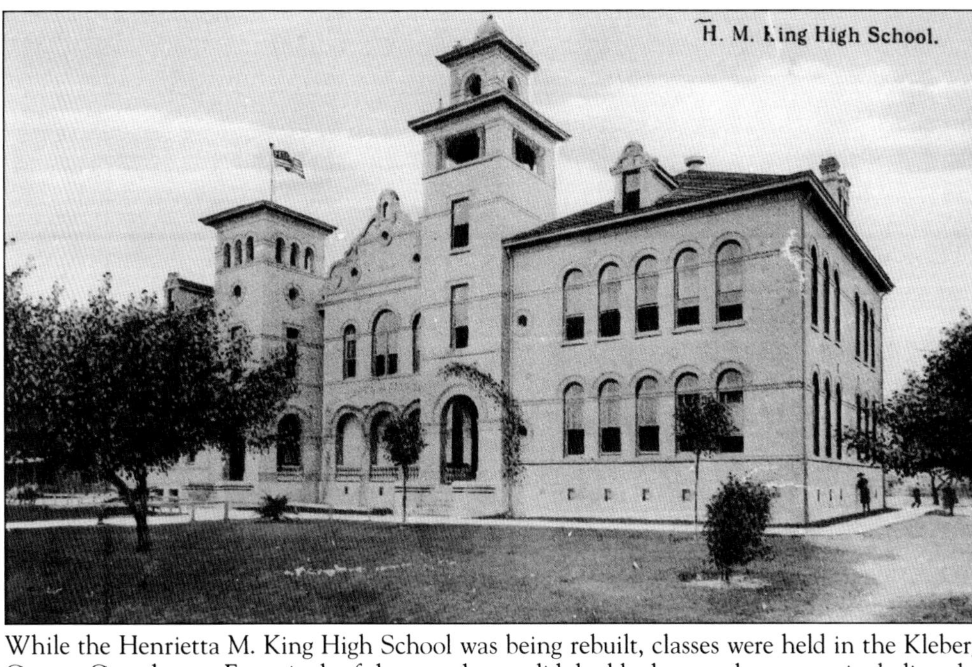

While the Henrietta M. King High School was being rebuilt, classes were held in the Kleberg County Courthouse. Every inch of the courthouse did double duty as classrooms, including the spacious courtroom and the clammy basement. A bond issue secured the funds for rebuilding, repairs were completed, and classes returned to the school building within a year. (Courtesy South Texas Archives, Texas A&M University-Kingsville.)

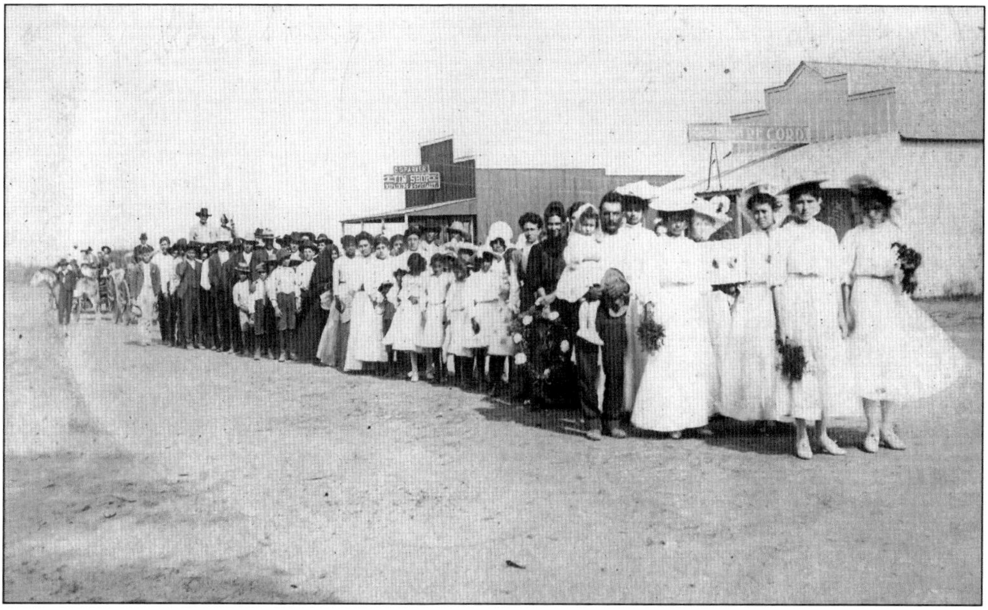

On April 15, 1909, most of Kingsville came out to attend a child's funeral. On the right, behind the funeral procession, is the Gulf Coast Record Building at 219 East Kleberg Avenue. A beautiful brick structure, the Toner/Finnegan Building, was erected at the site in later years. Toner took over editorship of the *Kingsville Record*. (Courtesy South Texas Archives, Texas A&M University-Kingsville.)

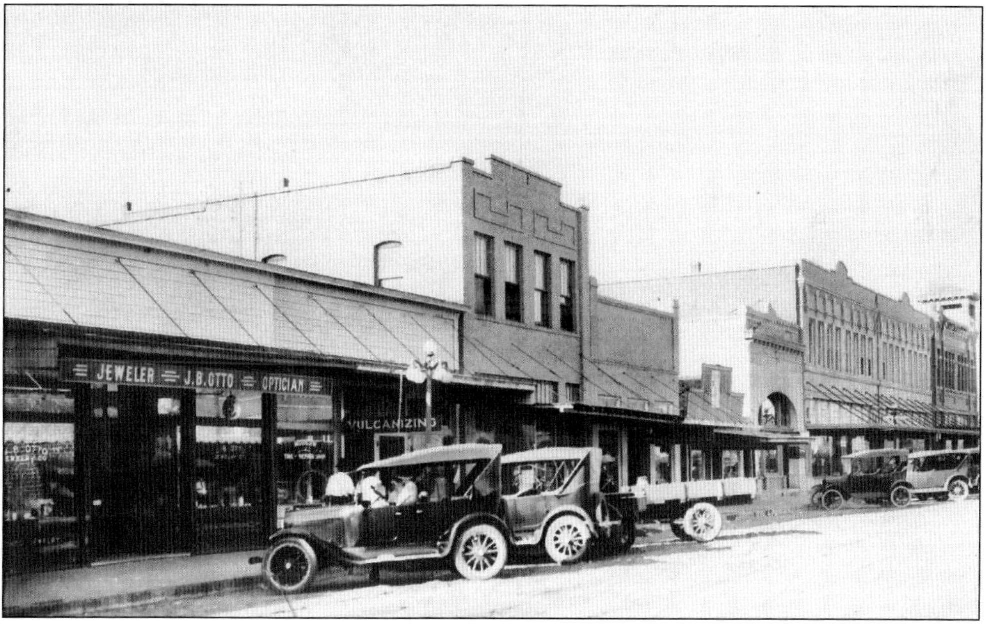

The two-story structure in the center of this picture is the Toner Building. It housed the *Kingsville Record* newspaper from 1909, when the building was constructed, until 1915, when the newspaper moved its office. In 1917, the growing city government needed more space, and the Toner Building began to serve as Kingsville City Hall. (Courtesy South Texas Archives, Texas A&M University-Kingsville.)

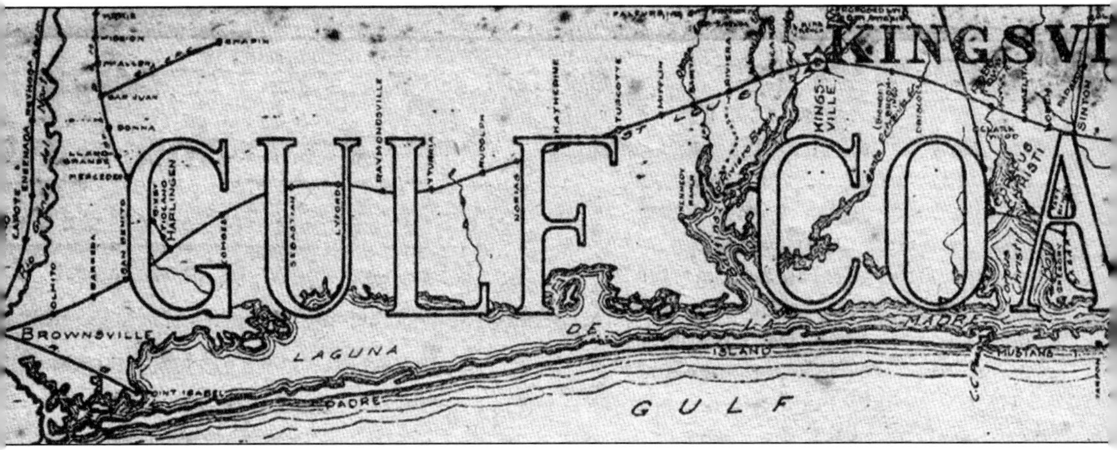

Small-town newspapers are the historic threads of a community and the link from a community's history to its present. This is especially true for the *Kingsville Record and Bishop News*, which started in 1906 as the *Gulf Coast Record*. After Kingsville voted to incorporate, the first official meeting of the incorporated town was held on November 28, 1911, and the *Gulf Coast Record* was made

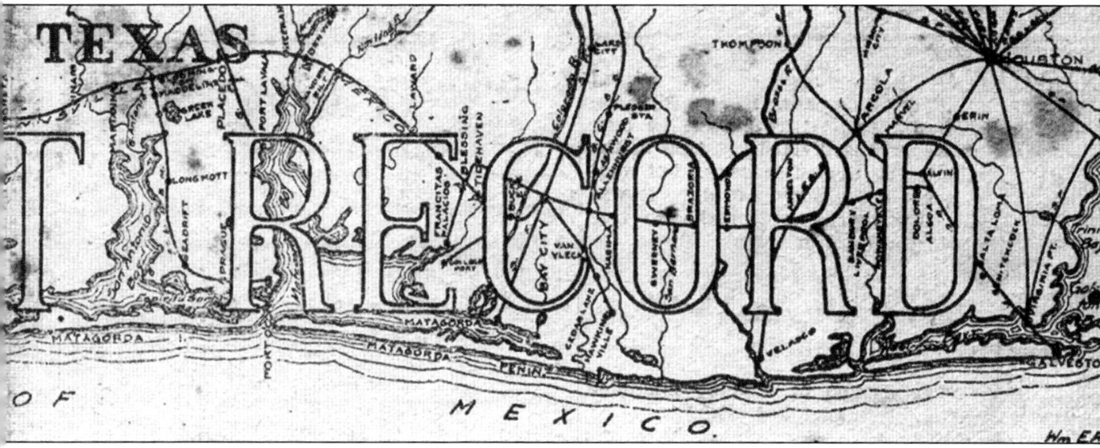

the official periodical of the town of Kingsville. With the exception of a few gaps caused by fire and other disasters, the *Kingsville Record* has recorded the history of the town. This beautiful banner was created for a special edition of the *Gulf Coast Record.* (Courtesy Kingsville Record and Bishop News.)

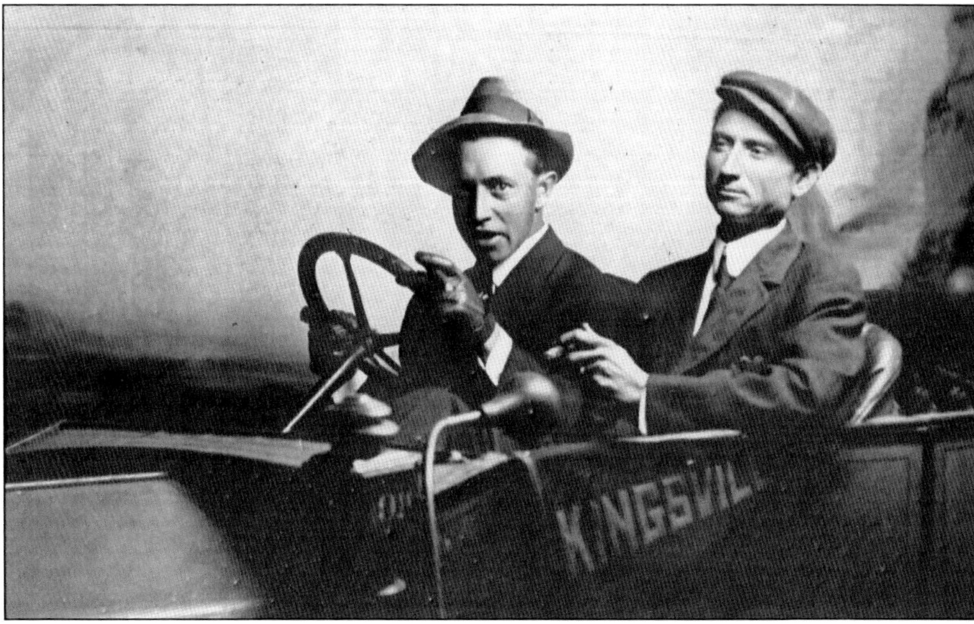

Ed Erard (left) is pictured here with Marcus Phillips. Erard was sometimes called "Mr. Kingsville" because of his persistent activities promoting the town. He started his career as a railroader, but a serious rail accident cut off half of his right arm and ended his railroading career. He was the editor of the *Kingsville Record* for decades. (Courtesy South Texas Archives, Texas A&M University-Kingsville.)

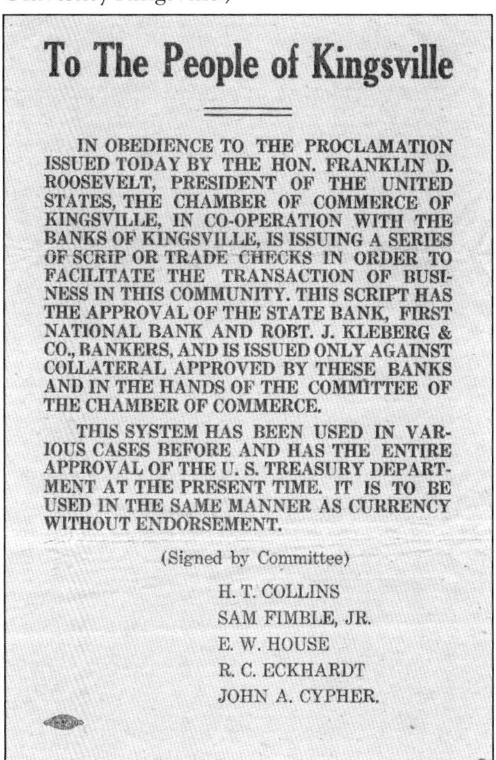

To The People of Kingsville

IN OBEDIENCE TO THE PROCLAMATION ISSUED TODAY BY THE HON. FRANKLIN D. ROOSEVELT, PRESIDENT OF THE UNITED STATES, THE CHAMBER OF COMMERCE OF KINGSVILLE, IN CO-OPERATION WITH THE BANKS OF KINGSVILLE, IS ISSUING A SERIES OF SCRIP OR TRADE CHECKS IN ORDER TO FACILITATE THE TRANSACTION OF BUSINESS IN THIS COMMUNITY. THIS SCRIPT HAS THE APPROVAL OF THE STATE BANK, FIRST NATIONAL BANK AND ROBT. J. KLEBERG & CO., BANKERS, AND IS ISSUED ONLY AGAINST COLLATERAL APPROVED BY THESE BANKS AND IN THE HANDS OF THE COMMITTEE OF THE CHAMBER OF COMMERCE.

THIS SYSTEM HAS BEEN USED IN VARIOUS CASES BEFORE AND HAS THE ENTIRE APPROVAL OF THE U. S. TREASURY DEPARTMENT AT THE PRESENT TIME. IT IS TO BE USED IN THE SAME MANNER AS CURRENCY WITHOUT ENDORSEMENT.

(Signed by Committee)

H. T. COLLINS
SAM FIMBLE, JR.
E. W. HOUSE
R. C. ECKHARDT
JOHN A. CYPHER.

The 1930s put the whole nation under stress. Ed Erard, editor of the *Kingsville Record*, came back from an Austin lobbying trip with the knowledge that the federal government would soon order a bank holiday. The city issued a proclamation, and the chamber of commerce printed trade scrip for businesses and individuals to use while the banks were closed. (Courtesy South Texas Archives, Texas A&M University-Kingsville.)

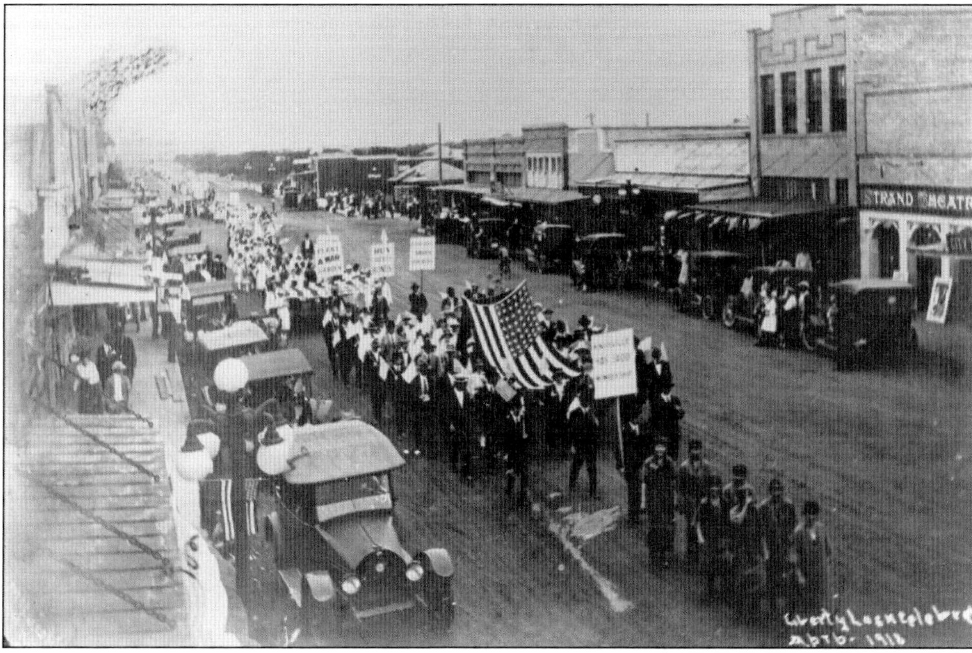

This photograph, titled "Liberty Loan Celebration," is dated April 6, 1918. The buildings at right, on the south side of the street, illustrate how the community had grown. The two-story structure is the Toner Building, which housed Kingsville City Hall. The Strand Theatre is next door. (Courtesy South Texas Archives, Texas A&M University-Kingsville.)

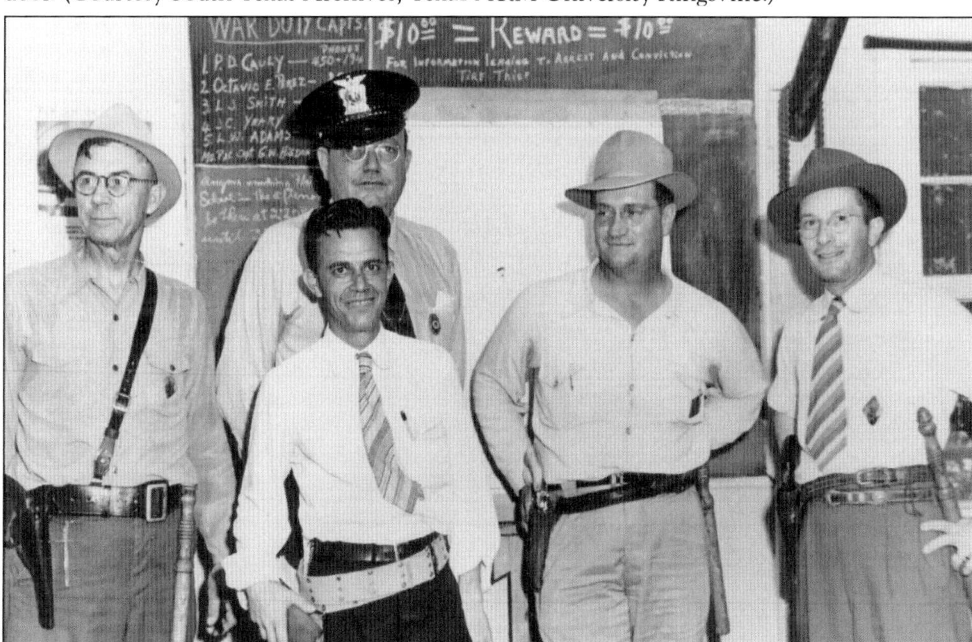

Kingsville was never shy about community defense. The World War II war-duty police pictured here, from left to right, are L.W. Adams Sr., W.E. "Shorty" Newton, J.C. "Cy" Yearly, Charles Flato III, and, in back, police chief Archie Goode. No one was going to mess with their town. (Courtesy South Texas Archives, Texas A&M University-Kingsville.)

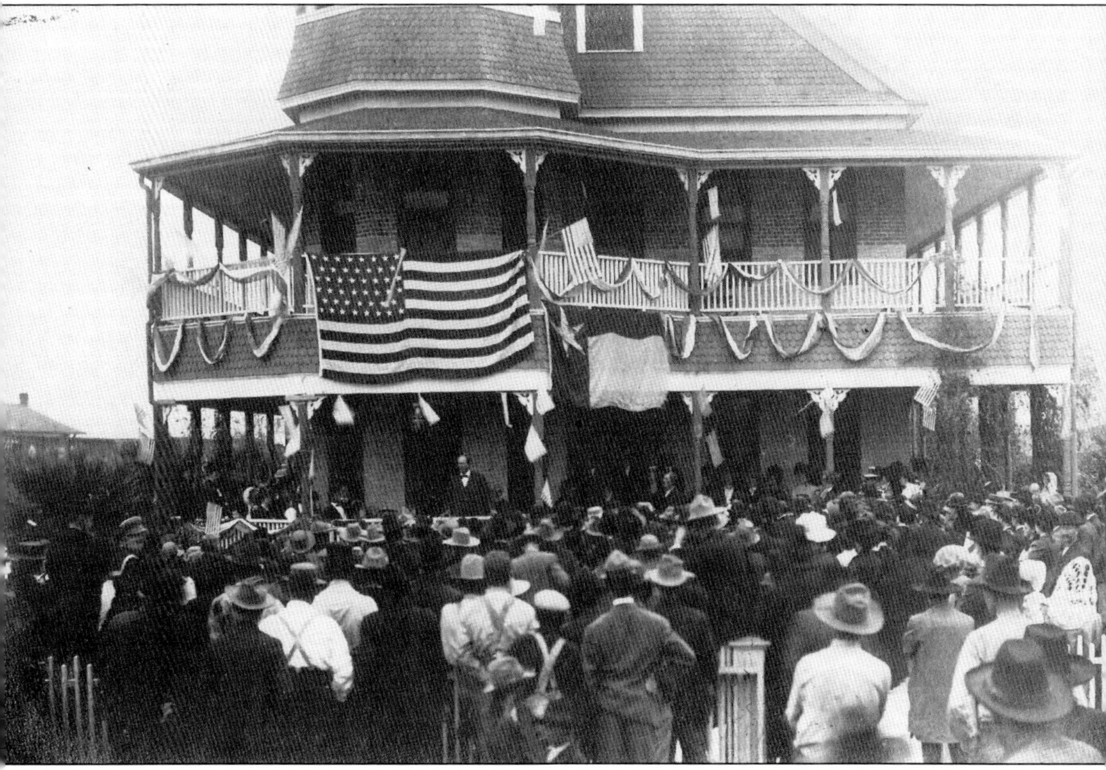

In this image from around 1910, folks gather at the King's Inn Hotel to hear a visiting speaker. Early newspaper articles described speakers at special events, complete with the text of their speeches. The speaker might be a community leader or a political candidate. Perhaps a visiting minister would give a rousing religious speech, or a visiting educator would encourage the community to closely tend to the education of their children. Businesspeople and railroad managers took turns at oratory in early Kingsville and always drew a crowd. (Courtesy South Texas Archives, Texas A&M University-Kingsville.)

Three

Churches and Schools

Kingsville was born in the age of racial segregation. There were three communities within one town—white, African American, and Hispanic. With such sentiments prominent, early brochures promoting the town used the careful racial segregation as a selling point in the same way they used the numerous churches in the community as a selling point for people to settle in Kingsville.

Henrietta King's influence in the town was strong. She encouraged congregations and churches by donating land to each Christian church wanting to build in Kingsville. She discouraged the use of alcoholic beverages by specifying in property deeds that the sale of alcohol on said property would result in that land's ownership reverting back to King Ranch. She also gave large amounts of money and land specifically for building schools and educational facilities.

Efforts were made early on by the local churches to have visiting congregations worship together to bridge the gaps caused by institutional segregation. The free market and specific encouragement from community leaders such as Luis and Manuela Fuentes, of the El Nuevo Mundo department store, and Charles Andrews helped with integration breakthroughs for local businesses.

Education was a big part of the community's history. Whole books could be written about the efforts of the different ethnic groups of people to provide a way for their children to get quality educations. The African American and Hispanic communities made heroic efforts to provide the best educations possible to their children. Hispanic students attended Henrietta M. King High School as early as the 1940s. The school board finally built a school in the African American community in 1913. It was replaced with a larger school, the Frederick Douglass School, in the 1940s, and that building remained in use by the town until 1969. On July 15, 1955, the Kingsville School Board unanimously voted to desegregate H.M. King High School, allowing all students to attend and complete their high school educations at the same school.

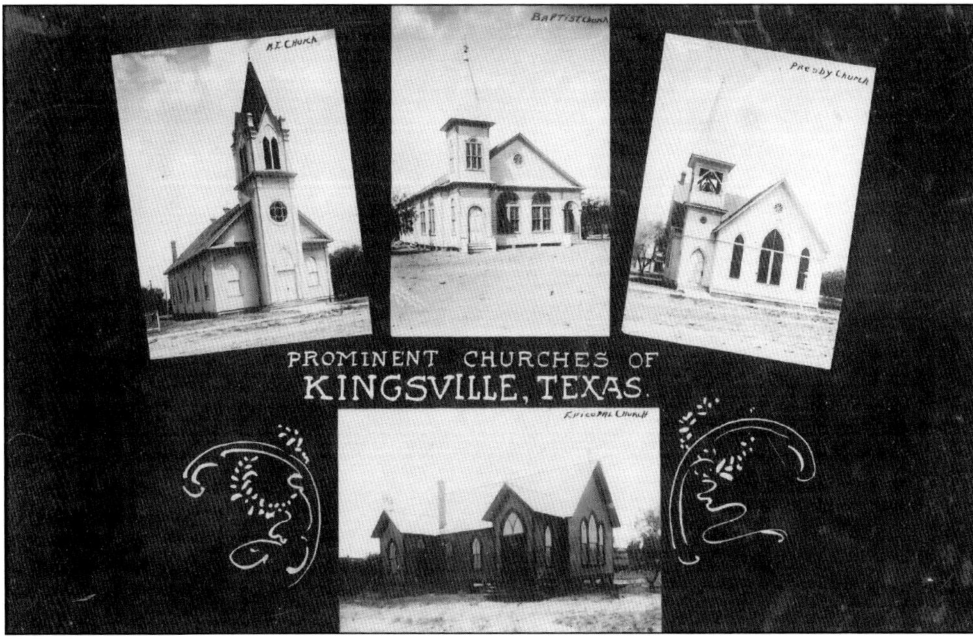

This photographic composite of prominent churches in early Kingsville was printed in a postcard format. Henrietta King wanted a strong Christian influence in town and made the building of churches as easy and welcome as possible. The many Christian denominations in early Kingsville became a selling point in enticing visitors to settle there. (Courtesy South Texas Archives, Texas A&M University-Kingsville.)

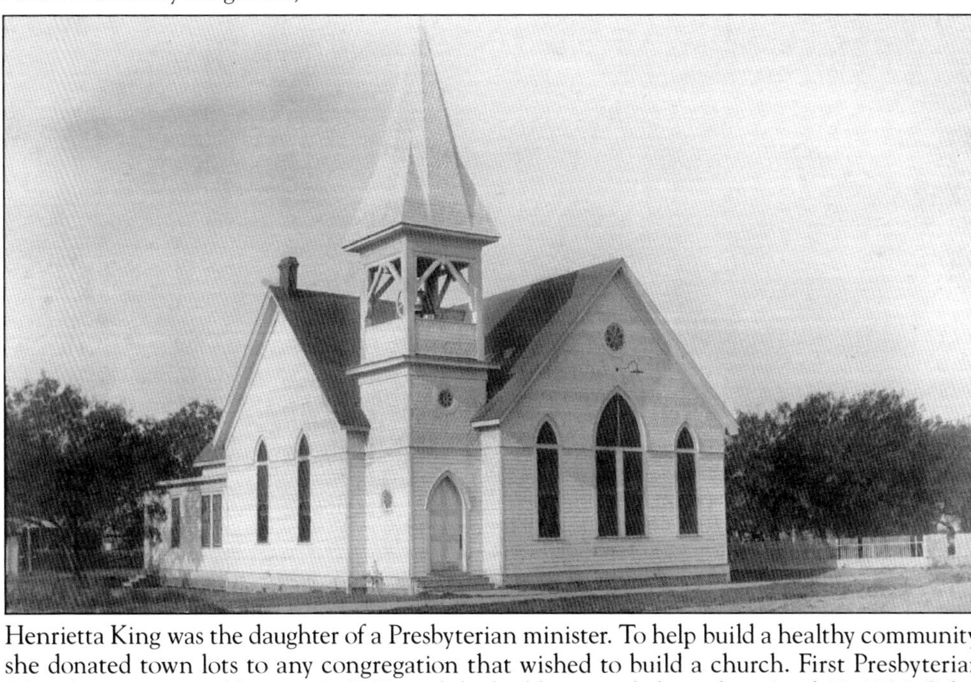

Henrietta King was the daughter of a Presbyterian minister. To help build a healthy community, she donated town lots to any congregation that wished to build a church. First Presbyterian Church was organized January 8, 1905, and the building was dedicated on April 18, 1906. Other congregations were welcome to use the church to conduct services while their own churches were being constructed. (Courtesy King Ranch, Inc., Kingsville, Texas.)

The first Methodist worship services were held in a grove of mesquite trees in March 1904. The beautiful First Methodist Church was erected in 1908 and hosted the congregation's first services in January 1909. This building was moved in 1950 and became Scott's Chapel Methodist Church, in the African American community. (Courtesy King Ranch, Inc., Kingsville, Texas.)

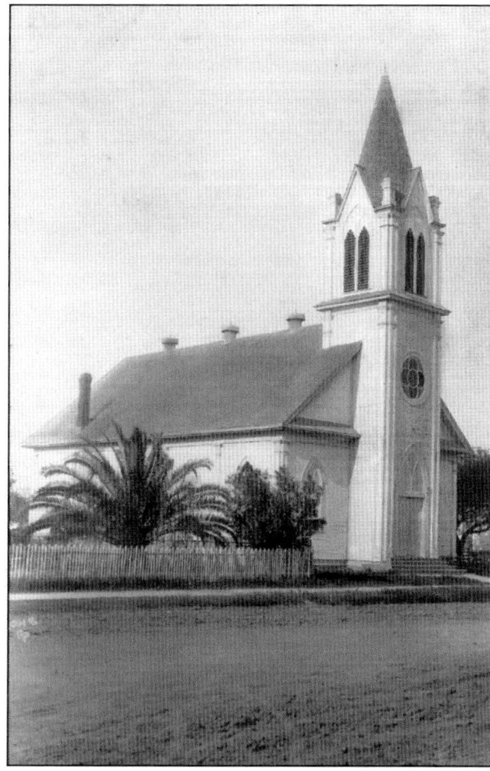

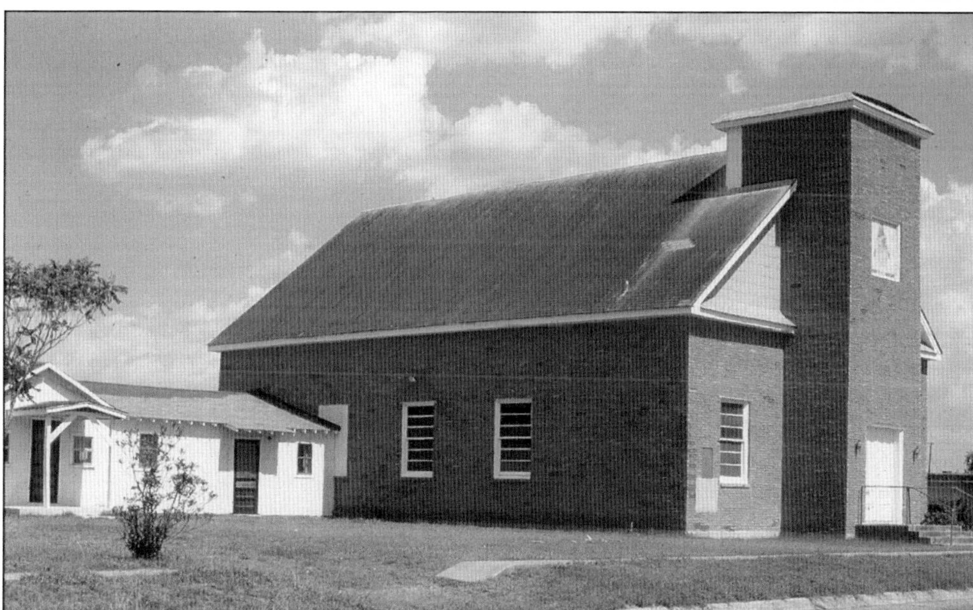

Scott's Chapel UMC is the Methodist church in the African American community known as The Quarters. It was established in 1908 and held services in various locations until First Methodist Church donated this structure to Scott's Chapel in 1950. The building had to be divided into two parts for the move to its present location. (Courtesy South Texas Archives, Texas A&M University-Kingsville.)

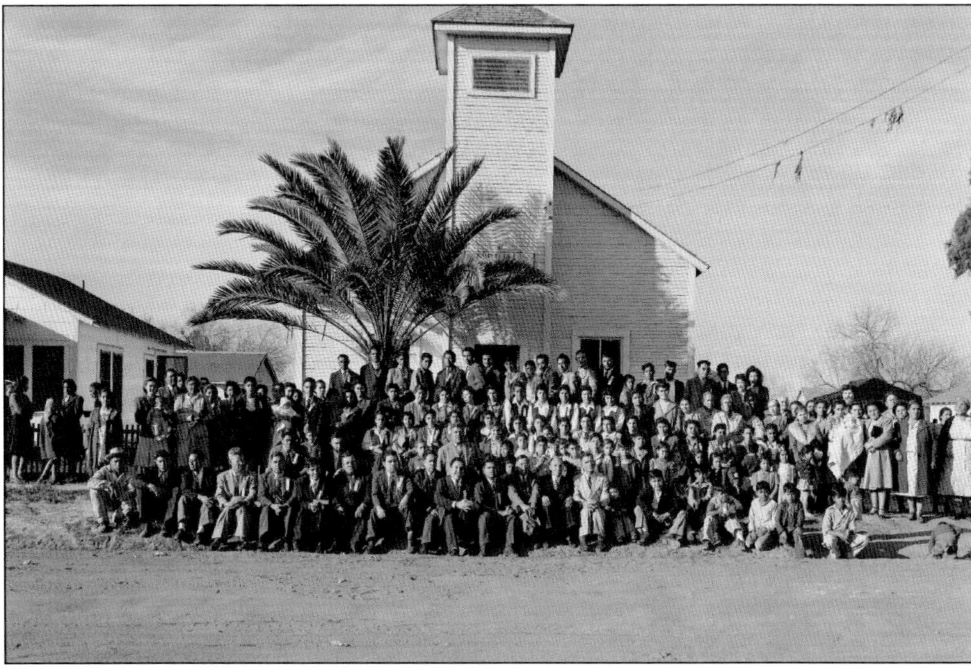

El Buen Pastor United Methodist Church, called the "Mexican Methodist Church" by the photographer, is located at Ninth Street and Alice Avenue. It was established in 1914 to serve the Spanish-speaking Methodist community. (Courtesy Dolph Briscoe Center for American History, The University of Texas at Austin, Mexican Methodist Church, Dodd (Jimmie) Photographic Collection, Creator: Dodd, Jimmie.)

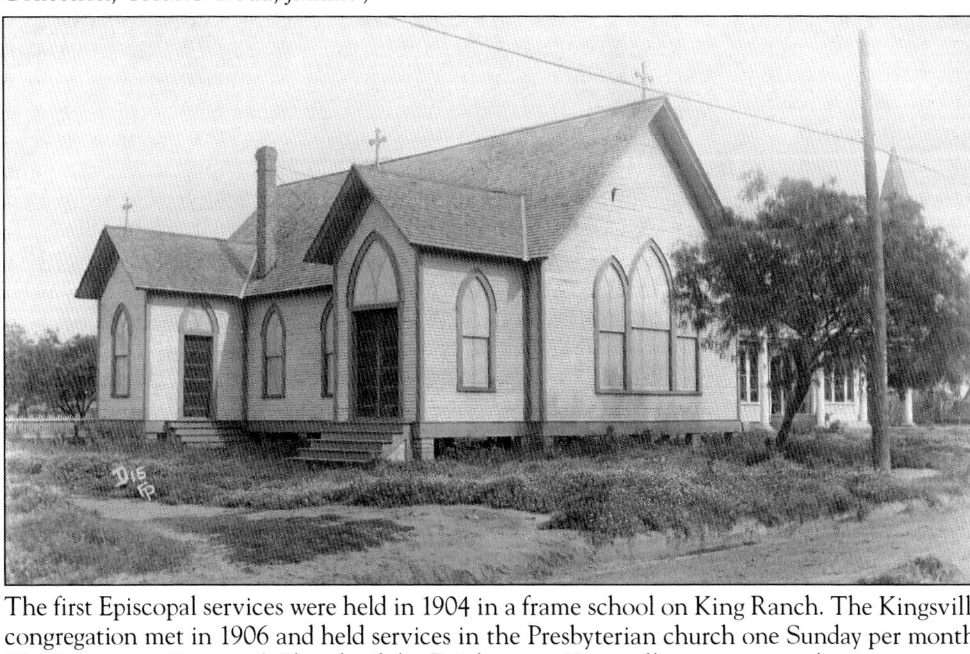

The first Episcopal services were held in 1904 in a frame school on King Ranch. The Kingsville congregation met in 1906 and held services in the Presbyterian church one Sunday per month. The Protestant Episcopal Church of the Epiphany in Kingsville was organized as a mission in 1908. The first services were held March 5, 1910, and the first church building was dedicated on January 23, 1912. (Courtesy King Ranch, Inc., Kingsville, Texas.)

The first Catholic services were held in the King's Inn Hotel in February 1908. The first church building for St. Gertrude's Catholic Church, seen here around 1908 or 1909, was on King Avenue and Seventh Street, but that structure was badly damaged in the 1916 hurricane and totally destroyed by the 1919 hurricane. The church was rebuilt. St. Gertrude's Catholic Church helped to establish St. Martin Catholic Church. (Courtesy King Ranch, Inc., Kingsville, Texas.)

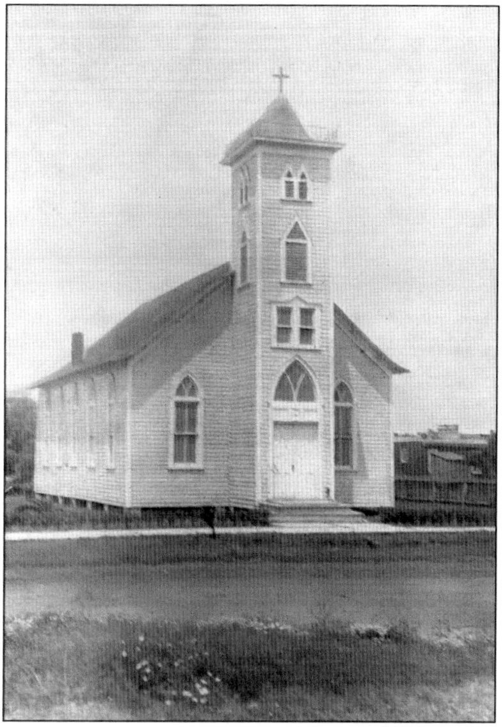

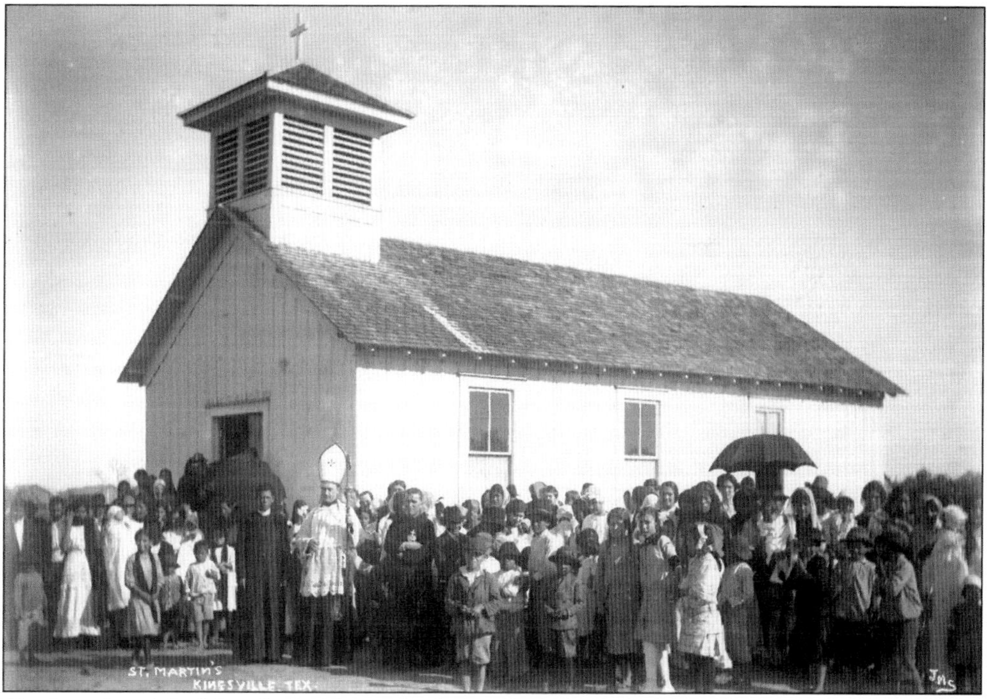

The first church building for St. Martin Catholic Church was constructed in 1914, and this picture shows the first communion, held in 1915. St. Martin was established to serve the Spanish-speaking Catholic community. The St. Martin parish developed a school that taught in Spanish for half the day and in English for half the day. (Courtesy St. Martin Catholic Church Collection.)

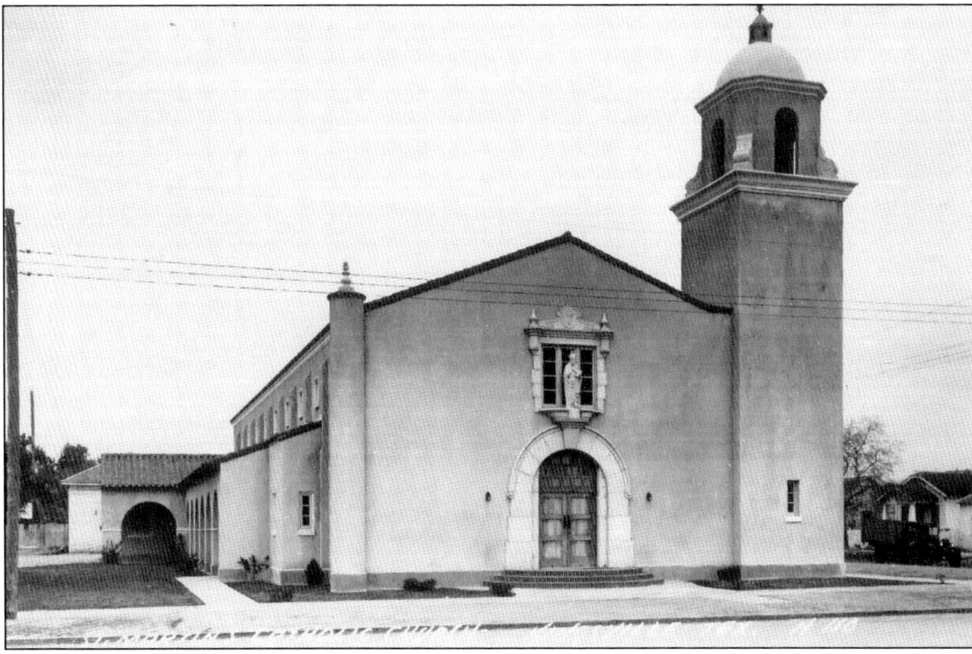

Over the years, there were three St. Martin Catholic Church buildings in Kingsville. The third and current home of the parish was built in 1946 and is located at 715 North Eighth Street. St. Martin is a vibrant focal point of Kingsville's Hispanic Community. (Courtesy King Ranch, Inc., Kingsville, Texas.)

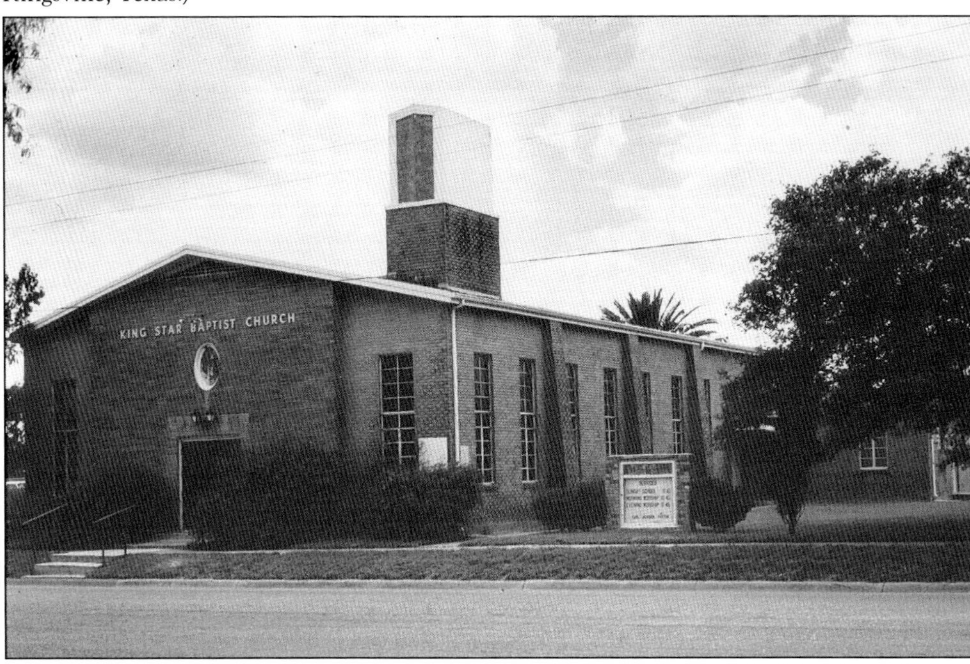

The new King Star Baptist Church is located close to the original church building. King Star was instrumental in the 1950s in bringing the segregated communities of Kingsville together. White and African American congregations would exchange members, visiting and worshiping in each other's churches. (Courtesy South Texas Archives, Texas A&M University-Kingsville.)

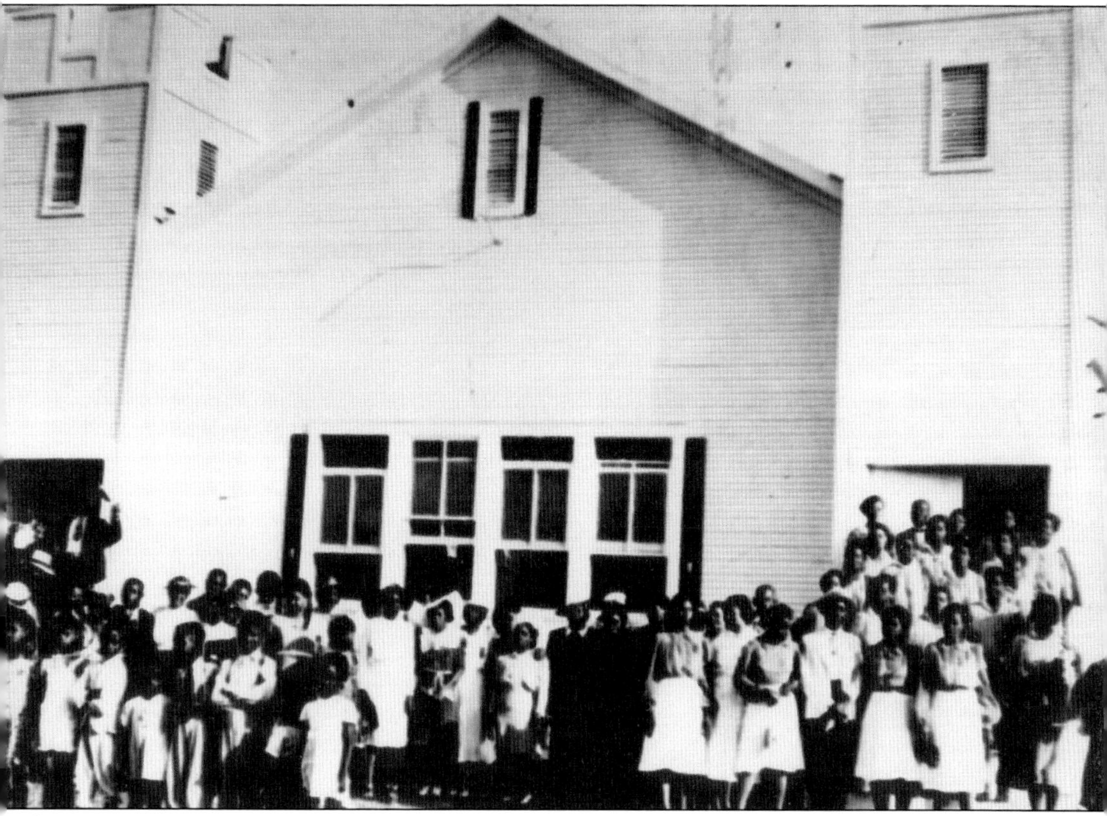

The King Star Baptist Church and congregation are pictured here in 1938. King Star, originally established as a Baptist mission with a traveling minister, was the first African American church in Kingsville. In 1908, the congregation built a church on Fordyce and Second Streets. Because of segregation in education, there was no school for African American children. The congregation insisted its children receive an education, so it took on the task of ensuring those educations by teaching classes and establishing a school within the church. In 1912, rather than build a separate school for a small number of students, the Kingsville School Board approved a payment of $5 per month to King Star Baptist Church for the use of the church facilities as a school. (Courtesy South Texas Archives, Texas A&M University-Kingsville.)

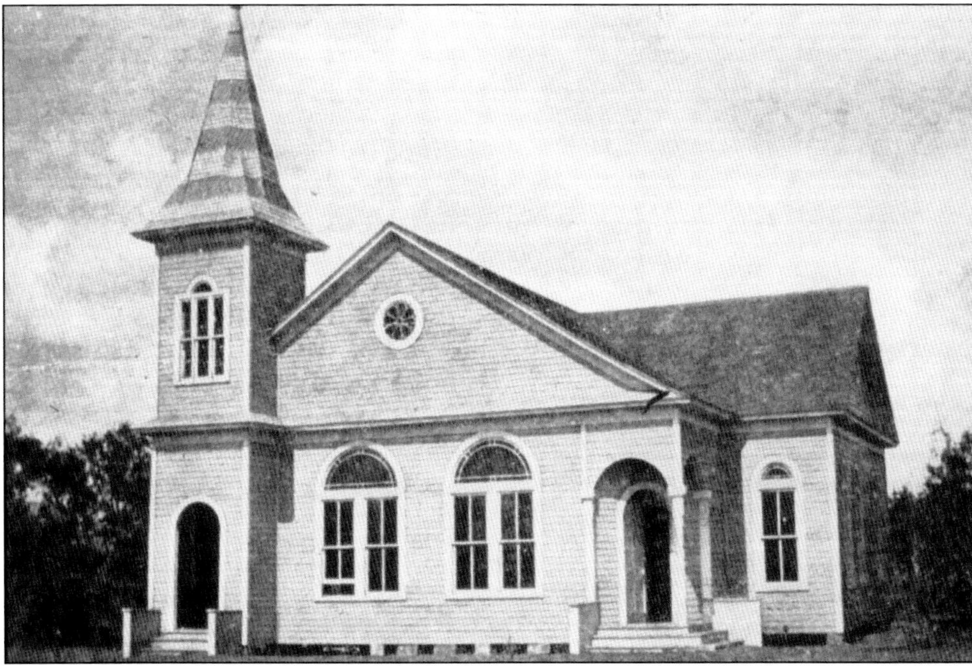

In August 1904, the First Baptist Church in Kingsville was organized by 12 members. This lovely building was constructed in 1907. Mission work was important to this church, and it helped establish the Retama Baptist Church, the University Baptist Church, and the Central Baptist Church. (Courtesy King Ranch, Inc., Kingsville, Texas.)

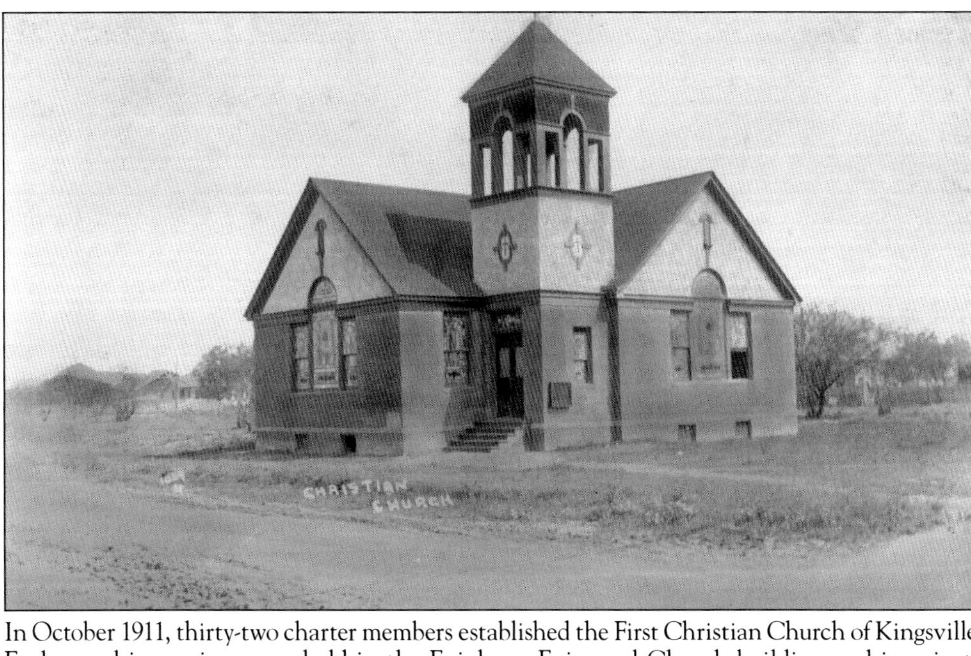

In October 1911, thirty-two charter members established the First Christian Church of Kingsville. Early worship services were held in the Epiphany Episcopal Church building and in private residences. In 1913, the corner of Seventh Street and East King Avenue became the home to the First Christian Church building. (Courtesy King Ranch, Inc., Kingsville, Texas.)

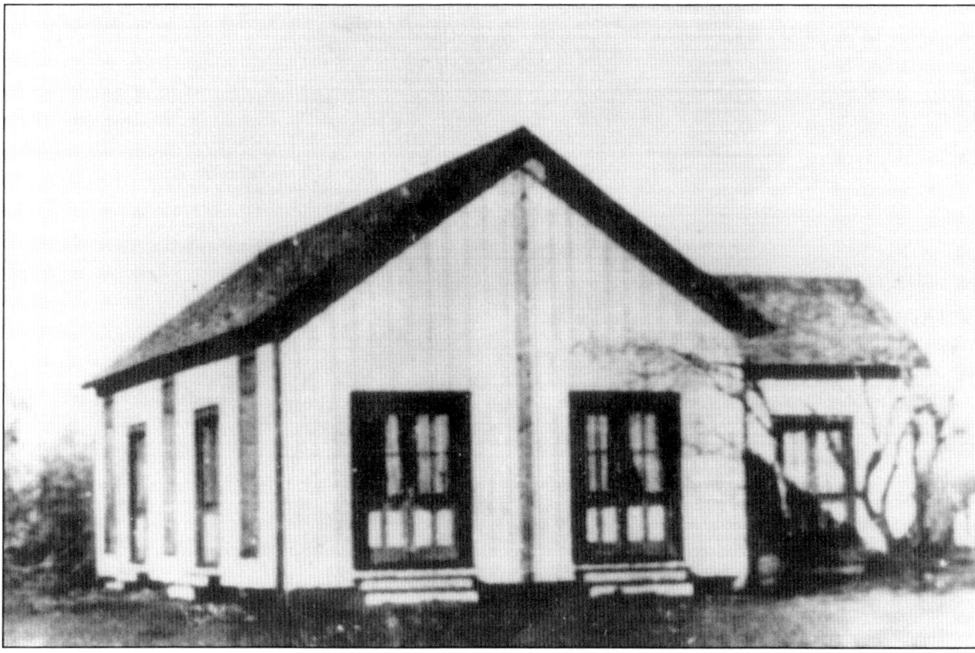

This frame building was Kingsville's first school, constructed in 1906 at a cost of $3,500. The entire staff consisted of three people: T. M. Colston, the first school superintendent, and two teachers. Kingsville's first school class contained 32 children, under the instruction of Elizabeth Turner in October 1905. (Courtesy South Texas Archives, Texas A&M University-Kingsville.)

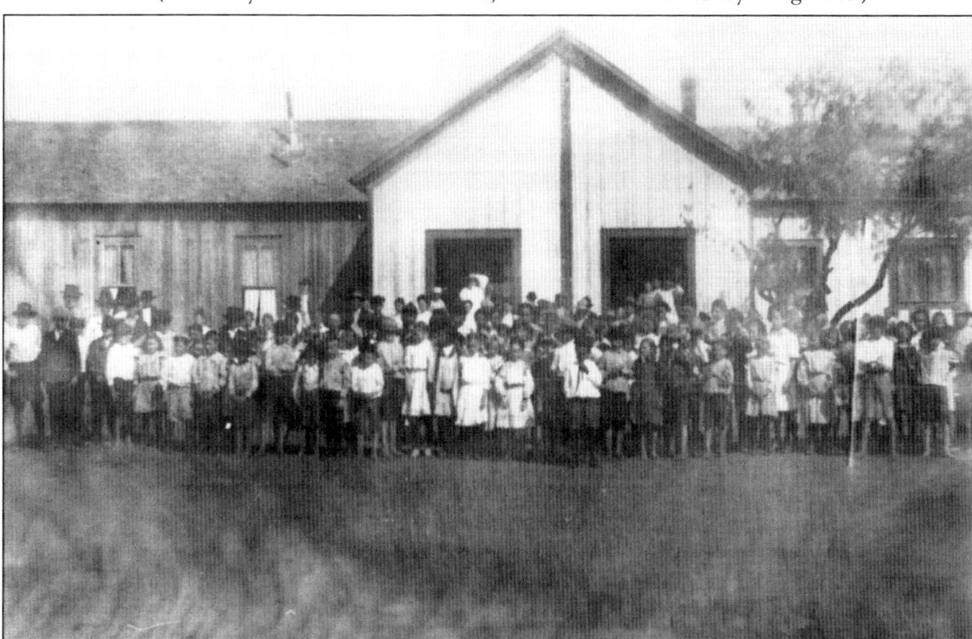

By 1908, additions had been made to the building and there were 125 students enrolled at the school, 80 of whom were first graders. Half of the first graders were Spanish-speakers and needed specific teaching efforts. Language in education has been a long-term issue in Kingsville. (Courtesy South Texas Archives, Texas A&M University-Kingsville.)

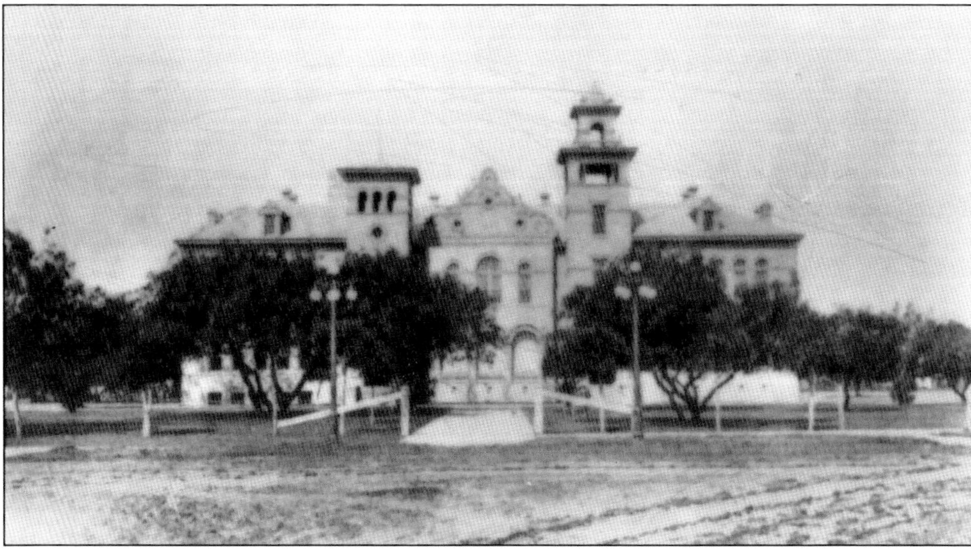

Henrietta King donated land and oversaw construction of the Henrietta M. King School in 1909. This two-story brick building was initially used for all grades; as the community grew, the facility became the town's high school. The grounds were fenced in 1909 to keep out stray King Ranch cattle. (Courtesy South Texas Archives, Texas A&M University-Kingsville.)

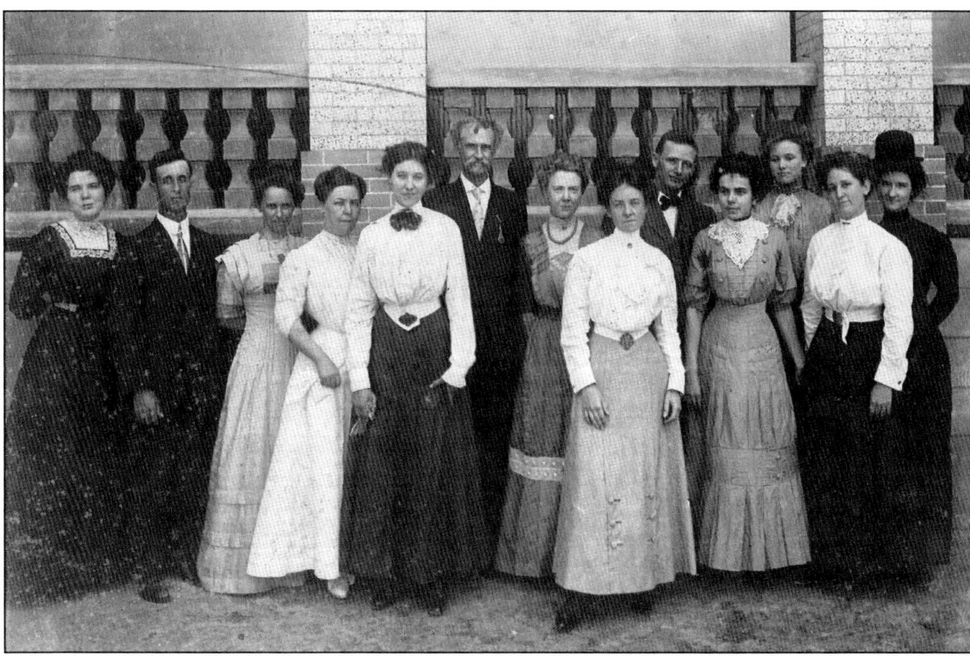

The first faculty at the new Henrietta M. King School is pictured here in 1909. By 1913, there were 700 students enrolled. By 1939, enrollment swelled to 2,584. Four ward schools were built to accommodate the lower grades, and the Kingsville School District had 61 instructors in 1939. After the four ward schools opened, the original school became Henrietta M. King High School. (Courtesy South Texas Archives, Texas A&M University-Kingsville.)

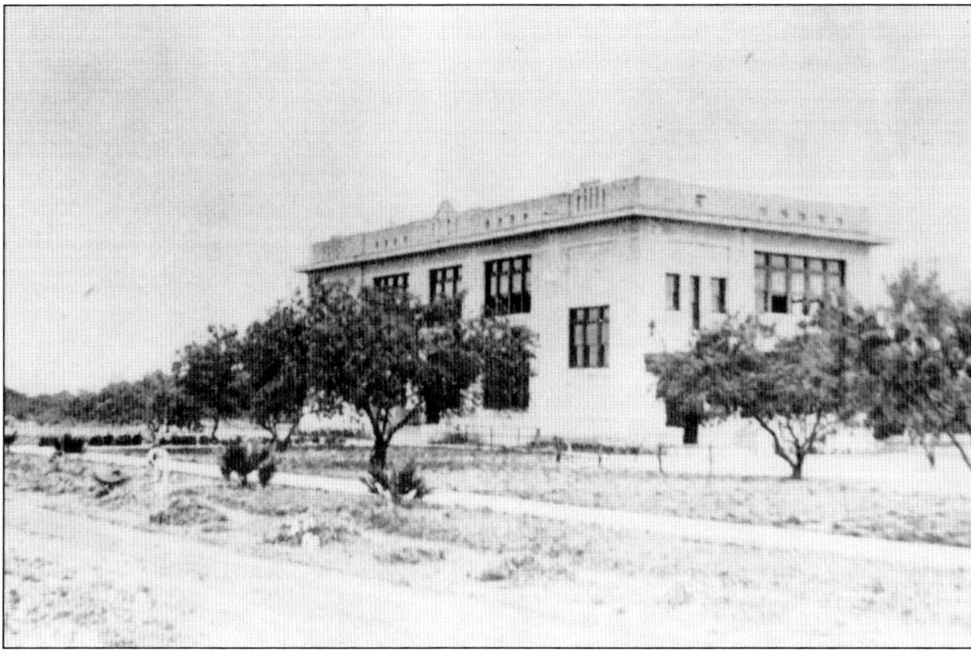

The "East Ward" school, Mirabeau B. Lamar Elementary, was located between Tenth and Twelfth Streets and East Fordyce and East Johnston Avenues. It was built in 1913. An identical school, Stephen F. Austin School, was constructed in the Hispanic community and called "North Ward." (Courtesy South Texas Archives, Texas A&M University-Kingsville.)

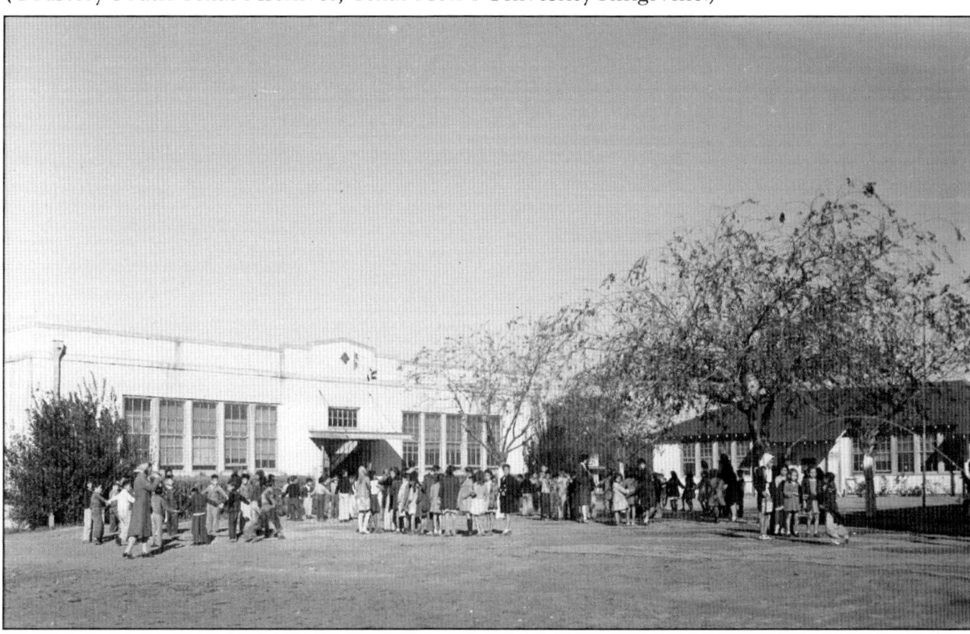

Stephen F. Austin School and the four-room stucco addition at right accommodated the increasing student population in the Mexican American part of Kingsville. In 1948, the old Kingsville Cotton Mill was renovated and turned into the Alice G.K. Kleberg Elementary School to meet classroom demands. (Courtesy Dolph Briscoe Center for American History, The University of Texas at Austin, Austin School, Dodd (Jimmie) Photographic Collection, Creator: Dodd, Jimmie.)

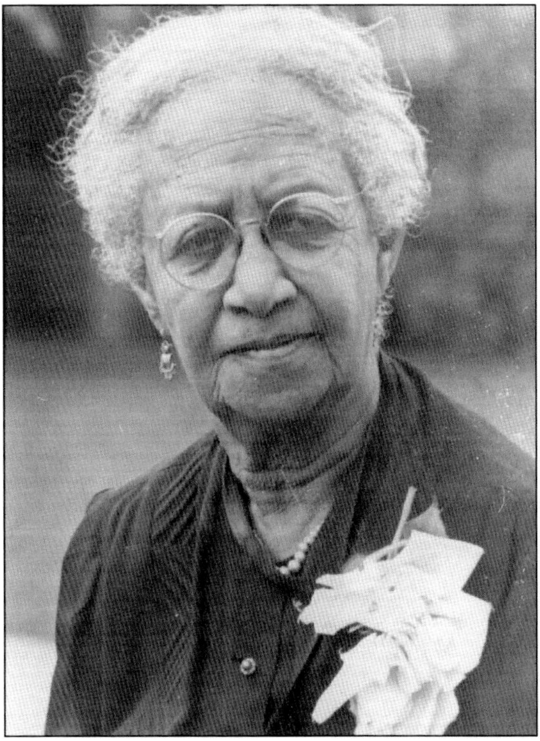

Jessie McDow was Kingsville's first African American schoolteacher. She was born in Corpus Christi, Texas, and taught for 36 years. McDow attended Tillotson College in Austin, Texas, receiving her teaching degree in 1902. She came to Kingsville in 1909 to teach at the school in King Star Baptist Church. (Courtesy South Texas Archives, Texas A&M University-Kingsville.)

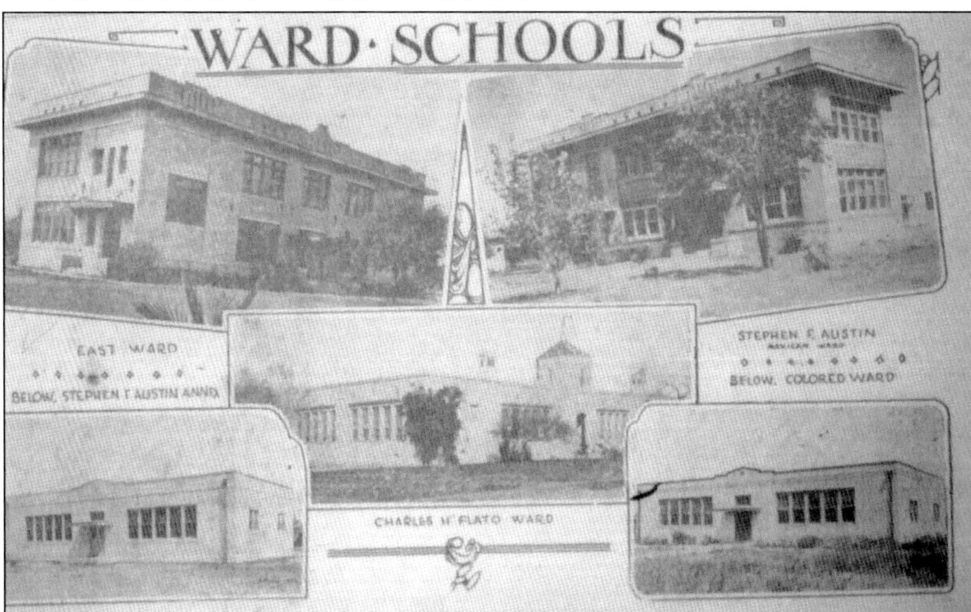

African American students attended school in the Colored Ward School, built in 1913. The name was eventually changed to Frederick Douglass School. In 1948, a larger Frederick Douglass School was built. Prior to 1950, African American students could not get an accredited high school diploma from Frederick Douglass School; they had to go to Corpus Christi to complete high school and receive a diploma. A composite photograph of the Ward Schools of Kingsville is printed in a postcard format. (Courtesy King Ranch, Inc., Kingsville, Texas.)

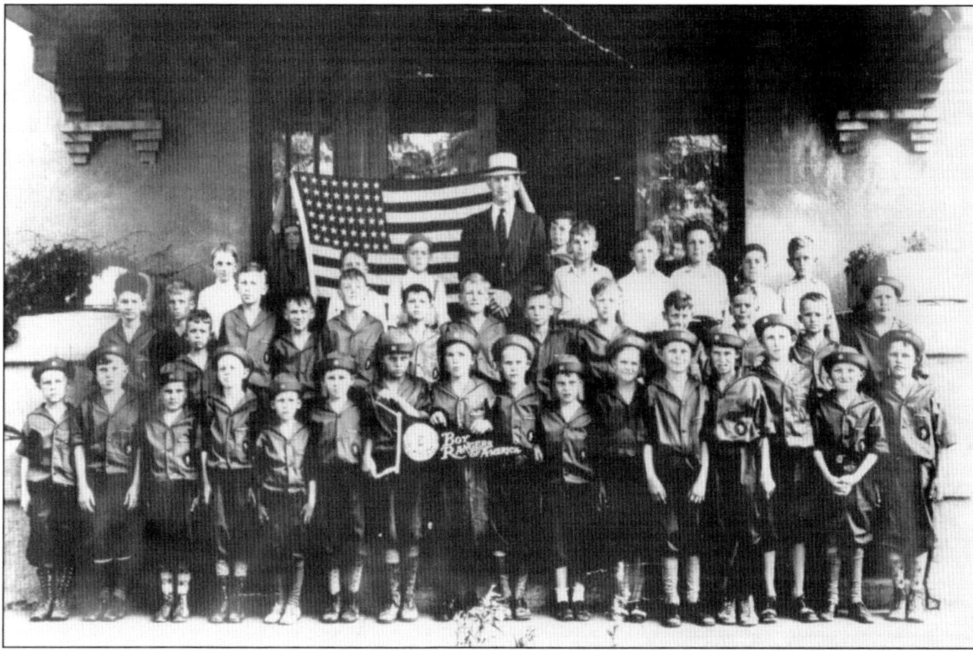

In this c. 1934 photograph, the Boy Rangers of America assemble in front of Lamar Elementary. Boy Rangers was originally a predecessor to the Cub Scouts; many Ranger groups overlapped with Cub Scout packs and were eventually absorbed by them. Scouting was an important part of the growing Kingsville community. (Courtesy South Texas Archives, Texas A&M University-Kingsville.)

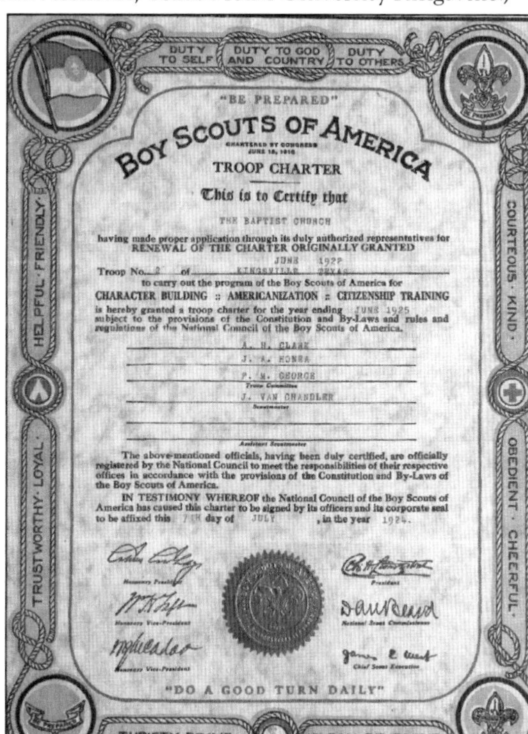

DUTY TO SELF · DUTY TO GOD AND COUNTRY · DUTY TO OTHERS

"BE PREPARED"

BOY SCOUTS OF AMERICA

TROOP CHARTER

This is to Certify that

THE BAPTIST CHURCH

having made proper application through its duly authorized representatives for RENEWAL OF THE CHARTER ORIGINALLY GRANTED JUNE 1922

Troop No. 2 of KINGSVILLE [illegible]

to carry out the program of the Boy Scouts of America for

CHARACTER BUILDING :: AMERICANIZATION :: CITIZENSHIP TRAINING

is hereby granted a troop charter for the year ending JUNE 1925 subject to the provisions of the Constitution and By-Laws and rules and regulations of the National Council of the Boy Scouts of America.

A. H. CLARK

J. A. HONRA

P. M. GEORGE

Troop Committee

J. VAN CHANDLER

Scoutmaster

Assistant Scoutmaster

The above-mentioned officials, having been duly certified, are officially registered by the National Council to meet the responsibilities of their respective offices in accordance with the provisions of the Constitution and By-Laws of the Boy Scouts of America.

IN TESTIMONY WHEREOF the National Council of the Boy Scouts of America has caused this charter to be signed by its officers and its corporate seal to be affixed this 7TH day of JULY, in the year 1924.

Honorary President · President

Honorary Vice-President · National Scout Commissioner

Honorary Vice-President · Chief Scout Executive

"DO A GOOD TURN DAILY"

HELPFUL · FRIENDLY · COURTEOUS · KIND · TRUSTWORTHY · LOYAL · OBEDIENT · CHEERFUL · THRIFTY · BRAVE · CLEAN · REVERENT ·

Boy Scouts of America Kingsville Troop 2 was called to help with community cleanup projects. Reports in the *Kingsville Record* commended the Scouts on their work, and the newspaper also reported when they went on local campouts. The Baptist Church first sponsored Troop 2 in 1922. (Courtesy South Texas Archives, Texas A&M University-Kingsville.)

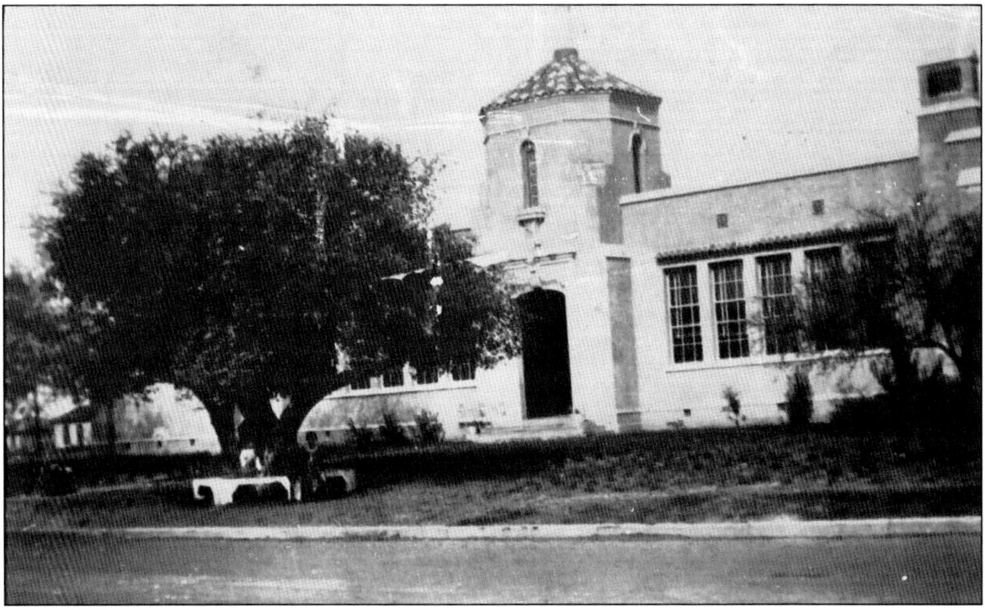

The Charles H. Flato Jr. Elementary School was opened in January 1925. Flato was elected the first school board president for Kingsville in 1906. The large tree in this 1928 picture was said to be the anacua tree where Henrietta King brought lunch to Richard King when he worked on that part of the King Ranch. (Courtesy South Texas Archives, Texas A&M University-Kingsville.)

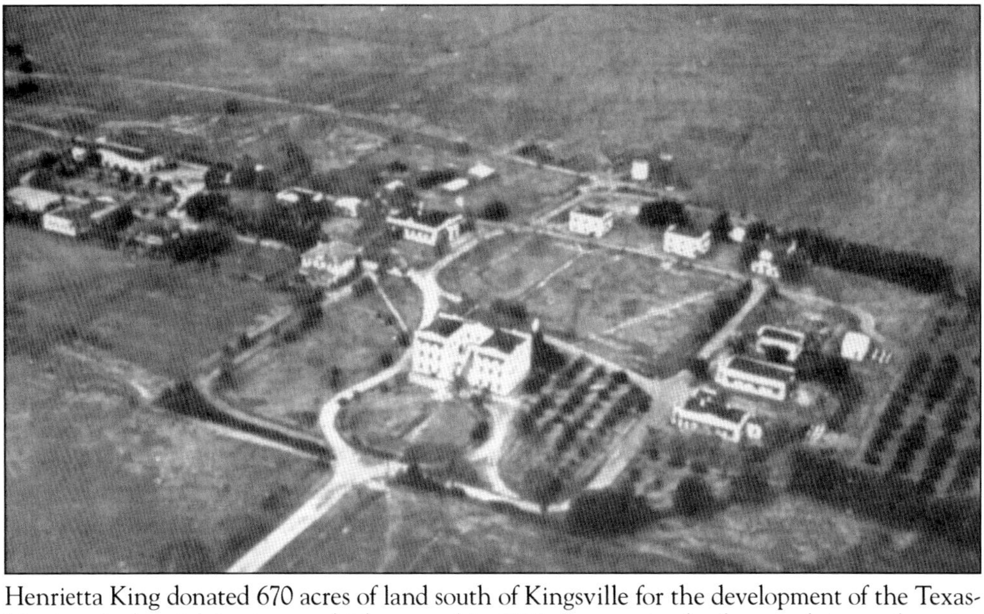

Henrietta King donated 670 acres of land south of Kingsville for the development of the Texas-Mexican Industrial Institute, which opened in 1912. It contained a farm, a dairy, and a print shop. The institute was established to meet the educational needs of Hispanic boys and offered schooling for grade levels 6 through 12 and eventually merged with the Presbyterian School for Mexican Girls to become the Presbyterian Pan American School. (Courtesy King Ranch, Inc., Kingsville, Texas.)

Construction of the Kingsville Cotton Mill began in March 1921. The total cost of building and equipment was $365,000, and the first cotton was put into the breakers on February 22, 1922. After World War II, the cotton mill was sold to the school district for $25,000 and became the Alice G.K. Kleberg Elementary School. (Courtesy South Texas Archives, Texas A&M University-Kingsville.)

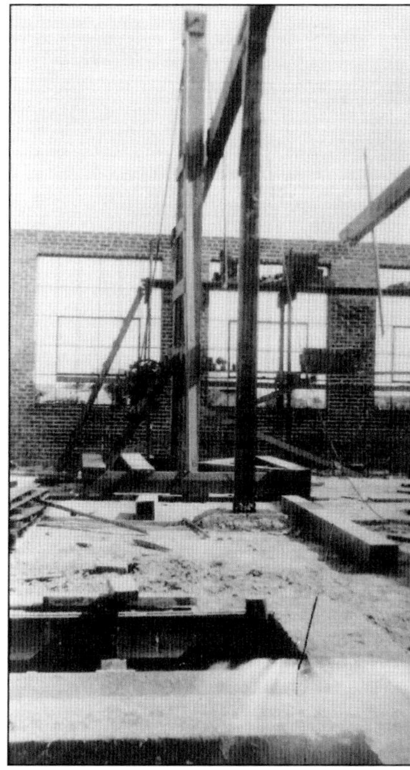

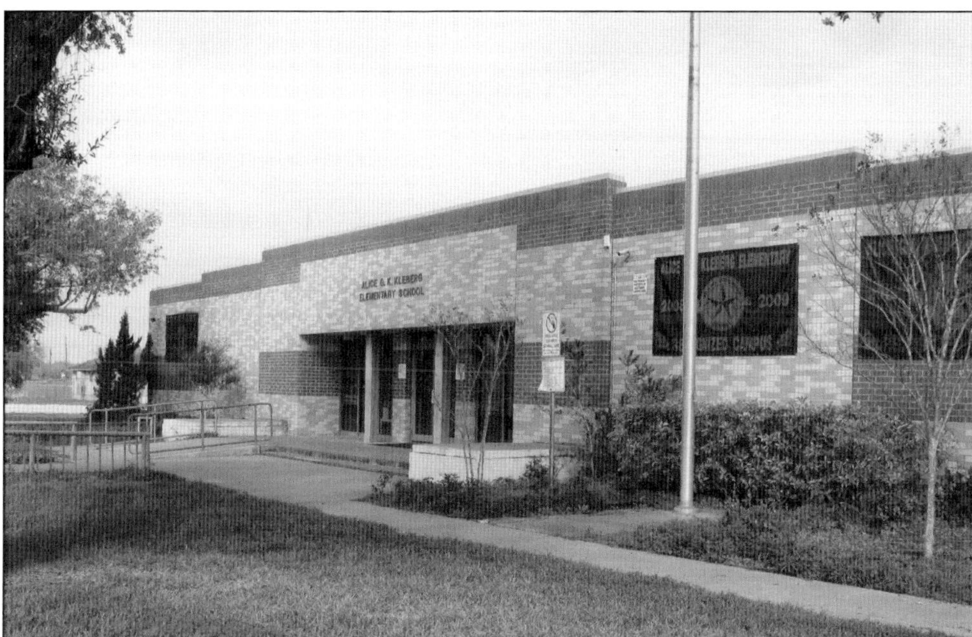

In fall 1946, the remodeled cotton mill was opened as the Alice G.K. Kleberg Elementary School. The school building was gutted by fire in 1988 and rebuilt with four inches of concrete added to the foundation. Some of the original red bricks were salvaged and used in the front wall of the structure. Insurance covered most of the rebuilding costs. (Photograph by the author.)

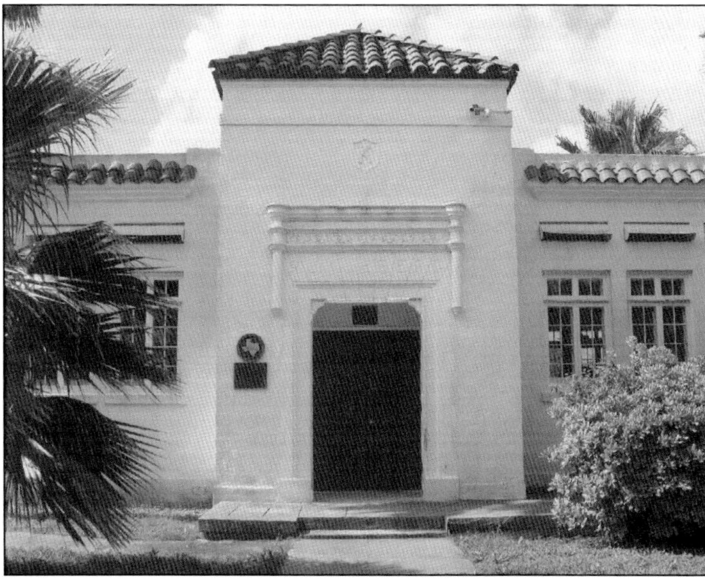

The Robert Kleberg Public Library was erected in 1925. The library had existed since the establishment of the Progressive Women's Club of Kingsville in 1909. It was the Women's Club that initiated the library and worked to expand it. The library bounced from one place to another until the construction of this building at Third Street and Yoakum Avenue. (Photograph by the author.)

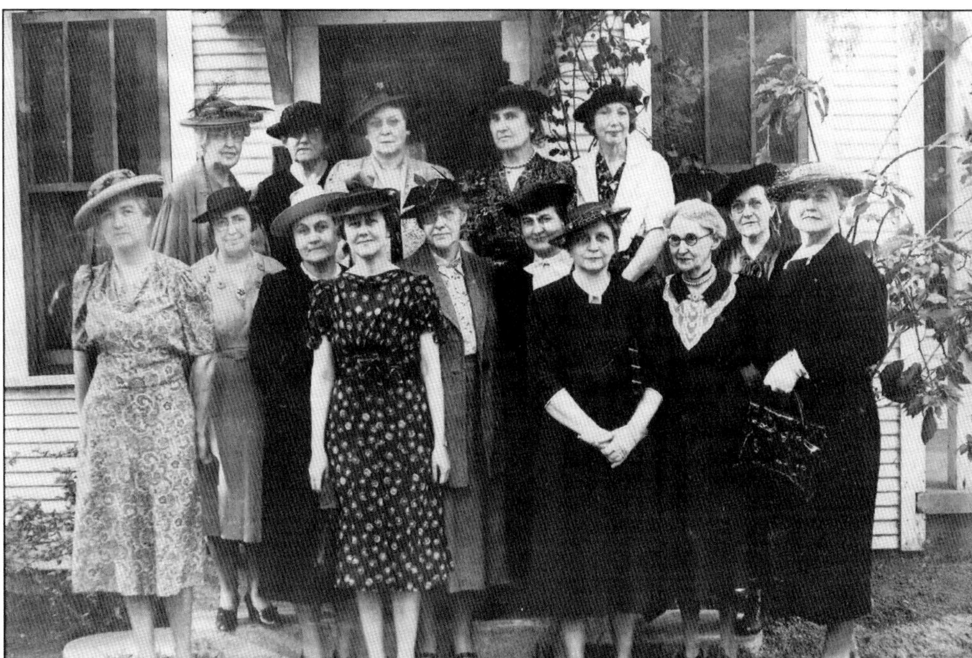

In 1939, the past presidents of the Progressive Women's Club pose for this photograph. The club was very active in early Kingsville and was responsible for establishing the town's public library. Books for the library were collected using a "book shower" put on by the members, and the community also donated books and funds. (Courtesy South Texas Archives, Texas A&M University-Kingsville.)

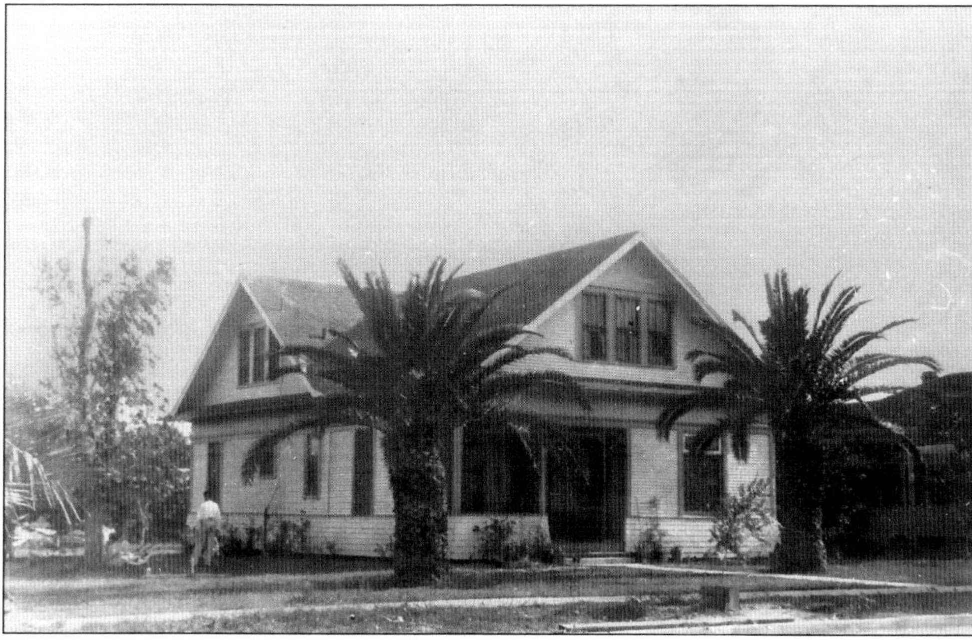

Kleberg County did not have a conventional hospital until 1914, so Dr. Hendry Allison used his house at 309 East Kenedy Avenue as a hospital. (Courtesy South Texas Archives, Texas A&M University-Kingsville.)

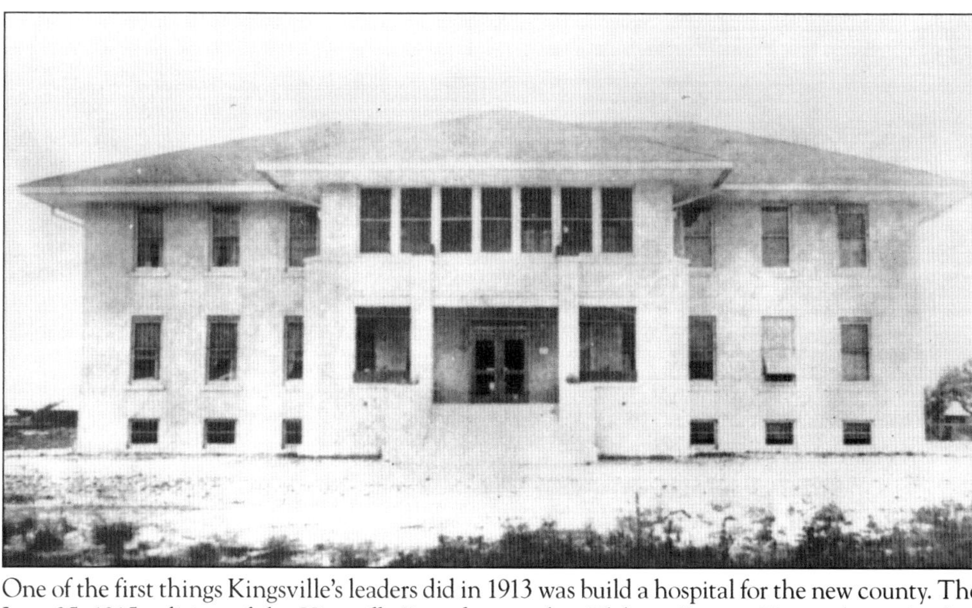

One of the first things Kingsville's leaders did in 1913 was build a hospital for the new county. The June 25, 1915, edition of the *Kingsville Record* states that Kleberg County Hospital was the first county hospital built under the McGregor-Colquitt Hospital Dispensary Law. The hospital could accommodate 50 patients and had modern X-ray equipment. (Courtesy South Texas Archives, Texas A&M University-Kingsville.)

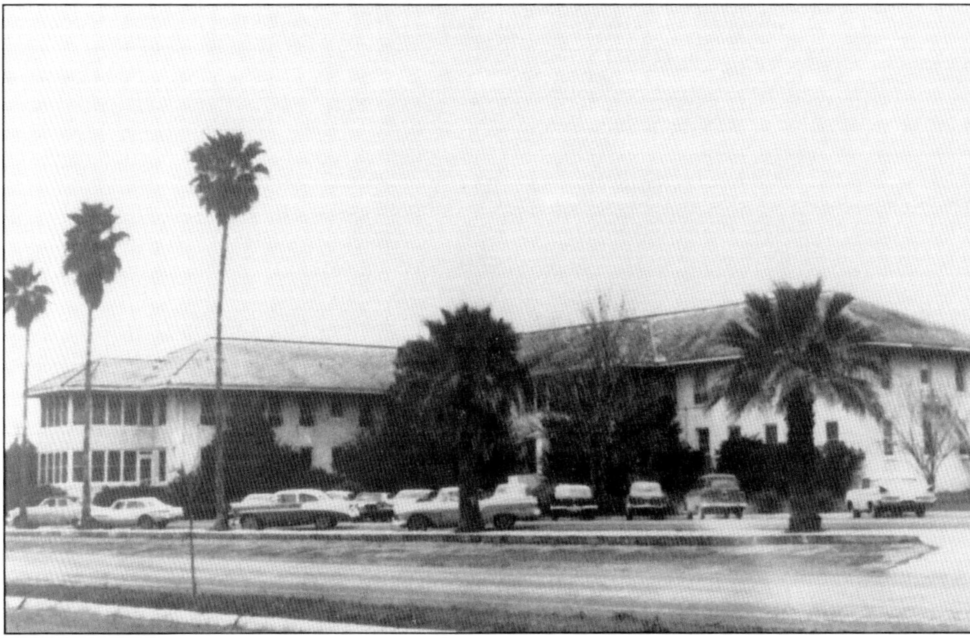

The Kleberg County Hospital was enlarged six times, eventually having 136 beds. Many of the rooms in the new wing of the hospital were furnished by contributions from local clubs and organizations. An iron lung was paid for with donations from a joint fundraising effort. (Courtesy South Texas Archives, Texas A&M University-Kingsville.)

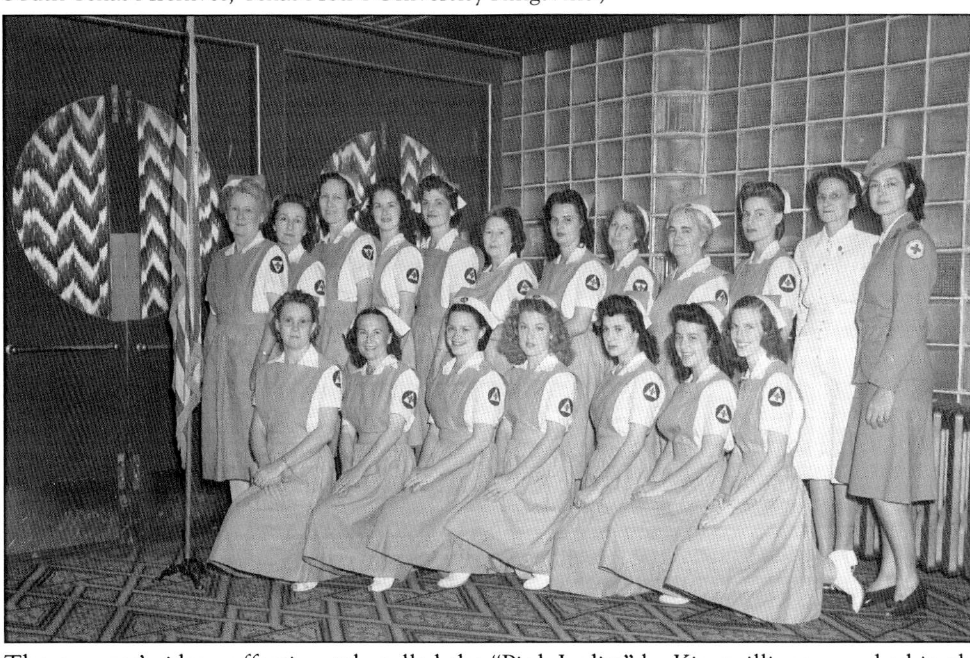

These nurses' aides—affectionately called the "Pink Ladies" by Kingsvillians—worked in the Kleberg County Hospital. Nurses' aides were indispensable in hospitals all over the nation. This picture was taken around the time that the hospital's new wing was added in 1946. (Courtesy Dolph Briscoe Center for American History, The University of Texas at Austin, [Pink Ladies], Dodd (Jimmie) Photographic Collection, Creator: Dodd, Jimmie.)

Four

The Unions and Railroad

Until the arrival of the South Texas State Teachers College in 1925, the railroad was Kingsville's only industry. The large ranches and farms were the main customers, and most of the town made its livelihood from the railroad. Along with the railroad came unions, including the Brotherhood of Locomotive Engineers, Brotherhood of Locomotive Firemen and Enginemen, Brotherhood of Boilermakers, Brotherhood Railway Carmen, International Association of Machinists, and others. The lure of unique employment possibilities with the St. Louis, Brownsville & Mexico Railway brought African American workers and their families to Kingsville.

The established unions did not accept African American trainmen in their ranks, so they were not represented in wage and working condition negotiations. To counter this, they created their own union, the Colored Trainmen of America (CTA), to represent their rights in negotiating with the rail companies. Their charter was filed with the State of Texas on June 13, 1918, and local no. 1 formed in Kingsville; local no. 2 formed in DeQuincy, Louisiana, in 1929. After World War II began, black workers migrated north to find employment in the war industries that offered better pay, and a lack of experienced labor in Kingsville became a serious problem for the railroad.

The railroad also established booster clubs to help promote Kingsville and community projects. A railroad baseball team regularly played against neighboring communities. Camaraderie was an important component of railroad work, and the workers often went on group outings.

As farming increased in the Rio Grande Valley, railroad freight traffic increased. The demand for ice to supply refrigerated cars became critical. The Kingsville Power Company, one of the area's first businesses, was established in 1904, and its main purpose at that time was the production of ice.

Over the years, five railroad companies controlled the Kingsville rails: the St. Louis, Brownsville & Mexico Railway (StLB&M); St. Louis-San Francisco Railway (Frisco); Gulf Coast Lines (GCL); Missouri Pacific Lines (MoPac); and Union Pacific. Each one has its own story about Kingsville.

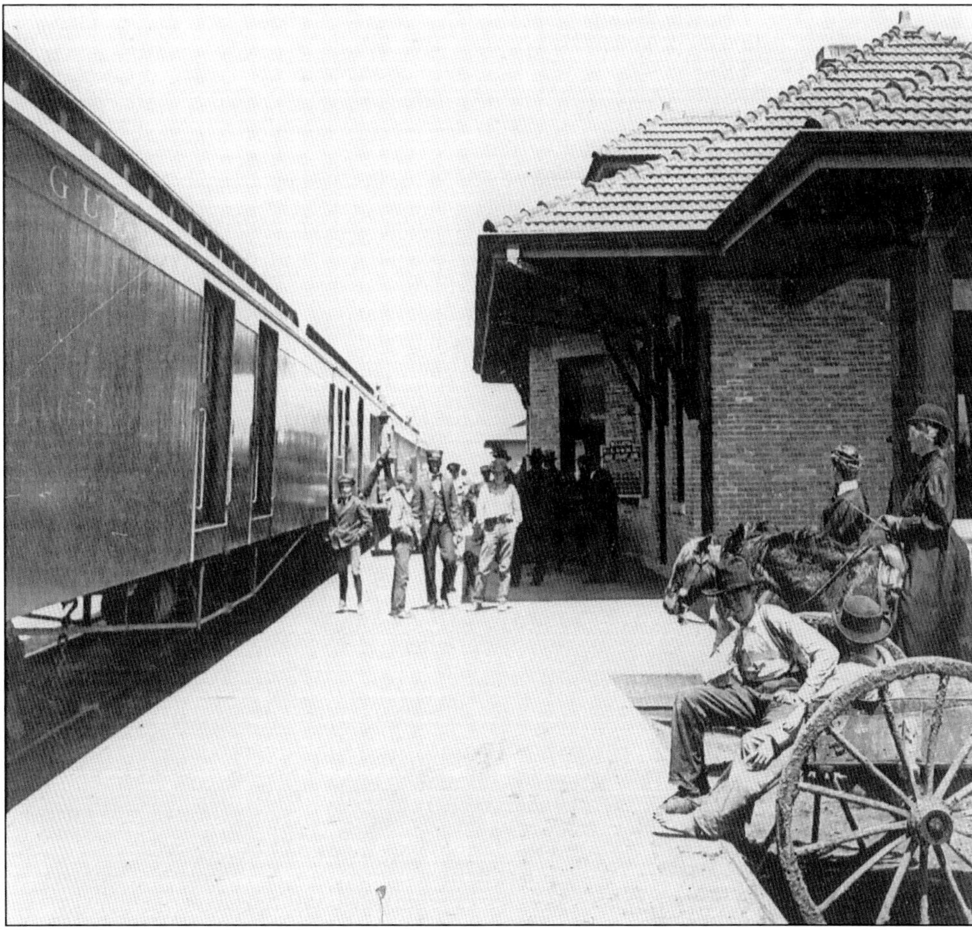

The passenger depot at Kingsville was always buzzing with activity. It was a popular pastime for locals to come to the depot to see who got on and off of the train. Passenger service was discontinued in 1966, but the depot has been beautifully restored and now serves as the 1904 Kingsville Train Depot Museum. (Courtesy King Ranch, Inc., Kingsville, Texas.)

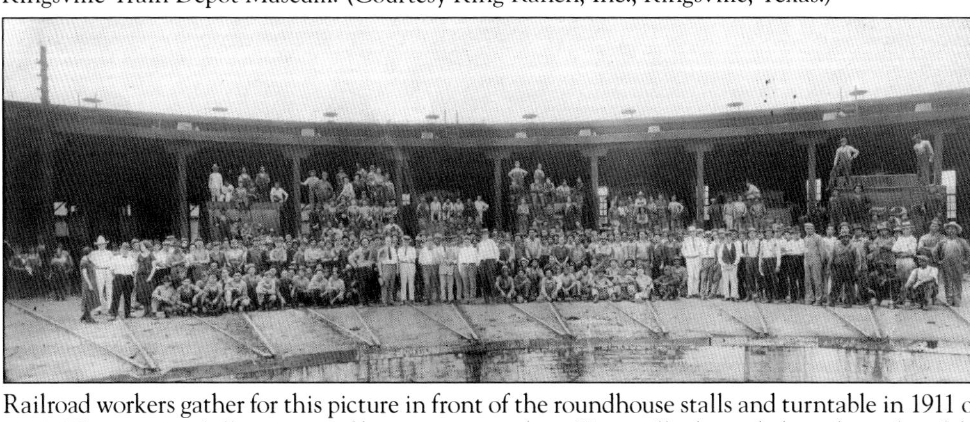

Railroad workers gather for this picture in front of the roundhouse stalls and turntable in 1911 or 1912. This is a good illustration of how many people in Kingsville depended on the railroad for their livelihoods. By 1913, the annual railroad payroll in Kleberg County was $390,000. (Courtesy South Texas Archives, Texas A&M University-Kingsville.)

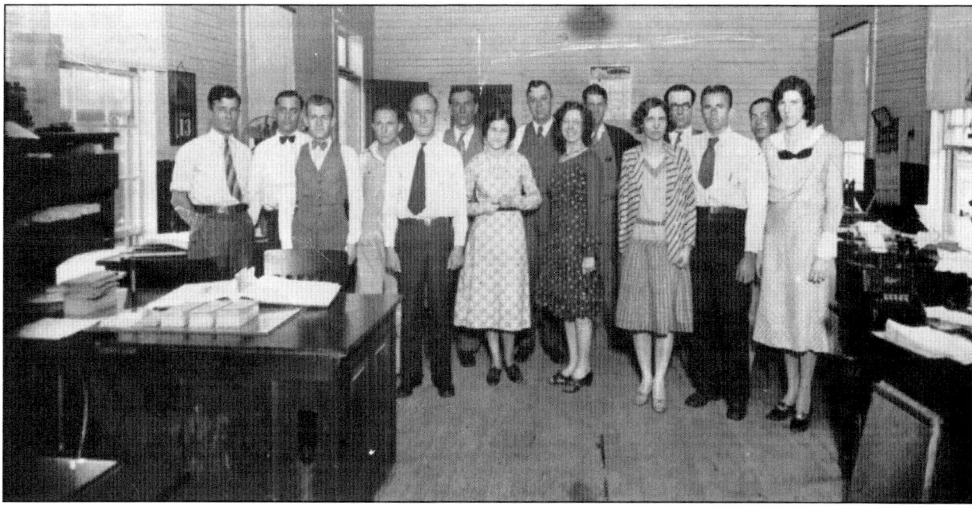

This 1929 photograph of the Missouri Pacific Lines clerical staff was taken in the storeroom and master mechanic office of the general office building. Pictured from left to right are Lee Skipper, E.O. Dube, Robert Stripling, Bill Kirby, A.B. Carmichael, ? Ellis, Emile Chesson, W.E. Hopkins, Ethel Knight, Joel Denham, Trula Wright, Dwight Brown, Eldridge Foster, M.A. Isdale, and Lila Hudspeth. (Courtesy South Texas Archives, Texas A&M University-Kingsville.)

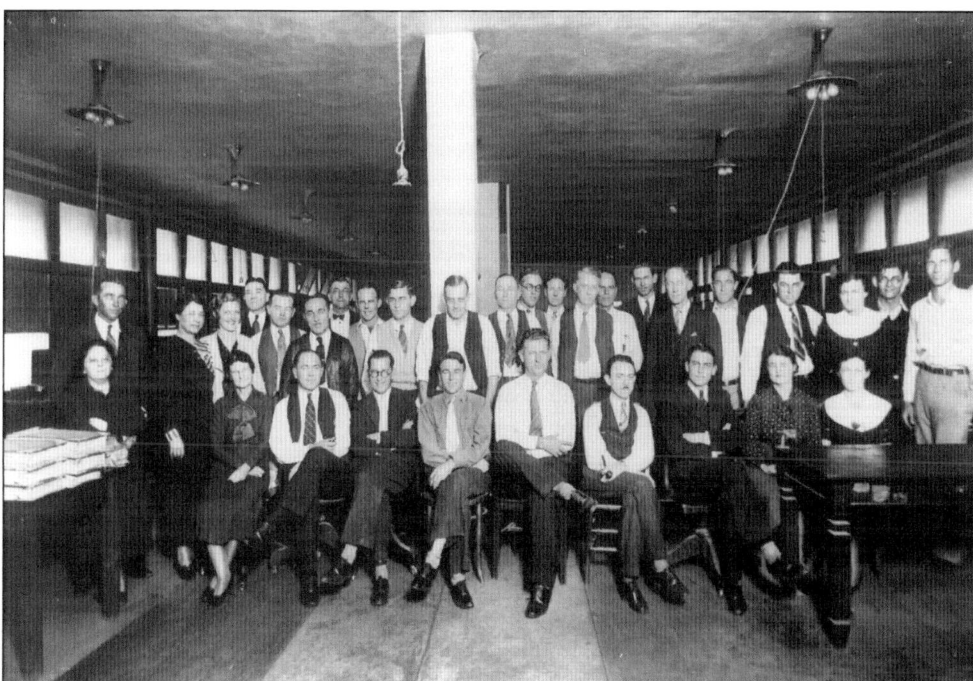

This picture from January 1936 depicts the staff of the Kingsville Auditor's Office of the Freight Interline, Freight Rechecker, Agent's Accounts, and Comptroller Departments and gives the viewer a peek into what the interior of the "General Office" building looked like. The employees are all named on page 156 of *Kleberg County Texas*. (Courtesy South Texas Archives, Texas A&M University-Kingsville.)

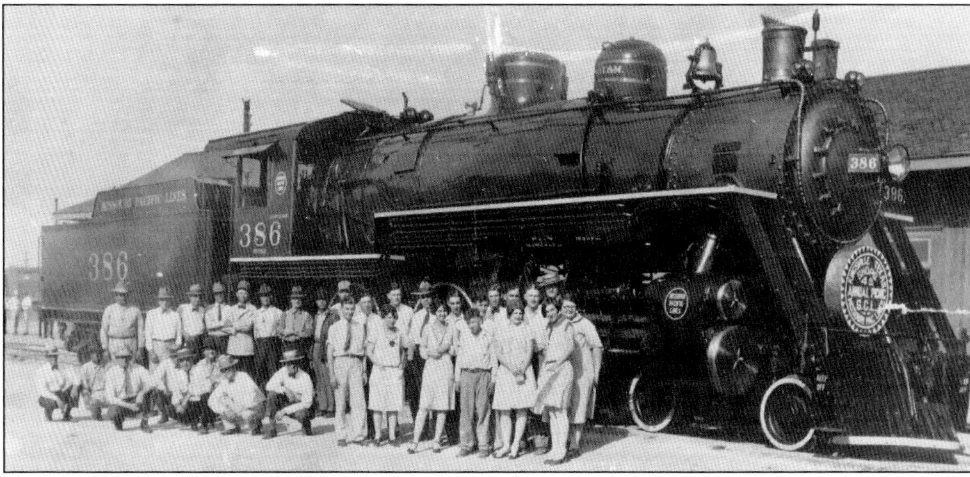

In 1927, these folks were headed to a picnic in New Braunfels until engine no. 386 broke down. Special trains were often used for picnics and important events. The sign on the front of no. 386 reads, "Kingsville Texas Shops 4th Annual Picnic G.C.L. Missouri Pacific Lines." (Courtesy South Texas Archives, Texas A&M University-Kingsville.)

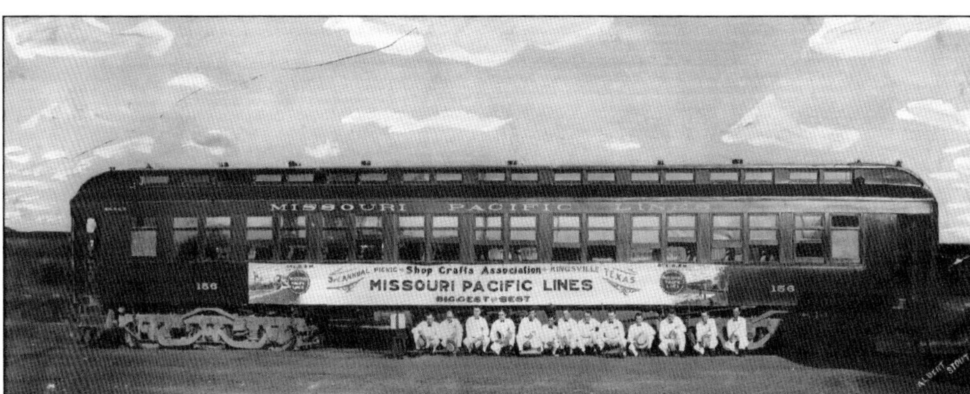

The railroad brought the unions to Kingsville, which also meant union booster clubs, union bands, union baseball teams, and union picnics. This c. 1927 image is from the era of Missouri Pacific Lines. This was the third annual picnic under MoPac control of the Kingsville railroad. (Courtesy South Texas Archives, Texas A&M University-Kingsville.)

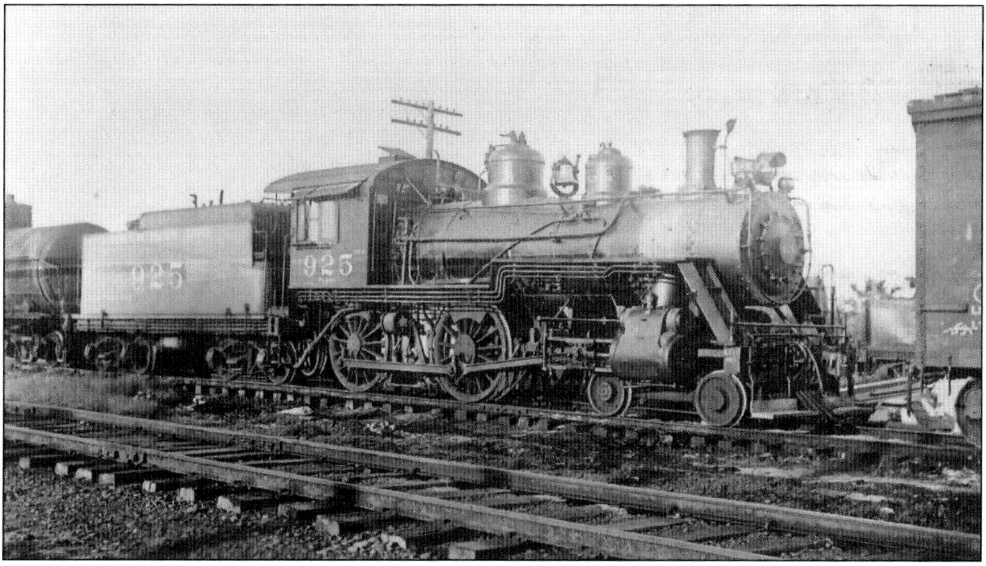

The original StLB&M locomotive no. 1 was repainted for Missouri Pacific Lines and rechristened no. 925. It was built by Baldwin in 1904 and was finally scrapped in Kingsville on February 6, 1936. It proudly ran under four of the five railroad companies that called Kingsville home. (Courtesy South Texas Archives, Texas A&M University-Kingsville.)

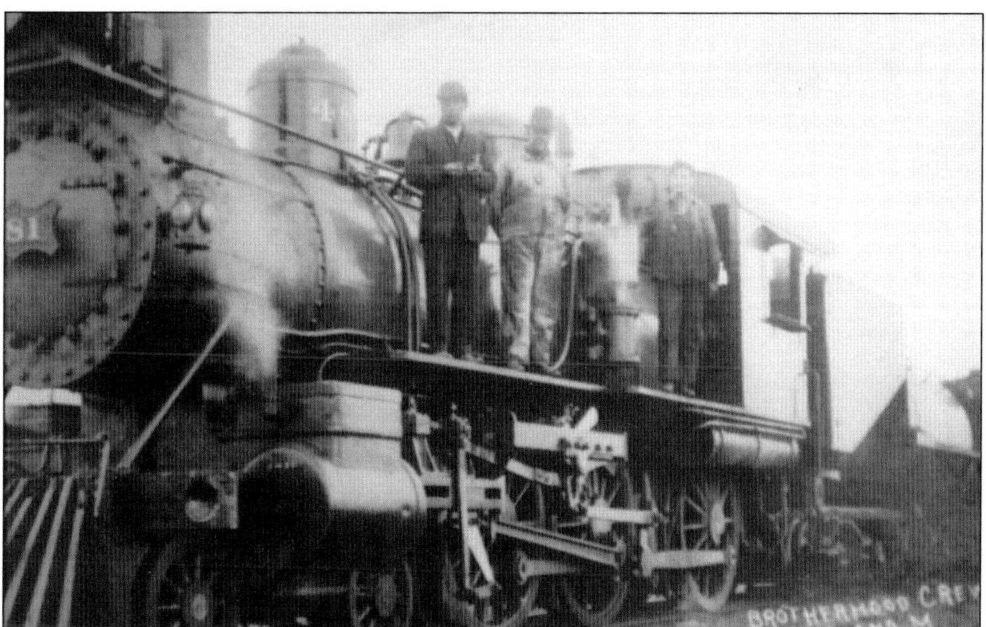

In the late 19th and early 20th centuries, railroad unions purposefully excluded African American workers. The Ku Klux Klan was a presence to be contended with in the 1920s and ran special trains carrying KKK members across the United States. (Courtesy South Texas Archives, Texas A&M University-Kingsville.)

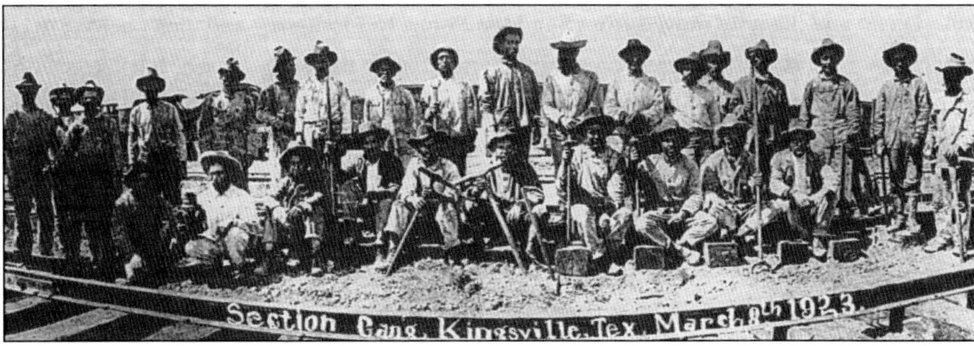

A Gulf Coast Lines section gang pauses for a picture in Kingsville on March 8, 1923. Section gangs were assigned a stretch of track to maintain and tended to employ Hispanic workers. When there was a train wreck, they would build a "shoo-fly," or temporary stretch of track, to take rail traffic around the accident. (Courtesy South Texas Archives, Texas A&M University-Kingsville.)

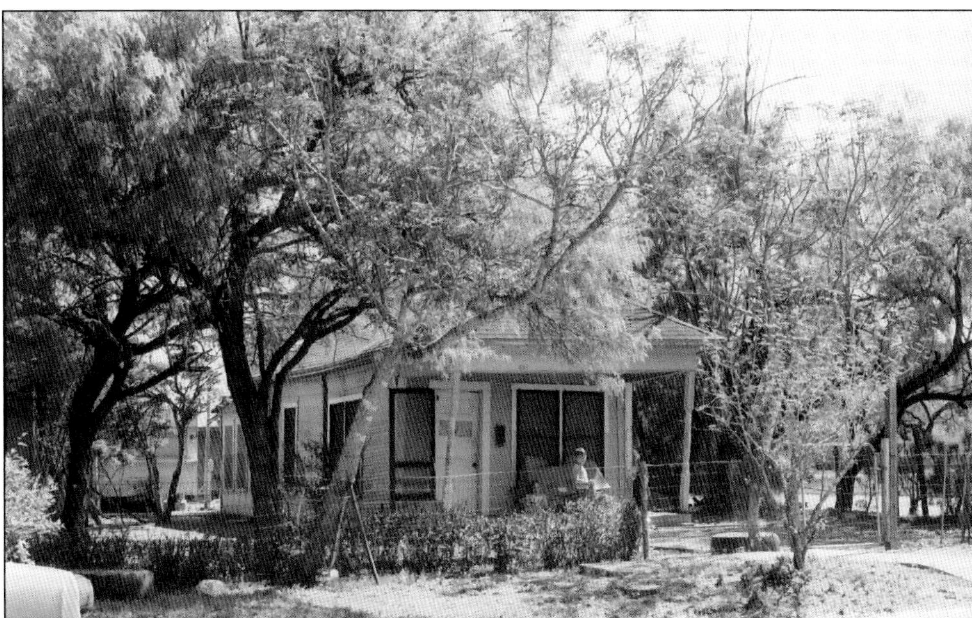

Housing was a problem in early Kingsville. Robert Kleberg realized a solution was needed for the basic comfort of railroad families. In 1913, houses were built by the Kleberg Town and Improvement Company and rented or sold to railroad employees. These homes were of a basic, narrow design known as a shotgun house. (Courtesy South Texas Archives, Texas A&M University-Kingsville.)

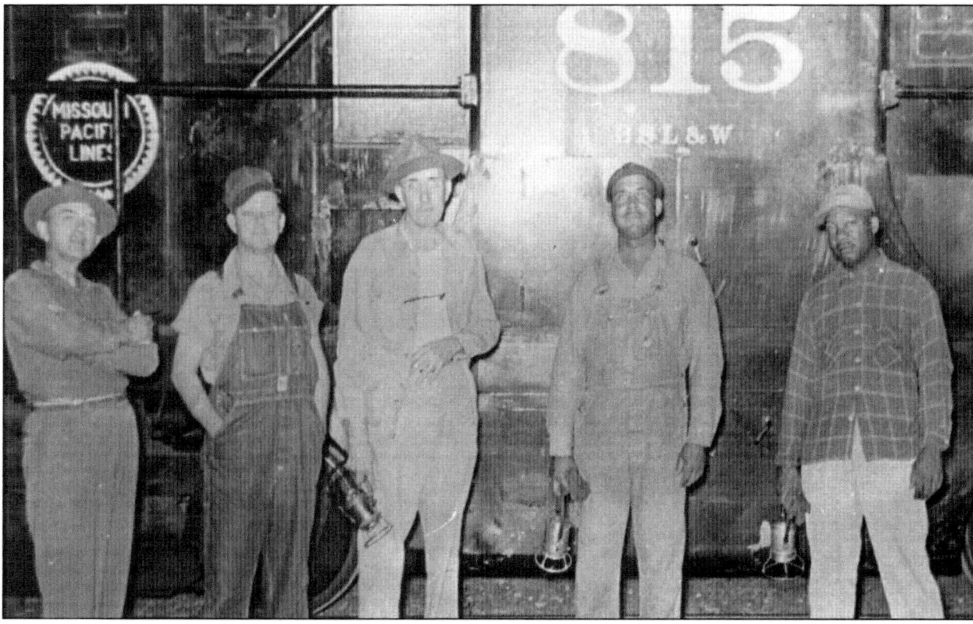

In 1918, African American railroad workers in Kingsville organized the Colored Trainmen of America union to promote better working conditions and the welfare of the African American trainmen. The union worked tirelessly for equal pay and equal working conditions for its members. The shrinking railroad industry of the 1940s deprived the CTA of most of its bargaining power. (Courtesy South Texas Archives, Texas A&M University-Kingsville.)

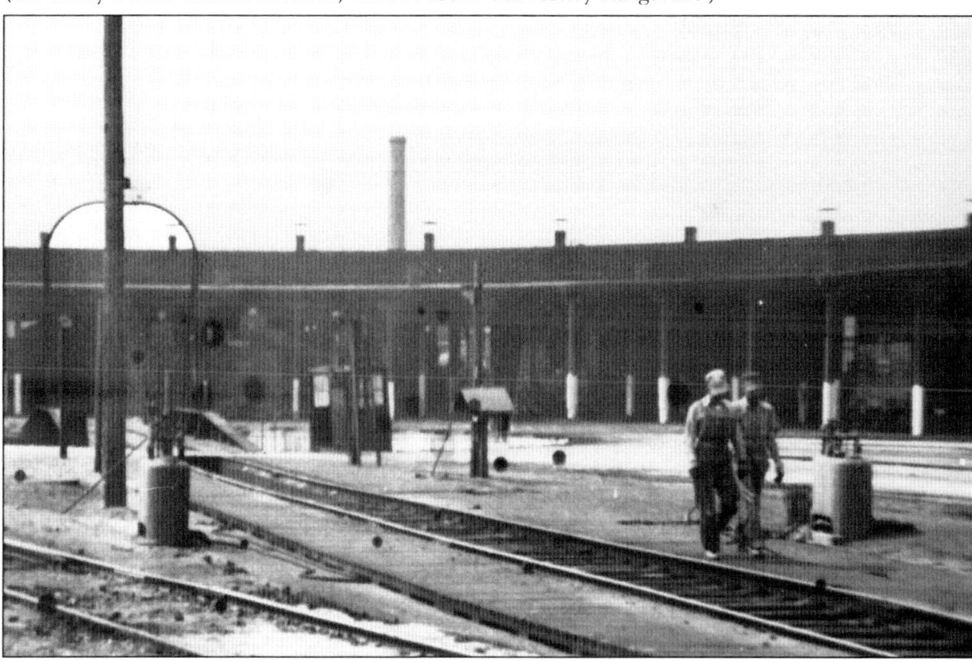

At the time of the October 1, 1920, fire, the Kingsville roundhouse had 15 stalls, which all had pits. When the roundhouse was rebuilt in 1921, one stall was added. The pit allowed workmen access under the engines. Tracks 5 through 9 opened through the roundhouse into the back shops. (Courtesy South Texas Archives, Texas A&M University-Kingsville.)

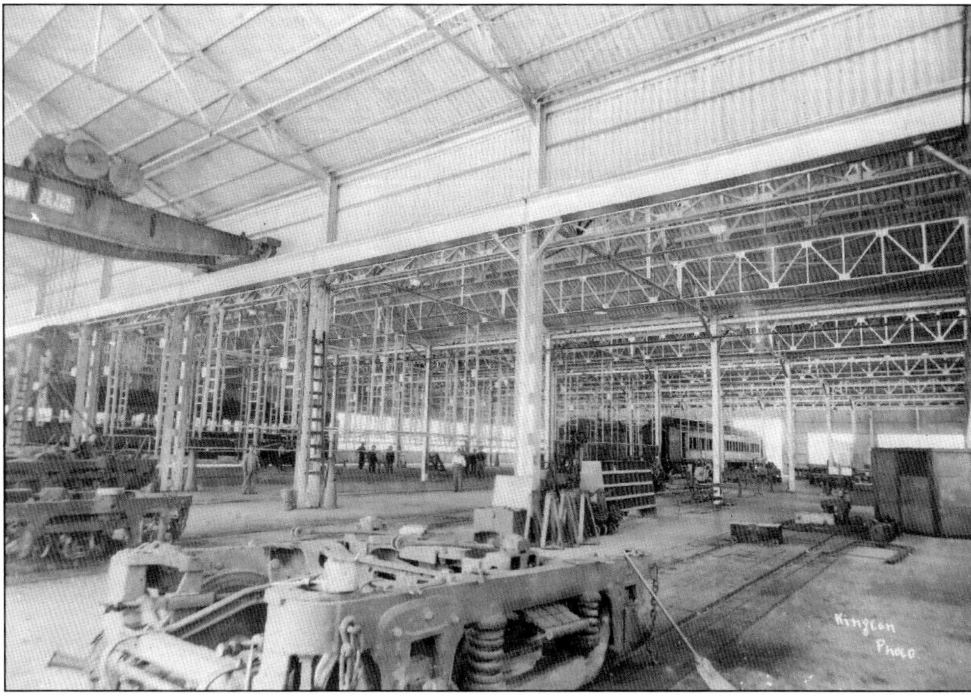

After the fire of 1920, the railroad shop was redesigned with the most modern equipment. It was then used to build and repair coaches, dining cars, and baggage cars. A significant amount of the work involved adding air-conditioning. (Courtesy King Ranch, Inc., Kingsville, Texas.)

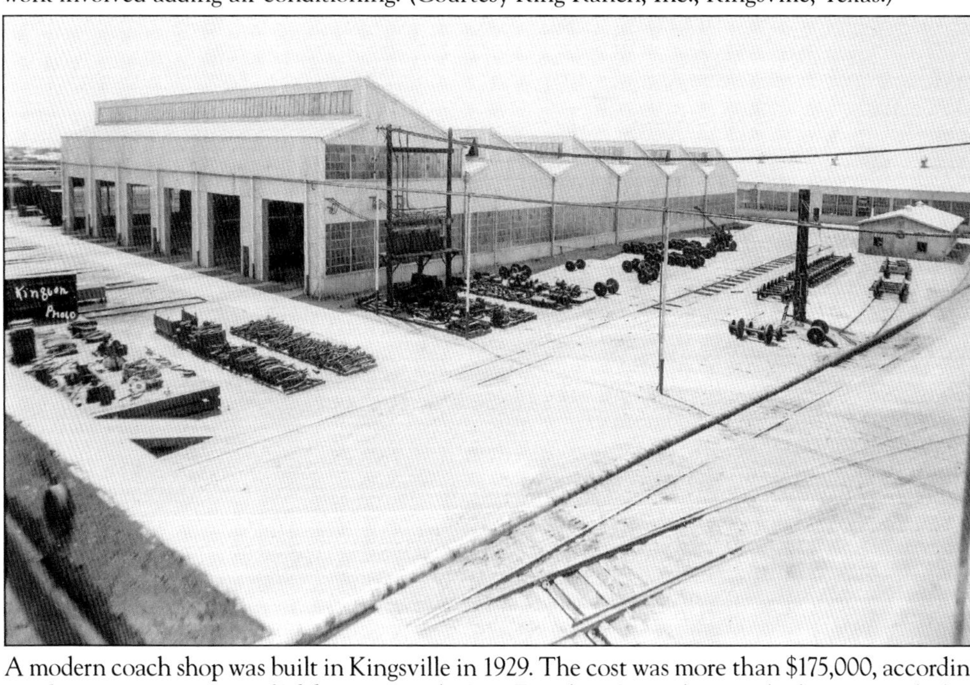

A modern coach shop was built in Kingsville in 1929. The cost was more than $175,000, according to *The Economic History of Kleberg County* by Ben F. Wilson Jr., and it was the largest coach shop south of St. Louis. The railroad shops employed about 400 workers. (Courtesy King Ranch, Inc., Kingsville, Texas.)

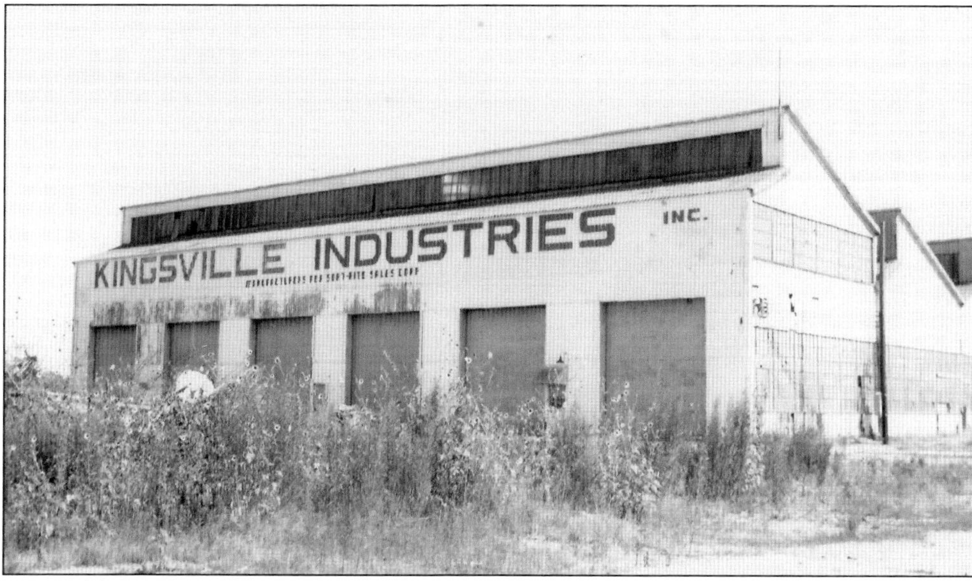

Pictured here on June 8, 1973, Kingsville Industries was the old coach shop for the railroad. Passenger service ended in 1966, and the car shop was closed soon after. Since then, the weeds have been cleared, and the building has been painted. In 2011, the old shop buildings were in use by Proco Inc. (Courtesy South Texas Archives, Texas A&M University-Kingsville.)

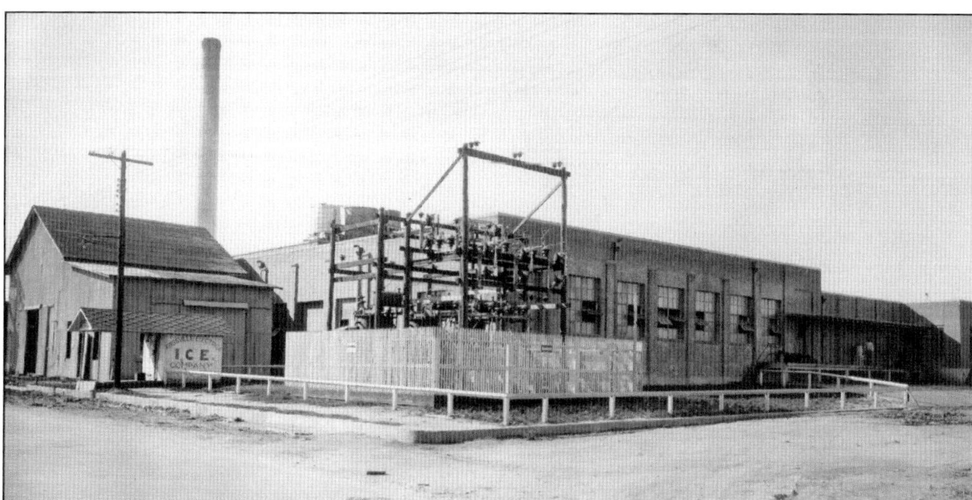

The Kingsville Power Company was established in 1904, and a power and ice plant was constructed in 1907. Ice became a critical commodity for the railroad as more and more produce was shipped out of the Rio Grande Valley. (Courtesy King Ranch, Inc., Kingsville, Texas.)

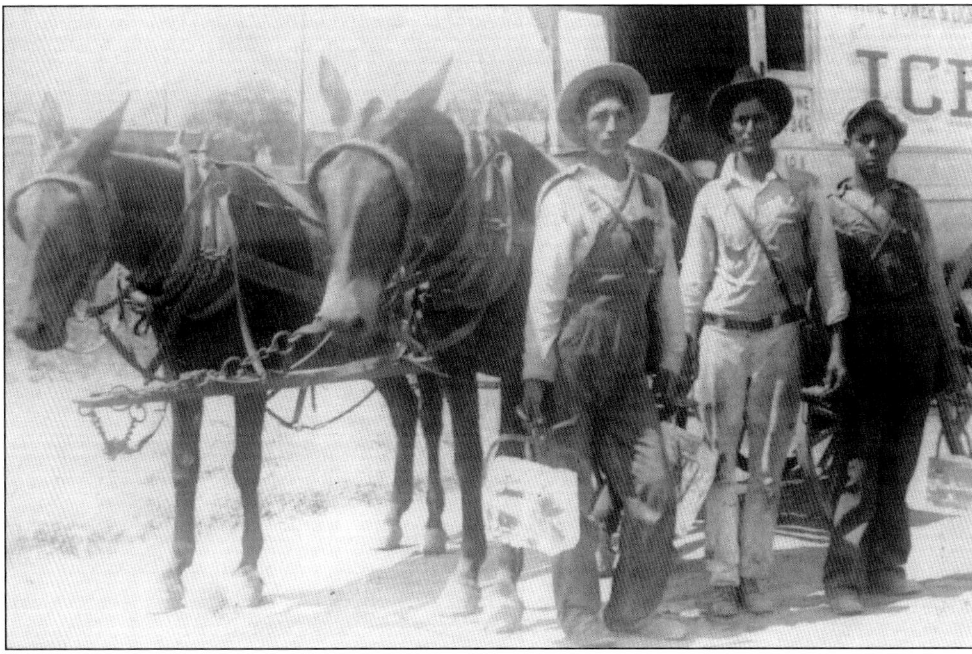

The mule- or horse-drawn ice truck was a welcome site on the dusty streets of early Kingsville. Ice blocks were frozen with scoring so that they could be broken into 25- and 50-pound blocks for use in home iceboxes. Residents would put a sign in the window to let the deliveryman know if they needed ice for the day. (Courtesy King Ranch, Inc., Kingsville, Texas.)

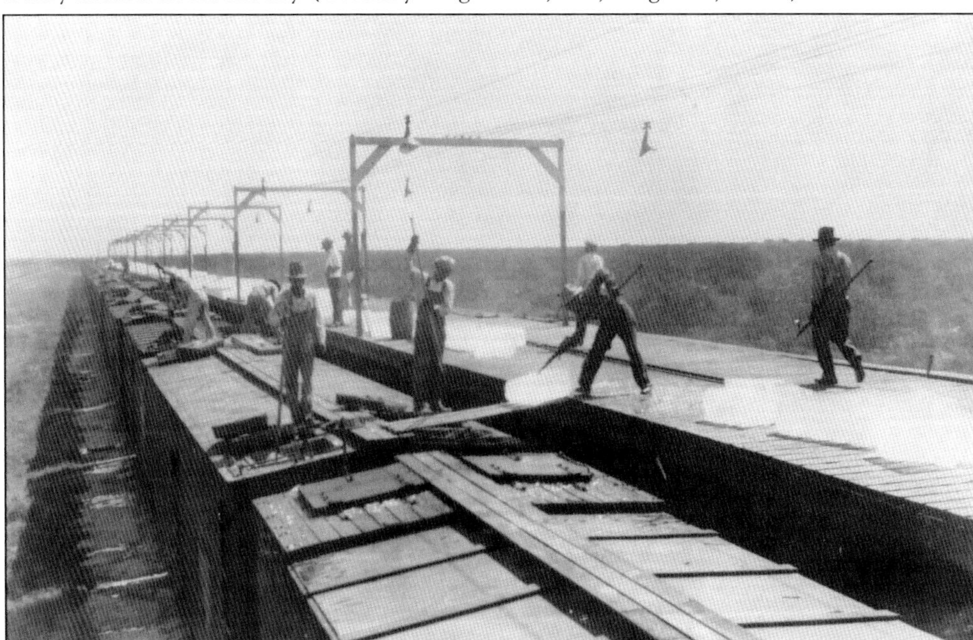

Refrigerator cars loaded with perishable fruits and vegetables needed ice to preserve freshness on the journey to distant markets. Here, workers load 300-pound blocks of ice into compartments on the tops of the cars, and the melting ice kept the produce cool. (Courtesy King Ranch, Inc., Kingsville, Texas.)

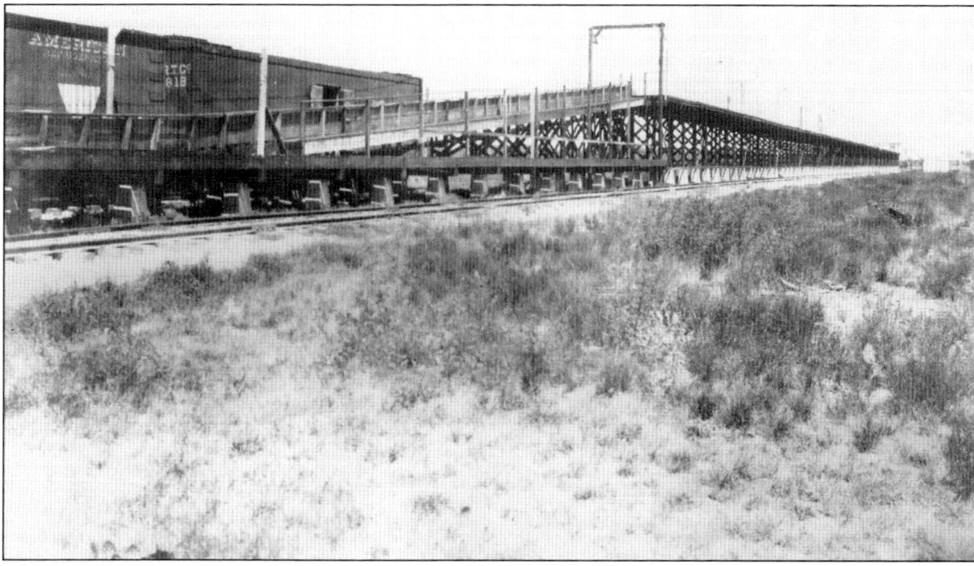

Kingsville was the main re-icing stop for produce coming out of the Rio Grande Valley. The west side of the ice factory contained an icing dock that could handle eight cars at a time. A second icing dock south of town contained storage for 1,000 tons of ice and could handle 40 cars of produce at a time. (Courtesy King Ranch, Inc., Kingsville, Texas.)

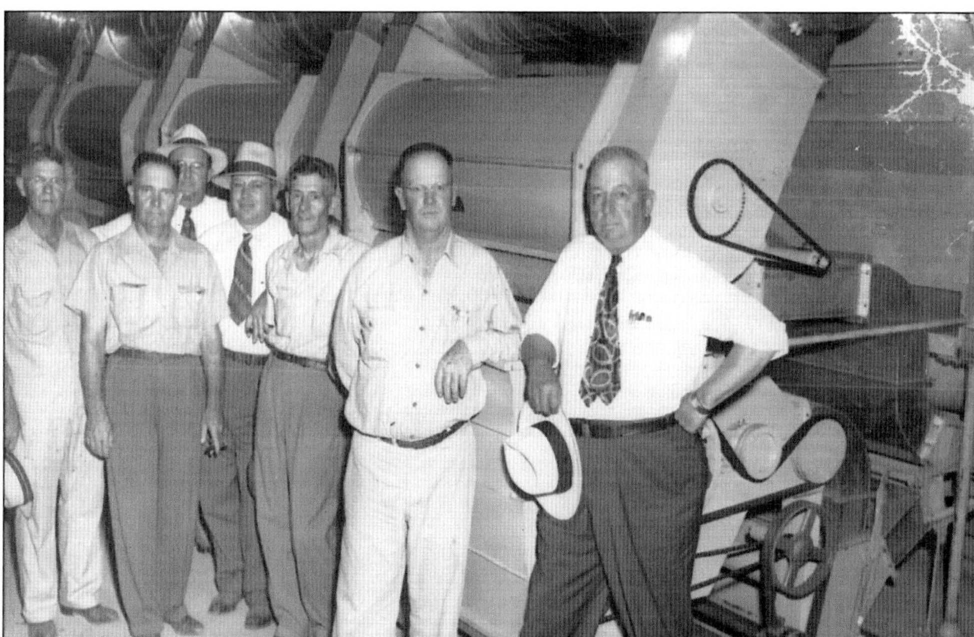

The manufacturing of ice was constantly being improved. Newspaper articles in 1915 reported that the ice plant was expanding from 20,000 pounds to 40,000 pounds of production per day. In 1925, another report told of an increase to 90,000 pounds a day. At its peak productivity, the ice plant could produce 110 tons of ice per day. (Courtesy King Ranch, Inc., Kingsville, Texas.)

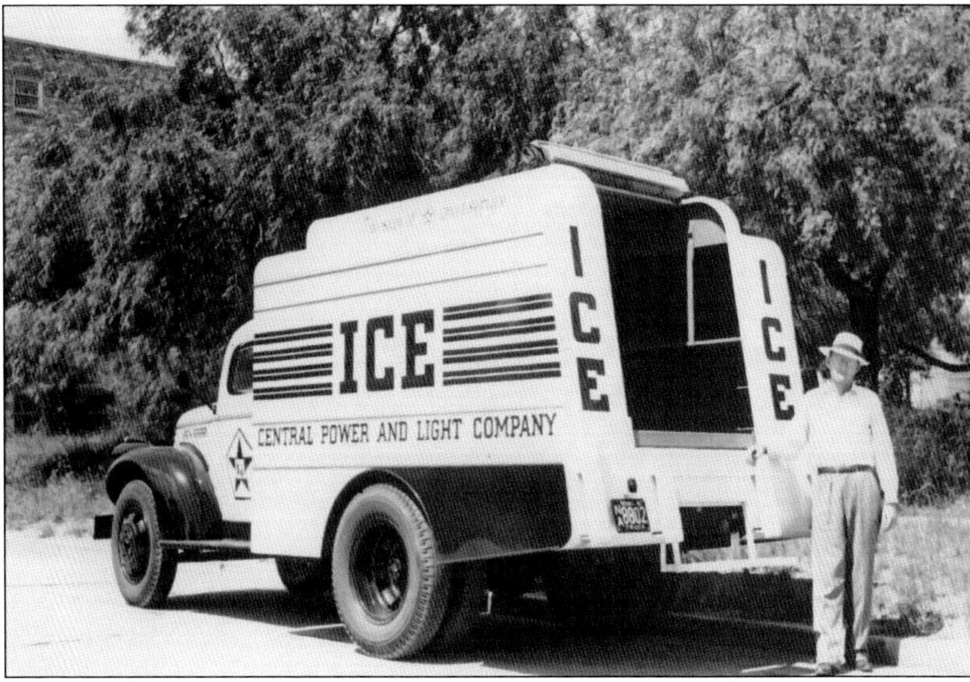

Home ice delivery entered the modern age before World War II with the use of this truck. After World War II, electric home refrigerators became popular, eliminating the need for such services. (Courtesy King Ranch, Inc., Kingsville, Texas.)

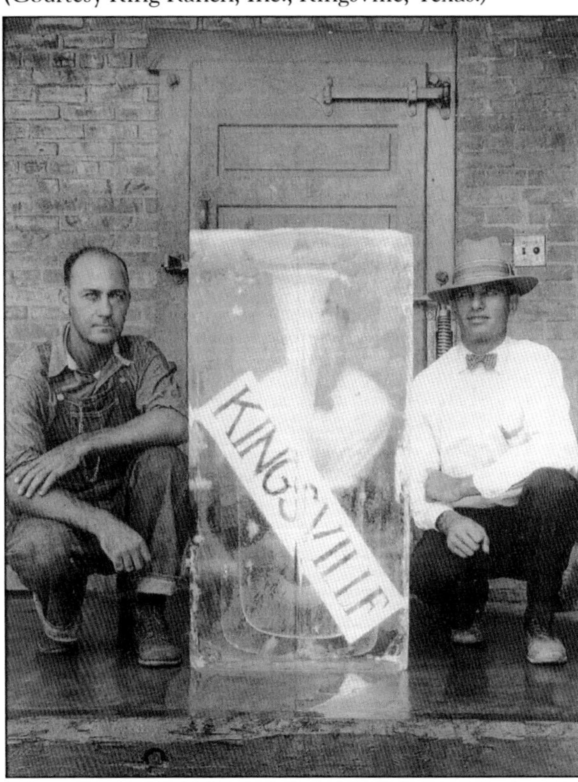

The ice factory manufactured 300-pound blocks of ice. This picture shows one of those blocks with an imbedded banner reading "Kingsville." Conveyor belts and ramps were needed to move the huge blocks from the manufacturing room to waiting railcars filled with produce. (Courtesy King Ranch, Inc., Kingsville, Texas.)

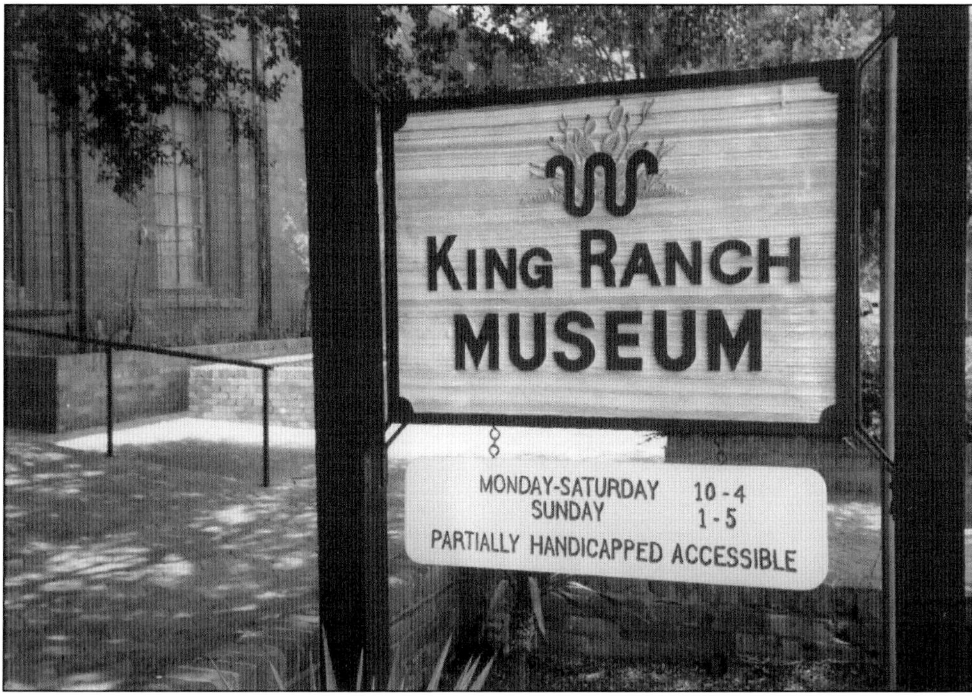

King Ranch purchased the old ice factory, the Central Power and Light Company Building, and began restoration in 1969. It was opened as a private family museum around 1976. In 1990, it opened to the public as the King Ranch Museum. On a hot summer day, the museum is a great place to visit and wonder how early Kingsvillians manufactured ice in the Wild Horse Desert. (Courtesy King Ranch, Inc., Kingsville, Texas.)

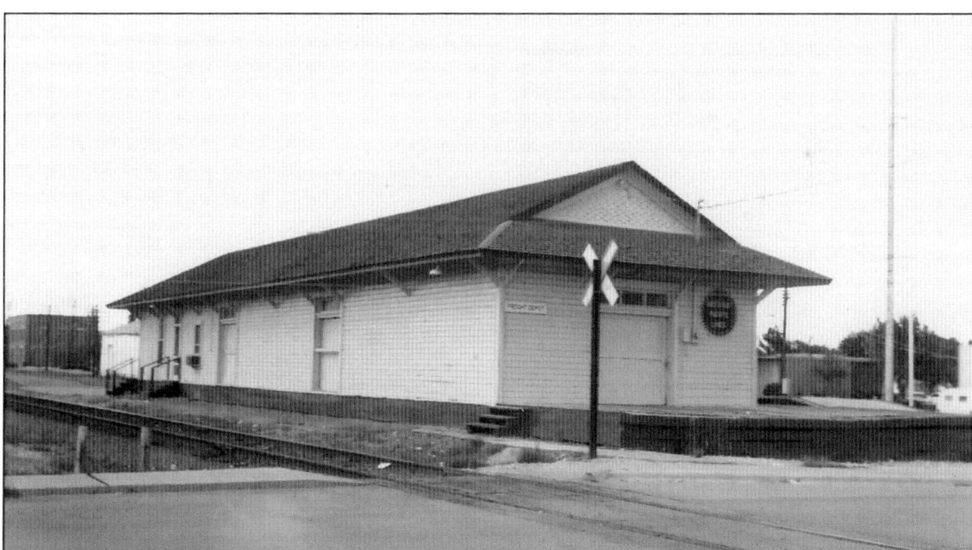

The Kingsville Freight Depot, with the ice factory in the background at left, is shown in this 1973 photograph. The frame building hugged the tracks at the intersection of the railroad and Yoakum Avenue. This structure changed little from the early days and was demolished in the late 1970s or early 1980s. (Courtesy South Texas Archives, Texas A&M University-Kingsville.)

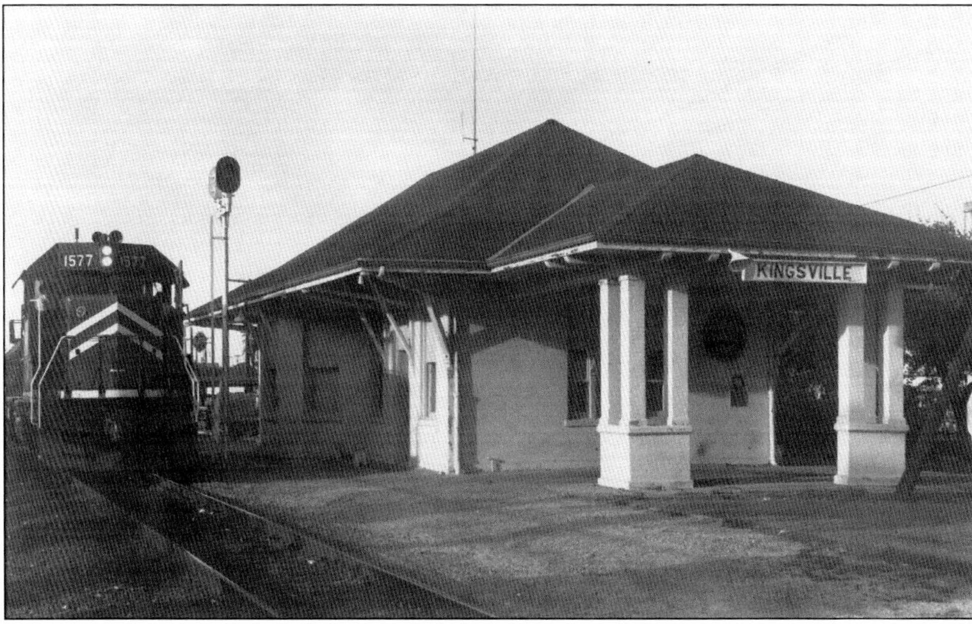

The diesel age did not alter the appearance of the passenger depot, but time changed its use. After passenger service ended, freight crews used the former passenger depot. There was an assignment board in the north waiting room for the crews. The front waiting room was turned into a locker area for crews staying in Kingsville. (Courtesy Vickie Lay Collection, 1904 Kingsville Train Depot Museum.)

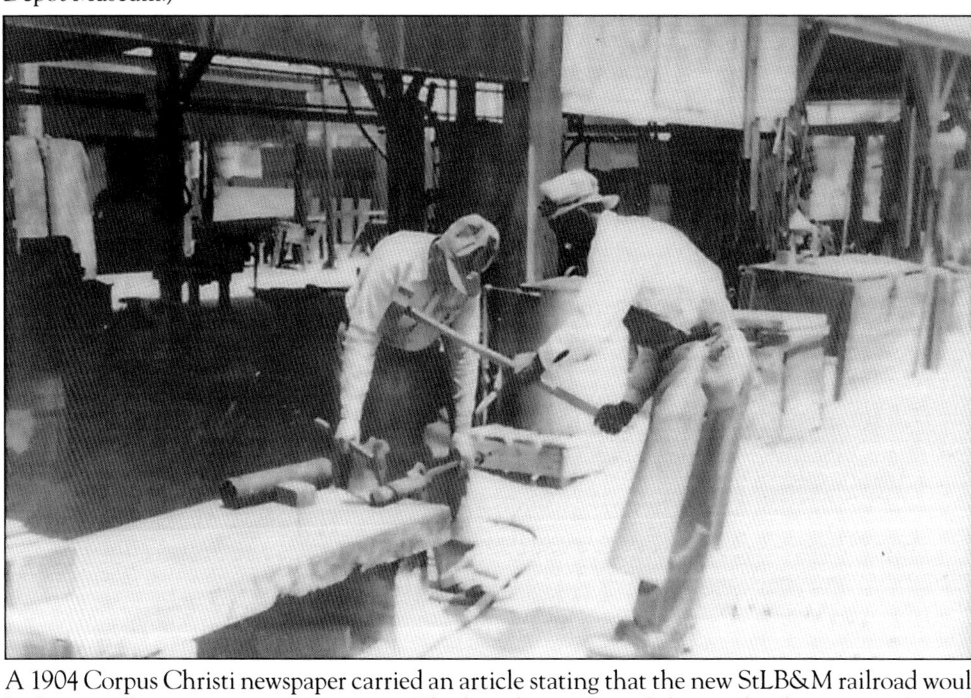

A 1904 Corpus Christi newspaper carried an article stating that the new StLB&M railroad would be hiring African American trainmen. The lengthy process of closing the shops started in July 1957. This photograph of shop workers is from the early 1970s. (Courtesy South Texas Archives, Texas A&M University-Kingsville.)

Five

Businesses and Entertainment

The business district is the heart of most communities. The main industry in Kingsville was the railroad, but a neighborhood developed to support the families who settled in the new community. Lumberyards, department stores, grocery stores, dry goods stores, restaurants, theaters, and pharmacies quickly appeared. Kingsville's prosperity drew doctors, lawyers, bankers, and real estate sales representatives to the town. Often, the prominent men of the community were involved in several enterprises concurrently.

In 1904, society in Texas was still segregated. In a sign of the times, one of the town's selling points was how carefully separated each group of people was from the others. Businesspeople in each group established businesses to serve their own communities. A "white" downtown developed first on Fifth Street and then moved to Kleberg Avenue after fire destroyed much of Fifth Street. The Hispanic downtown developed on Richard Avenue. In the 1950s, Luis and Manuela Fuentes opened the El Nueva Mundo department store, the first Hispanic business on Kleberg Avenue. African American railroad workers often supplemented their income by opening small businesses in The Quarters, at the intersection of Huisache Avenue and Second Street. The Quarters contained grocery stores, barbershops, and a taxi company.

Entertainment was an important community effort. The first movie in Kingsville was shown at the Kingsville Lumber Company on a canvas tarp serving as a makeshift screen. Movie houses soon popped up all over town. Theaters in the Hispanic community brought in popular Spanish-language movies from Mexico. El Teatro Iris and El Jardin (before it became a restaurant) hosted boxing and wrestling exhibitions.

Music also was an important part of early Kingsville. Many bands and musical groups were organized over the years to entertain the townspeople. The bandstand in Miller Park hosted a wide variety of shows.

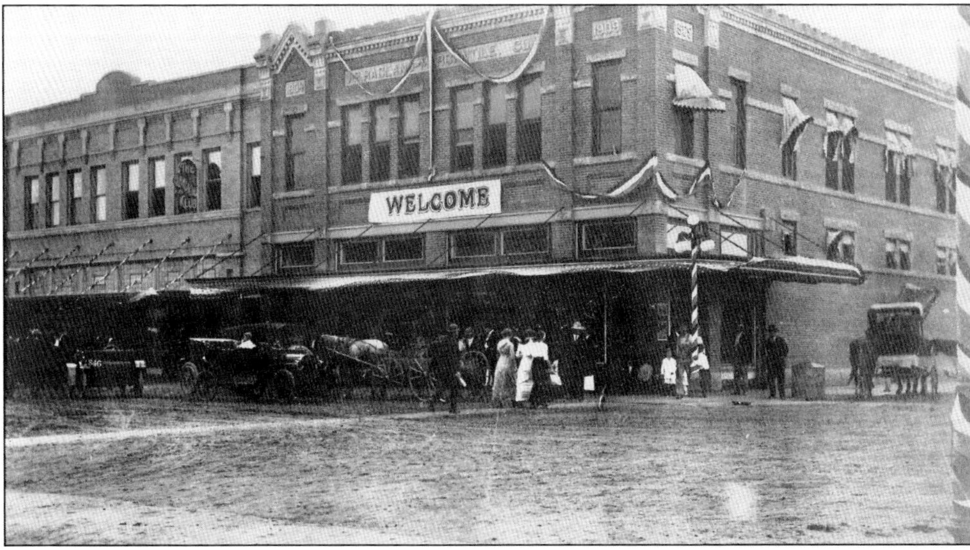

This welcome banner hangs on the side of the John B. Ragland Mercantile Company, locally referred to as "Raglands," about 1915. The unpaved streets were either dusty or muddy. Downtown buildings sported awnings to shade pedestrians. People would browse the stores and grab a meal or snack in one of the numerous restaurants—much like walking through modern shopping malls. (Courtesy South Texas Archives, Texas A&M University-Kingsville.)

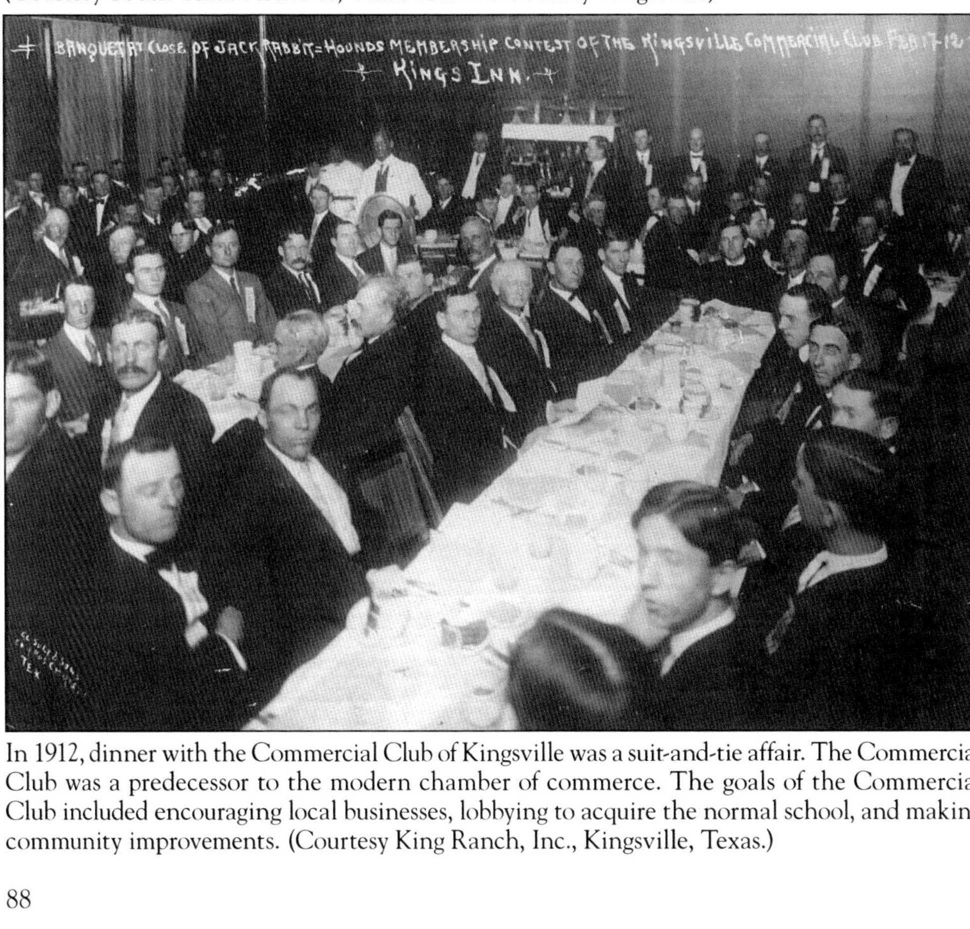

In 1912, dinner with the Commercial Club of Kingsville was a suit-and-tie affair. The Commercial Club was a predecessor to the modern chamber of commerce. The goals of the Commercial Club included encouraging local businesses, lobbying to acquire the normal school, and making community improvements. (Courtesy King Ranch, Inc., Kingsville, Texas.)

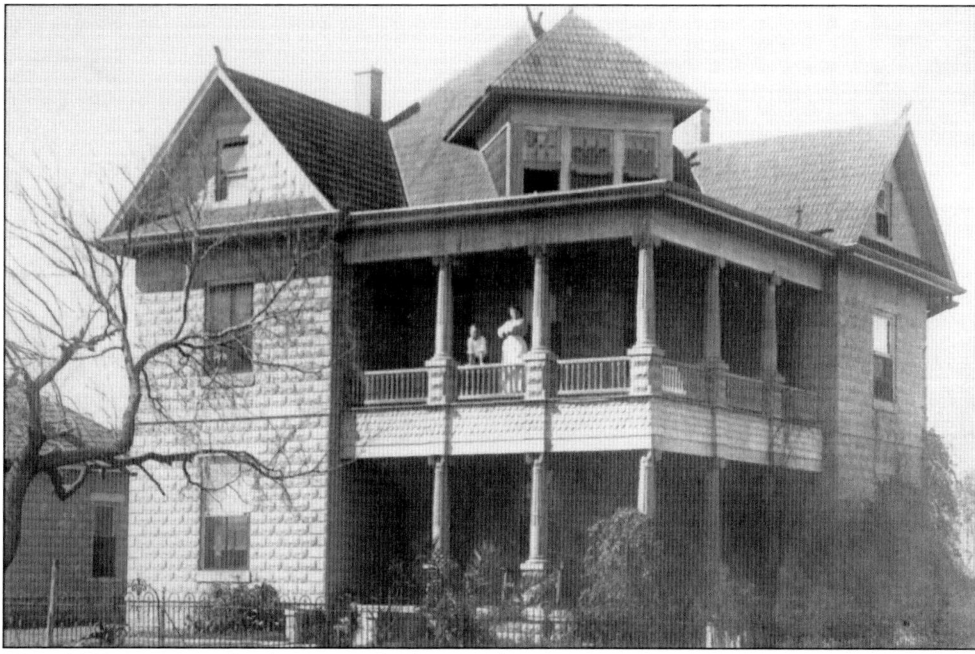

The old Watson Boardinghouse was built around 1906 to accommodate railroaders and visitors. Kingsville's first hotel and restaurant were located in a tent run by Mrs. Watson. Mr. Watson worked as a railroad pumper, filling the steam engines with needed water. This image is from 1915. (Courtesy South Texas Archives, Texas A&M University-Kingsville.)

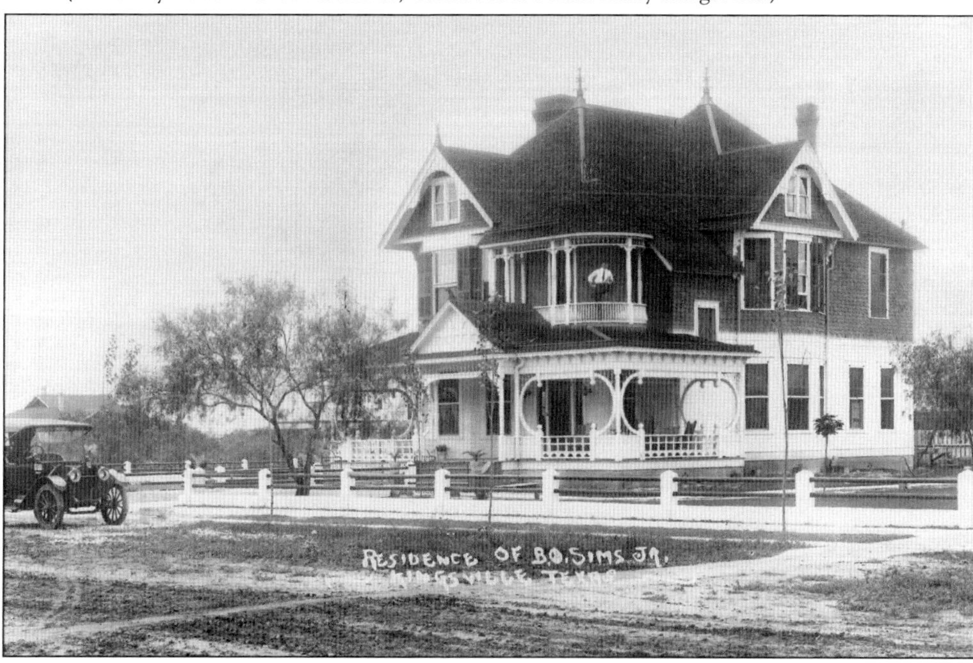

The B.O. Sims Jr. residence was one of the homes featured in the December 13, 1912, issue of the *Kingsville Record*. The article was titled "Kingsville: The Gem City of Southwest Texas." The lengthy feature described the progress of the new town in the eight short years of its existence. (Courtesy King Ranch, Inc., Kingsville, Texas.)

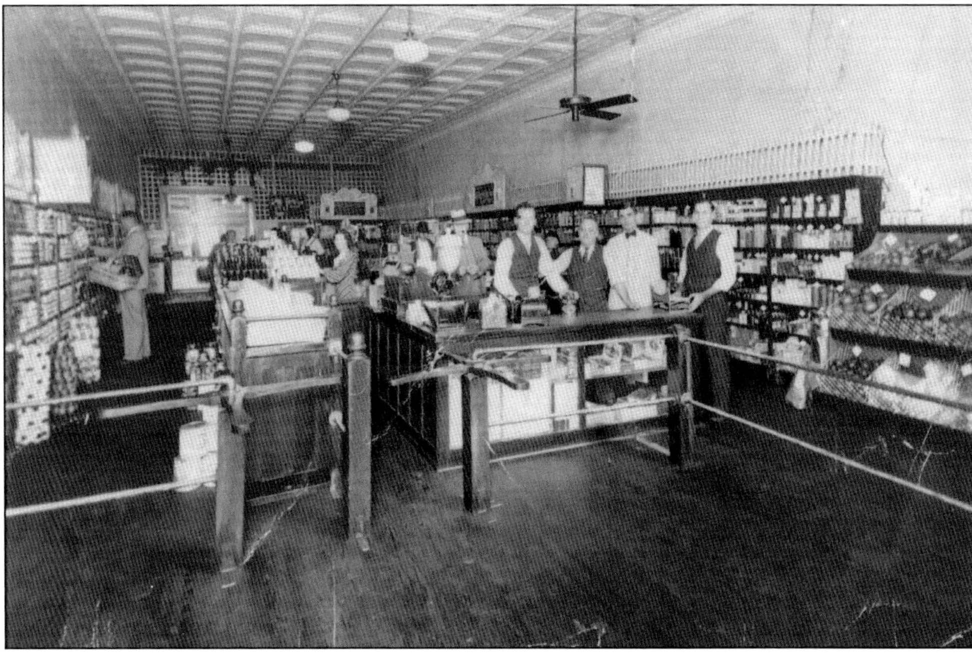

A 1930 photograph of Kingsville's Piggly Wiggly store shows four men standing at the checkout counter. They are, from left to right, owners Paul Moore and Bill Edgar, butcher Arthur Klare, and Rex Wright. This was a typical setup for a grocery store of the era, with hardwood floors and turnstile entrances and exits. (Courtesy South Texas Archives, Texas A&M University-Kingsville.)

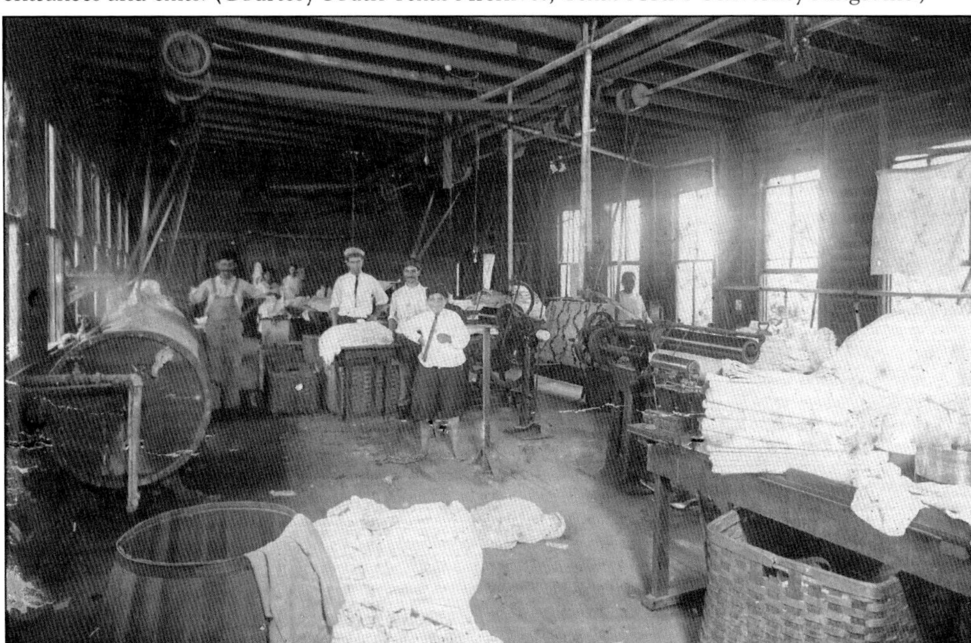

Kingsville's Steam Laundry was frequently advertised in the *Kingsville Record*. Steam power was used to drive the belts to run the laundry equipment. This image may be the only picture of the interior. The building has been restored and is currently home to the Hall of Frames picture-framing shop in 2011. (Courtesy South Texas Archives, Texas A&M University-Kingsville.)

The Kingsville Bottling Company started out as the Bishop Bottling Company. Joseph William Garrison purchased the business and moved it in 1915 to the building seen here on West Alice Avenue in Kingsville. Cecil and Joe Garrison owned and managed the company after their father died. A modern structure, erected in 1938, later became a Dr. Pepper franchise and is currently used as the Kingsville Recycling Center. This picture offers a look at street conditions around 1915. (Courtesy South Texas Archives, Texas A&M University-Kingsville.)

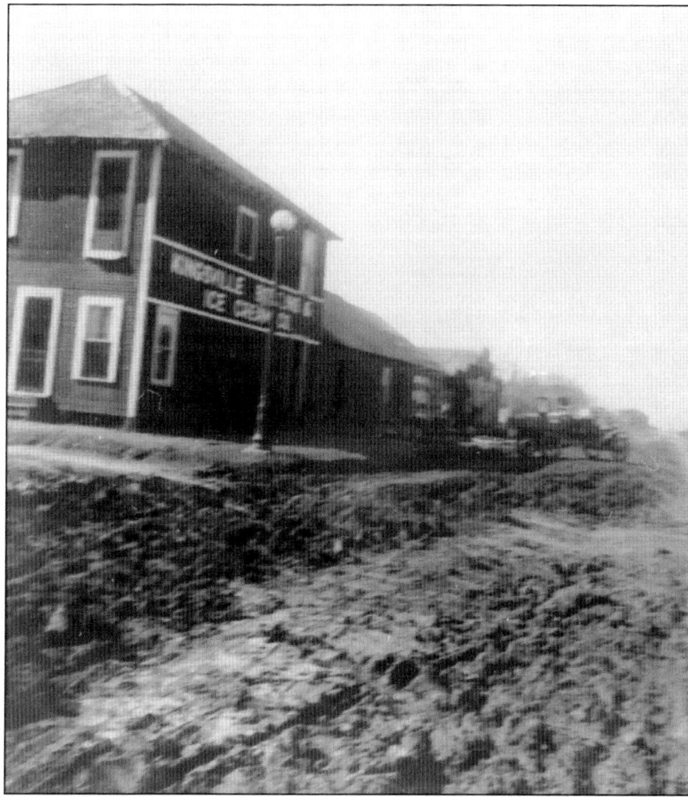

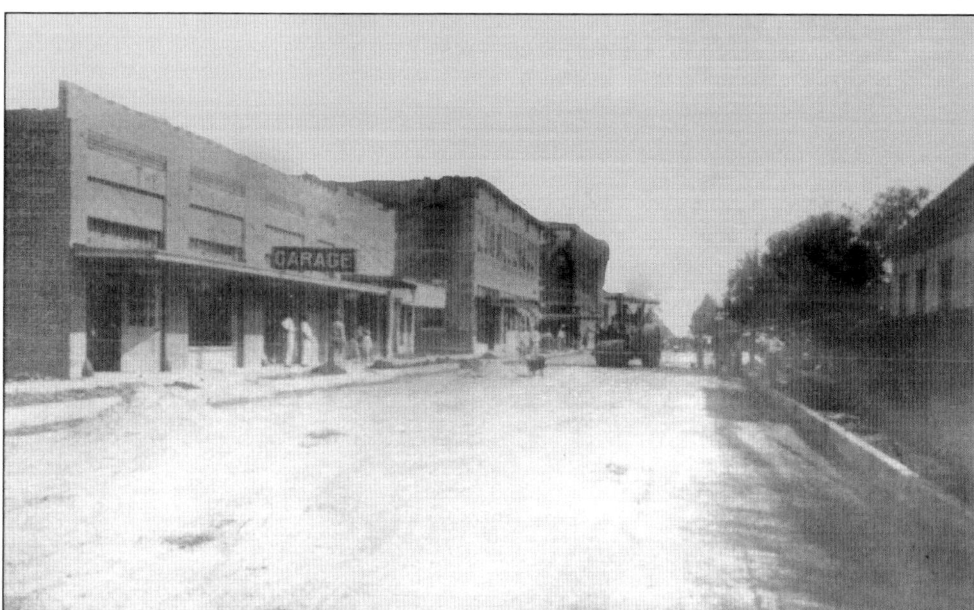

Street paving was a challenge for Kingsville. By 1916, citizens were clamoring for a solution to the generally dusty and sometimes very muddy streets of the new community. Tarvia (the brand name of a road-surfacing material) was one of the first methods of paving tested. (Courtesy South Texas Archives, Texas A&M University-Kingsville.)

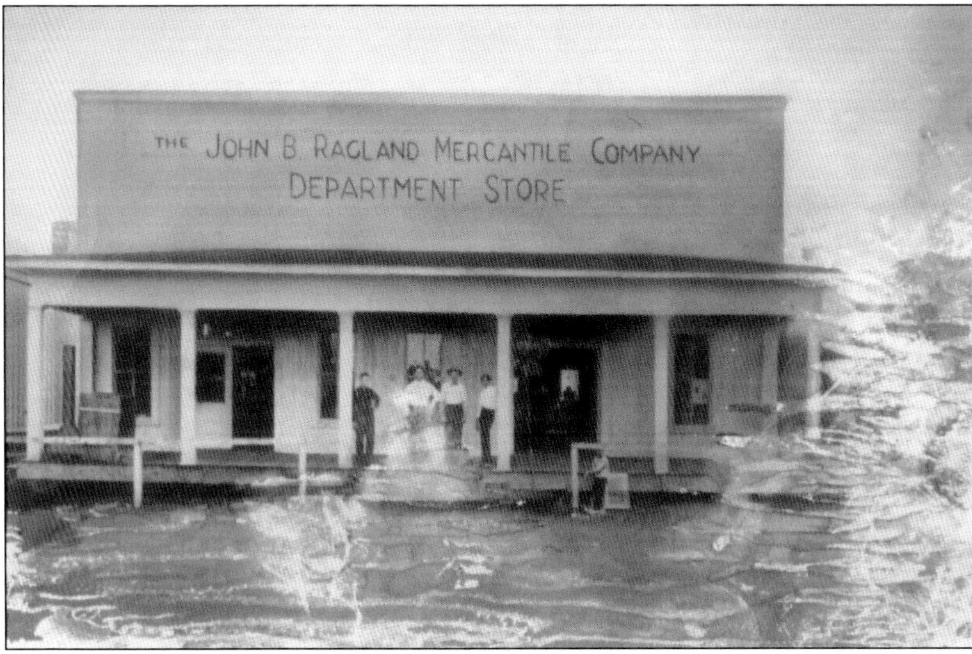

John B. Ragland constructed Kingsville's original John B. Ragland Mercantile Company store in October 1904. It was a frame, one-story structure that was 15 feet by 40 feet in size. Ragland had a store in Alice, Texas, and Robert Kleberg persuaded him to come to Kingsville and build one here. (Courtesy King Ranch, Inc., Kingsville, Texas.)

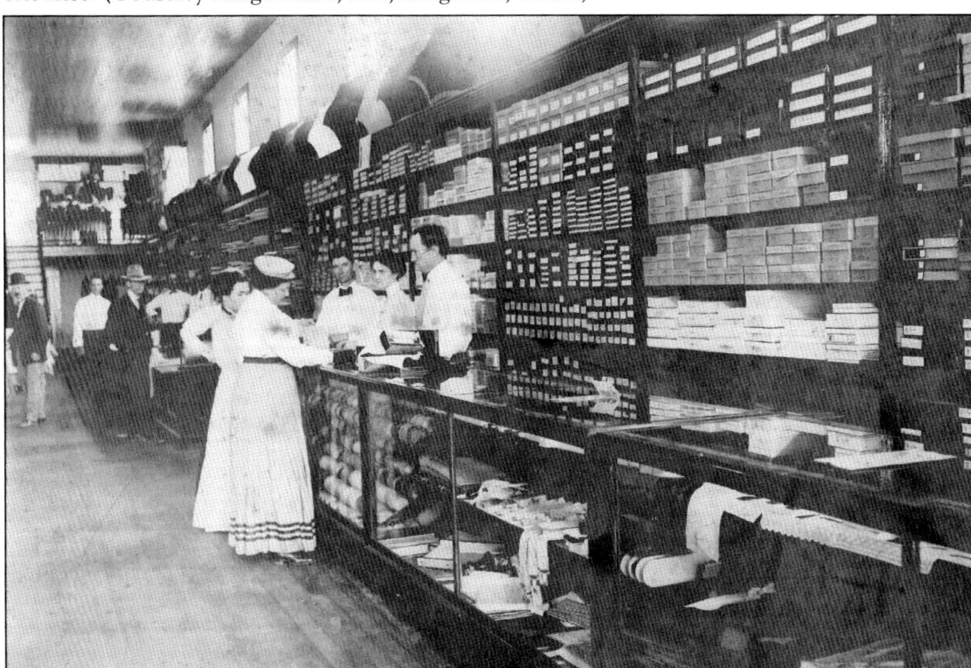

Looking at this photograph of the interior of Ragland's store, one can almost hear the creak of the hardwood floors. The store clerks were ready to open cases or pull down boxes for shoppers to view the goods more closely. (Courtesy South Texas Archives, Texas A&M University-Kingsville.)

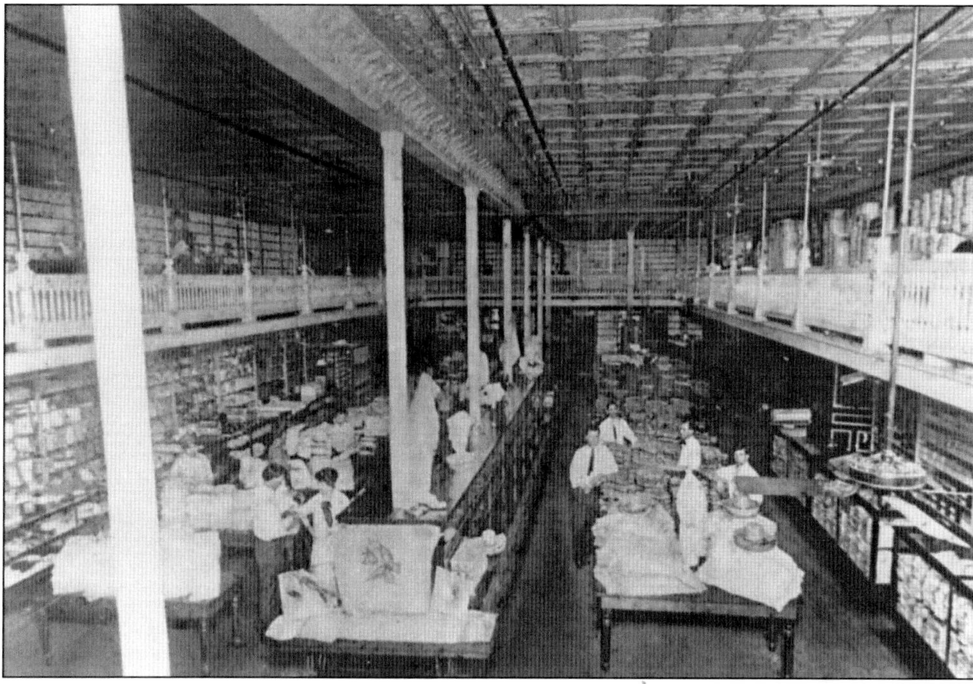

Fire safety was an important issue. The John B. Ragland Mercantile Company building was designed with an early sprinkler system to fight any blazes that might start in the structure. In this c. 1915 photograph, the sprinkler system can be seen running the length of the building, just below the pressed-tin ceiling tiles. (Courtesy King Ranch, Inc., Kingsville, Texas.)

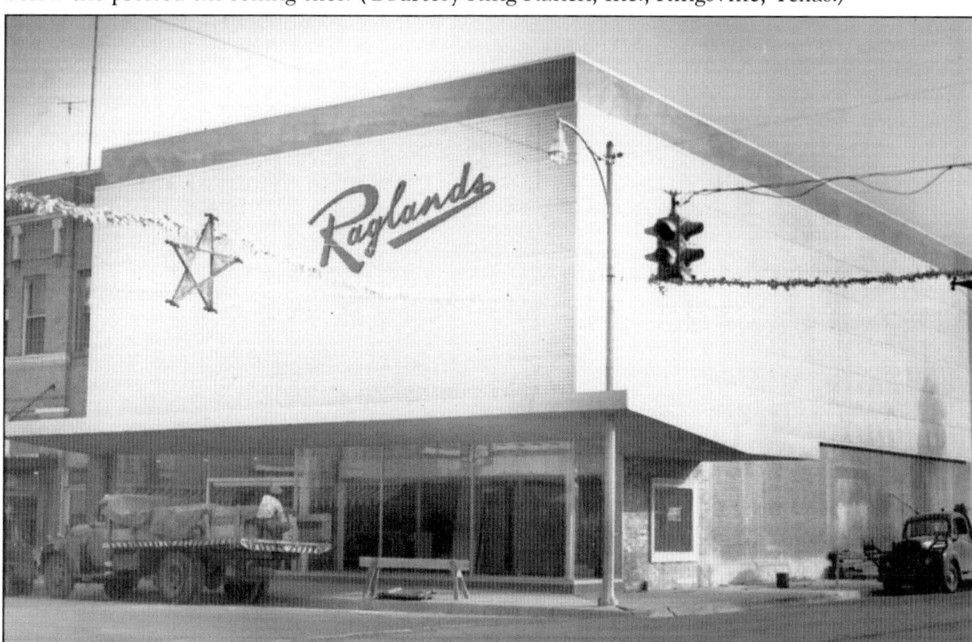

It was important for stores to put on a modern face in the 1950s. Raglands did just that by placing a veneer over the brickwork of the original building. The familiar cupola was removed when the new facade was added. (Courtesy King Ranch, Inc., Kingsville, Texas.)

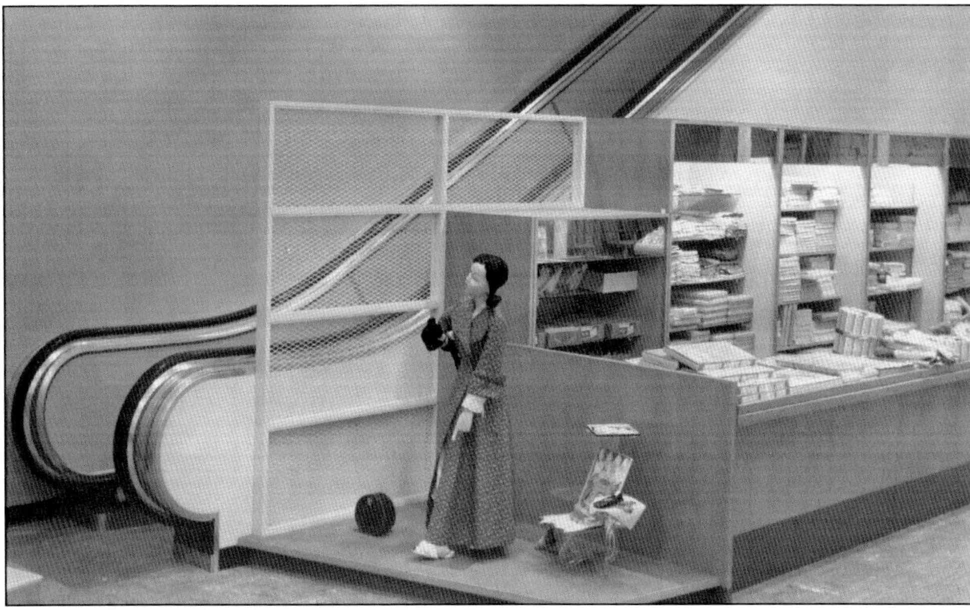

John B. Ragland Mercantile Company was the most popular department store in South Texas. It was also a business that stayed on the cutting edge by installing the first escalator in the region. Many Kingsvillians have fond childhood memories of riding up and down the escalator while their parents shopped at Raglands. (Courtesy King Ranch, Inc., Kingsville, Texas.)

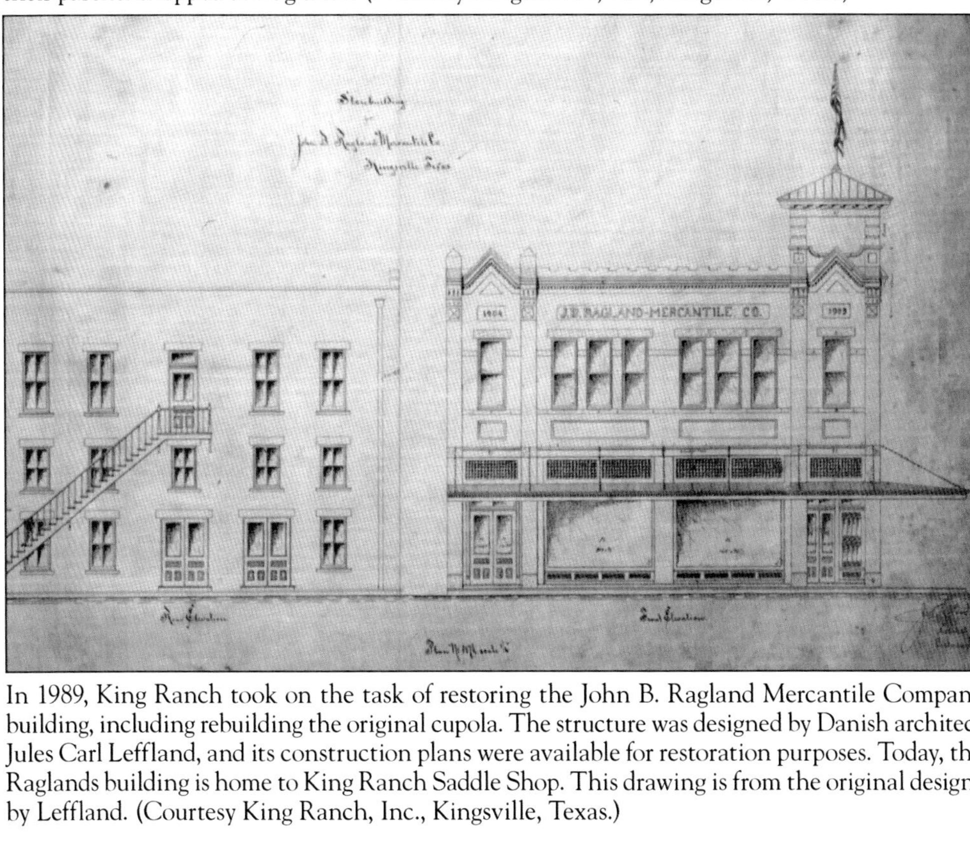

In 1989, King Ranch took on the task of restoring the John B. Ragland Mercantile Company building, including rebuilding the original cupola. The structure was designed by Danish architect Jules Carl Leffland, and its construction plans were available for restoration purposes. Today, the Raglands building is home to King Ranch Saddle Shop. This drawing is from the original designs by Leffland. (Courtesy King Ranch, Inc., Kingsville, Texas.)

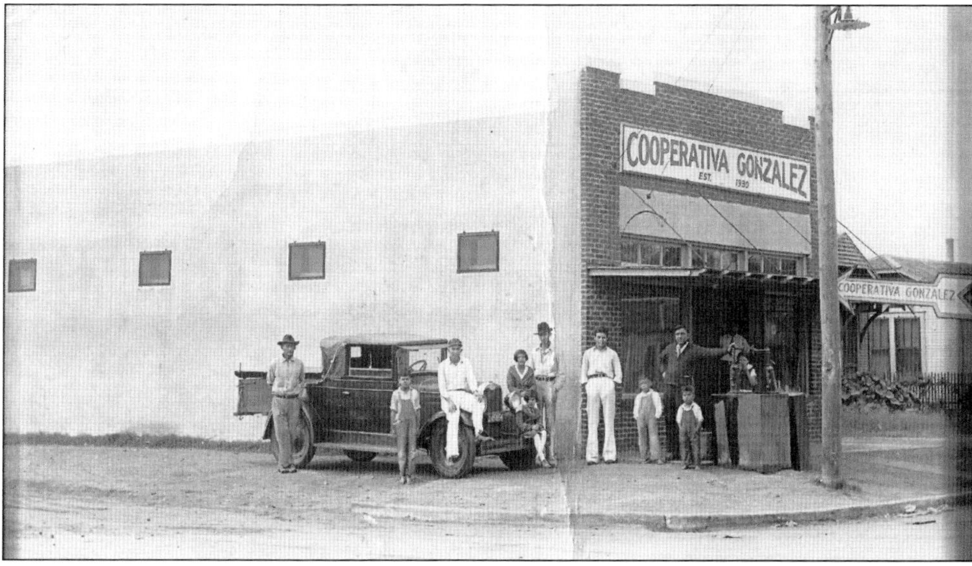

Originally, this photograph was printed in a postcard format. The Cooperativa Gonzalez on Richard Avenue served the Hispanic community in Kingsville. The store sold basic groceries such as eggs, bread, lard, beans, coffee, vegetables, and fruits. Foods were sold by weight and never prepackaged. (Courtesy South Texas Archives, Texas A&M University-Kingsville.)

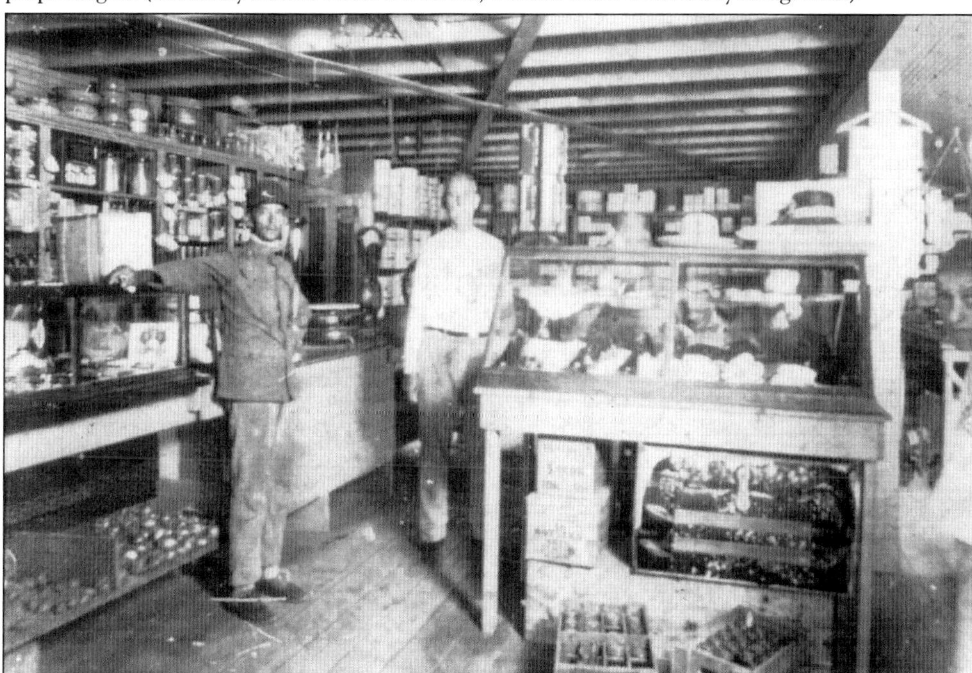

In 1919, Vicente Salazar came to Kingsville from Falfurrias, Texas, where he had run a clothing store, and established the Salazar Clothing and Grocery Store. The original building, a frame structure, had been a restaurant. Salazar's sons—Edwardo, Nicolas, and José—maintained the family business until 1965, when they were forced to close due to health issues. In 1927, they built a cement structure, the V. Salazar Building, on Richard Avenue and Sixth Street. (Courtesy South Texas Archives, Texas A&M University-Kingsville.)

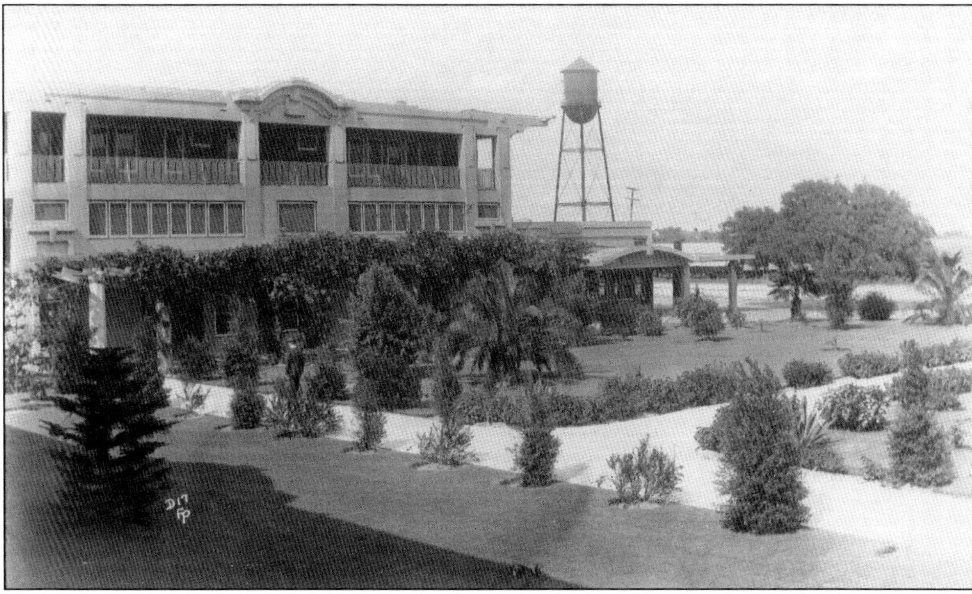

The Casa Ricardo Hotel grounds were beautifully landscaped with local and imported plants. Everything was an attempt to make visitors feel that they were in a special place. (Courtesy King Ranch, Inc., Kingsville, Texas.)

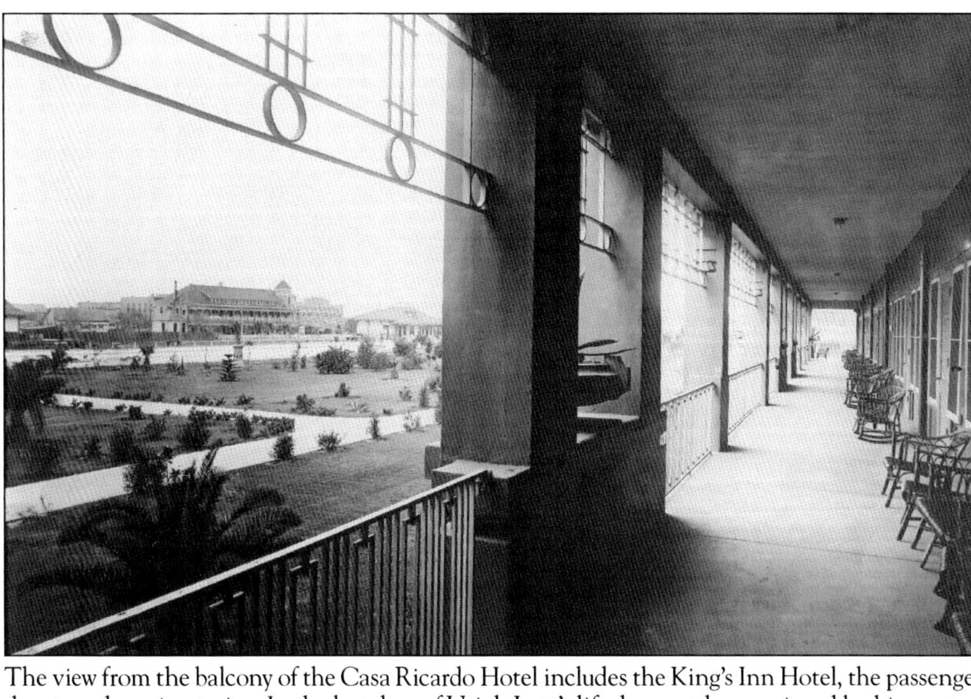

The view from the balcony of the Casa Ricardo Hotel includes the King's Inn Hotel, the passenger depot, and passing trains. In the last days of Uriah Lott's life, he must have enjoyed looking out at the railroad that he loved; the great railroad builder died penniless at the Casa Ricardo in 1915, and Kingsville mourned his passing. (Courtesy King Ranch, Inc., Kingsville, Texas.)

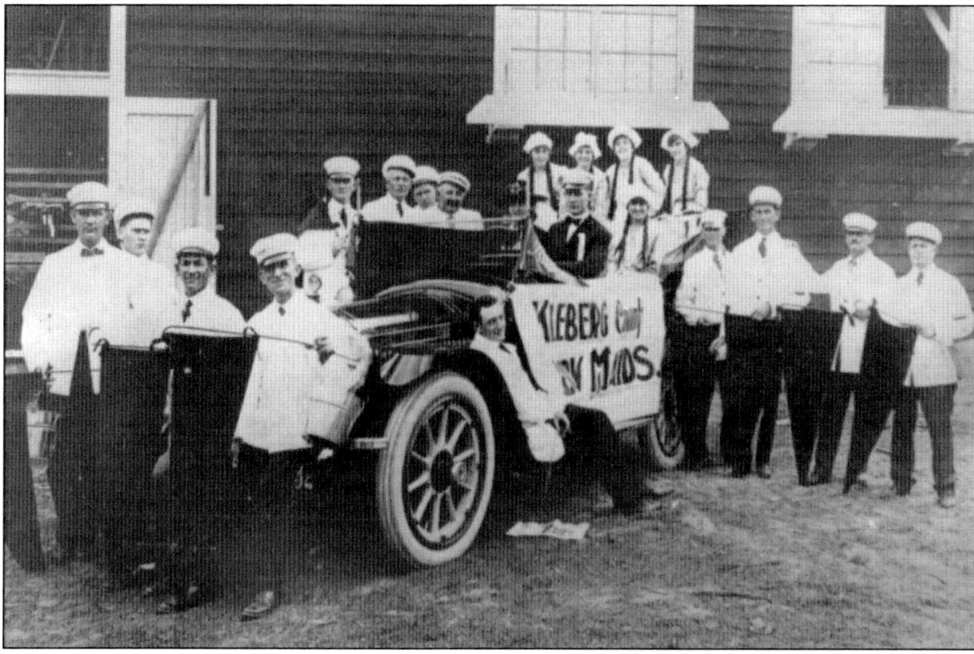

When one thinks of modern Kingsville and the region around Kleberg County, one does not think of the dairy industry. However, in 1910, King Ranch imported a herd of dairy cows from the Isle of Jersey and began serious efforts to cultivate a dairy industry. The Dairy Products Company was started as a cooperative for farmers to market their dairy products. (Courtesy King Ranch, Inc., Kingsville, Texas.)

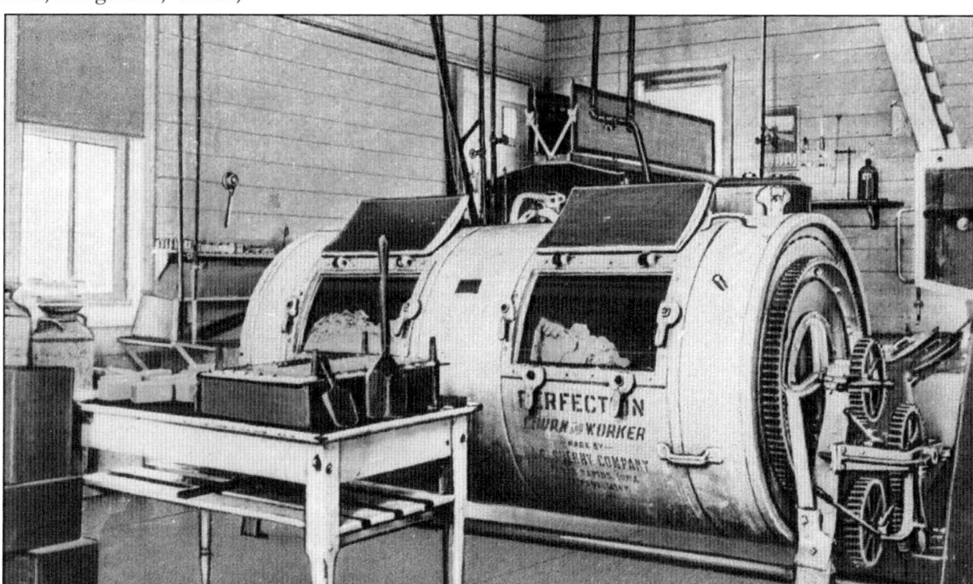

This 1919 photograph of the Dairy Products Company of Kingsville's butter churn was used in a promotional brochure. In 1913, butter was the company's only product, and 52,000 pounds was manufactured. In 1939, the company employed 25 people and produced 400,000 pounds of butter. Efforts were made after World War I to diversify the product line to include poultry and other items. (Courtesy South Texas Archives, Texas A&M University-Kingsville.)

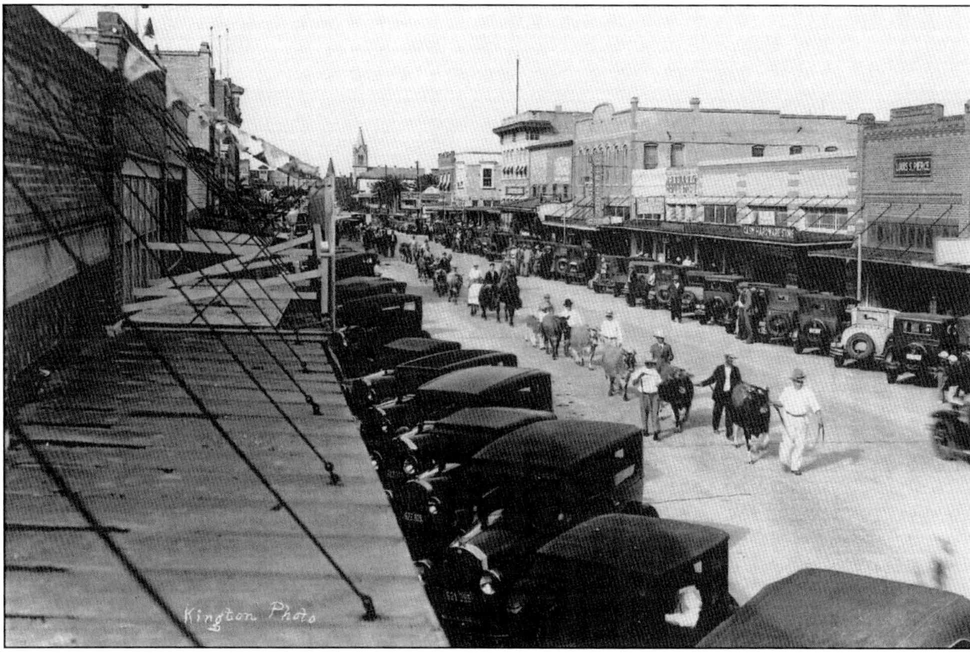

To encourage the dairy industry in Kleberg County, King Ranch worked with local farmers to improve the quality of dairy herds. Robert Kleberg developed a plan to sell registered King Ranch Jersey bulls at a fraction of their real value. Here, Librado Maldonado of King Ranch leads a parade of Jersey cattle down Kleberg Avenue. (Courtesy King Ranch, Inc., Kingsville, Texas.)

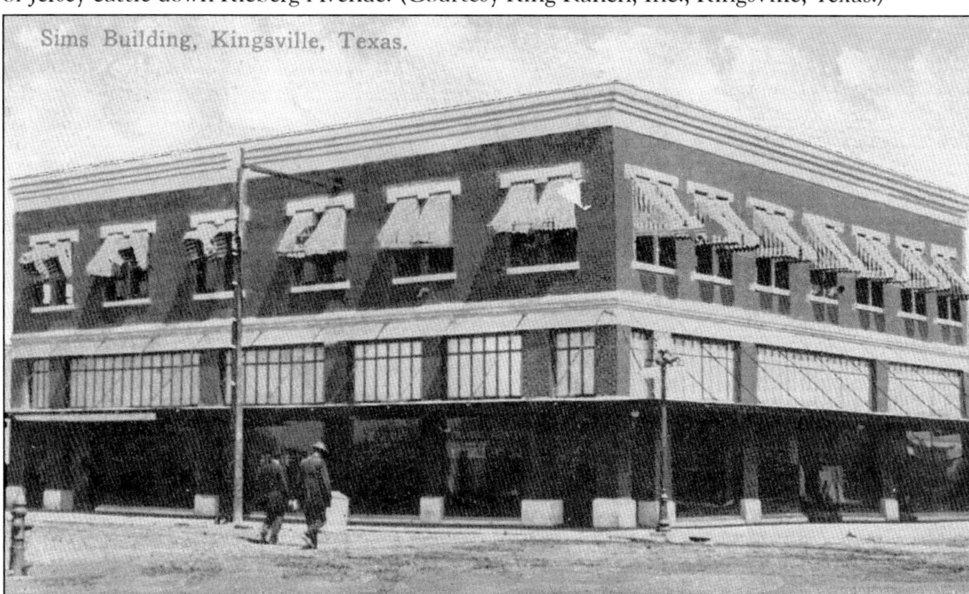

This early photograph of the B.O. Sims Building was printed in a postcard format. Located at the corner of Kleberg Avenue and Seventh Street, the structure housed the offices of B.O. Sims and a dry goods store; the First National Bank operated from the first floor. A J.C. Penney store eventually occupied the entire building. (Courtesy South Texas Archives, Texas A&M University-Kingsville.)

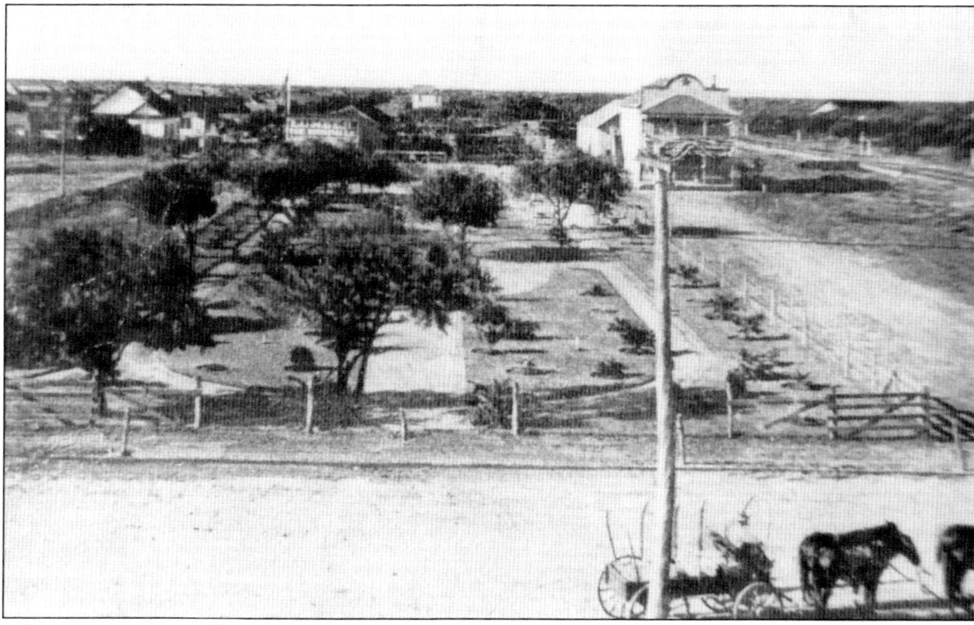

This c. 1906 image shows Caesar Park, which was sometimes called Artesian Park because the artesian well for the railroad was located here. For a period of time, there was a pond that attracted many toads that would sing at night. The community had to do away with the pond in order to get a restful night's sleep. (Courtesy South Texas Archives, Texas A&M University-Kingsville.)

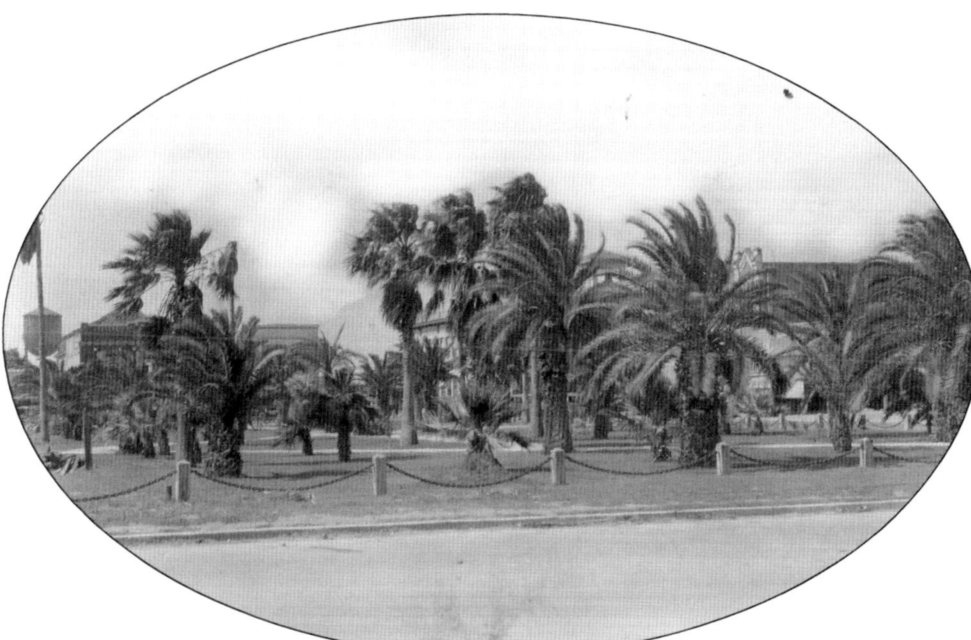

Kingsville was proud of Caesar Park. It was kept neat and welcoming for visitors to the town, and over 60 different kinds of palm trees were planted in the park. This eventually became the site of the post office. (Courtesy King Ranch, Inc., Kingsville, Texas.)

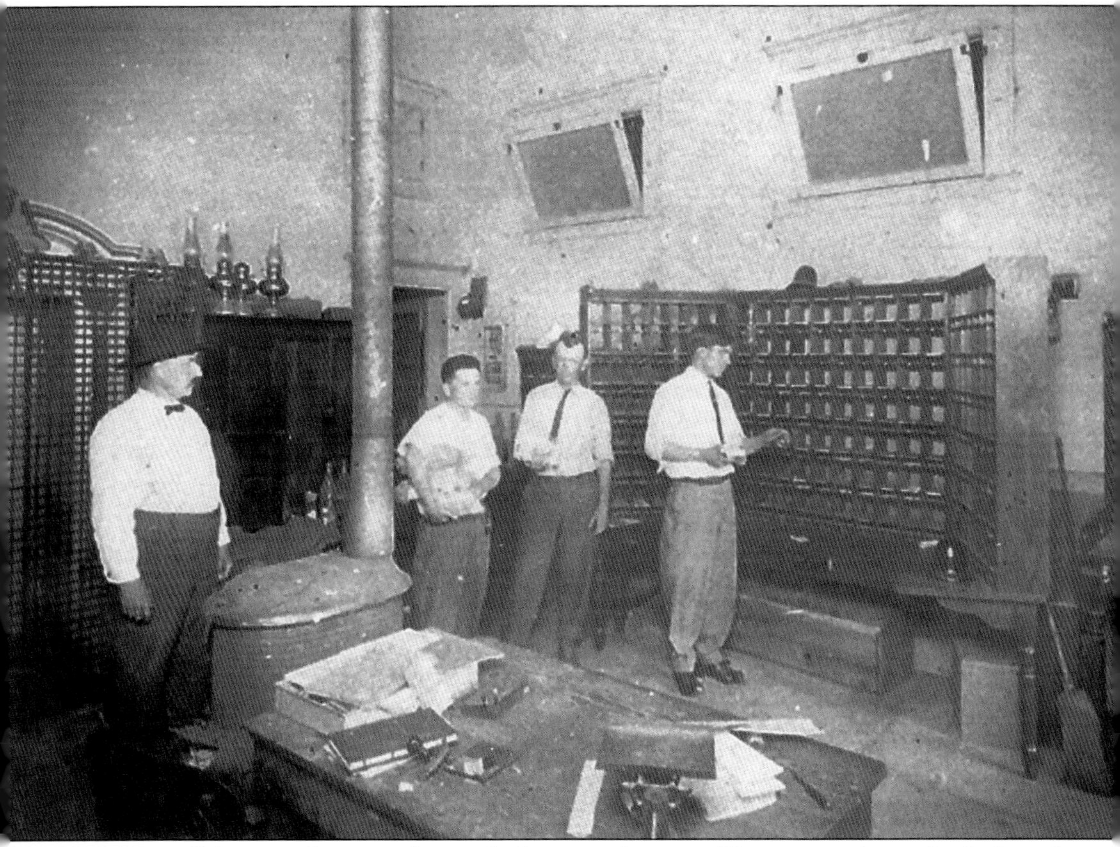

Kingsville's post office moved around often over the years. This picture shows the facility when it was in the rebuilt Kleberg Bank Building in 1912. Everyone in town had to come to the post office to pick up their mail, as there was no home delivery at that time. Pictured here are, from left to right, Ray Schmidt, Raleigh Crane, James Doss, and postmaster J.S. House. The Post Office Department designated Kingsville for free mail delivery in the city limits, which was formally inaugurated on October 1, 1926. Residents had to have sidewalk and house numbering in order to get mail delivered to their homes. (Courtesy South Texas Archives, Texas A&M University-Kingsville.)

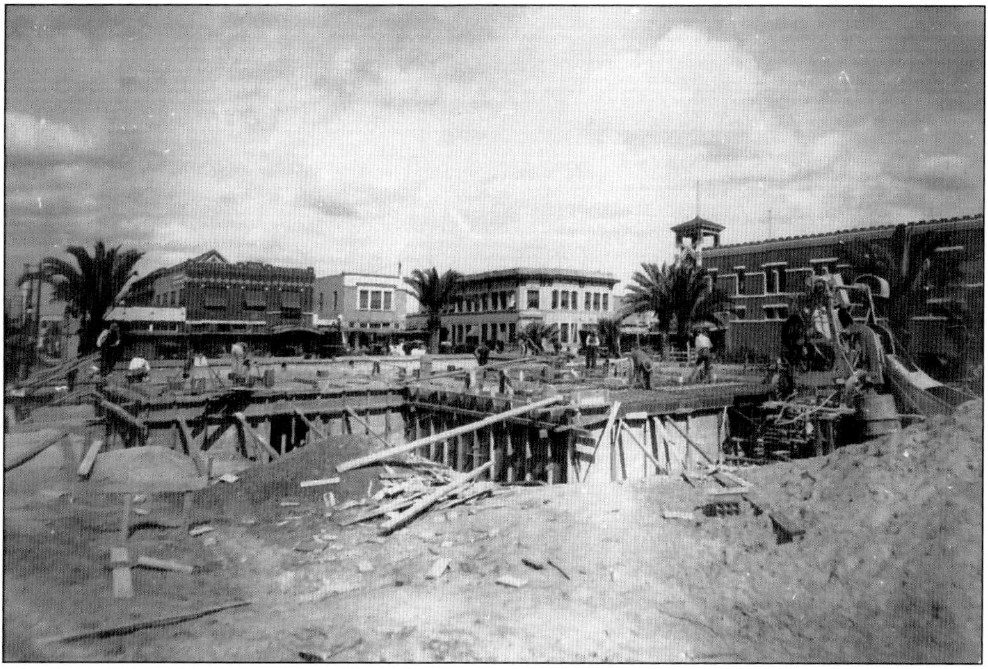

The foundation for the new federal post office building was poured in 1934. The beloved palm trees of Caesar Park were removed. With construction in the area by this time, the King's Inn Hotel, in the background at left, is no longer a part of the downtown view as it had been in the c. 1910 view on page 43. (Courtesy South Texas Archives, Texas A&M University-Kingsville.)

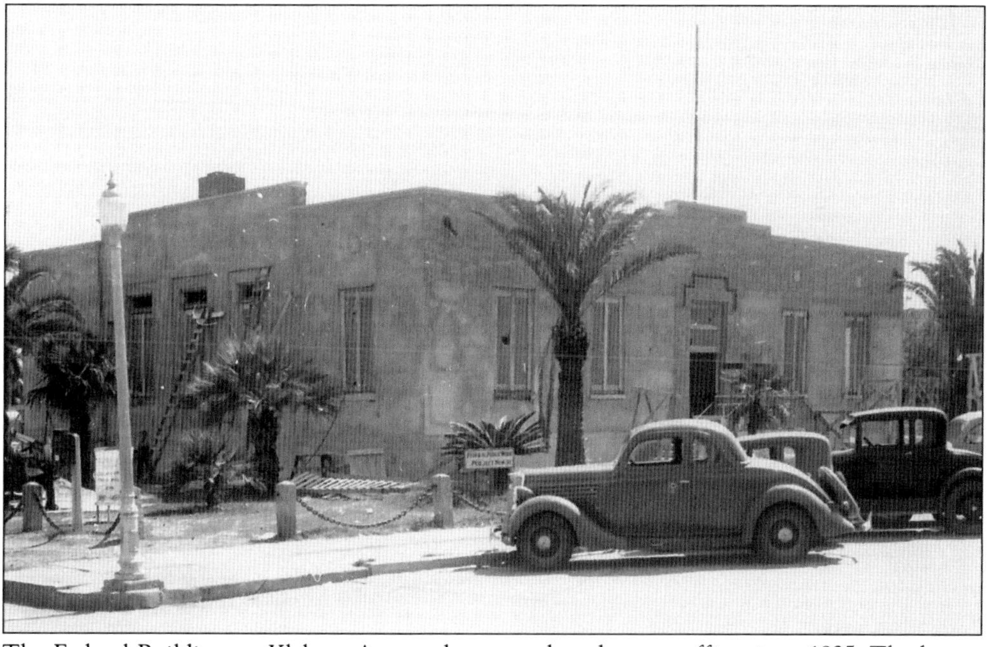

The Federal Building on Kleberg Avenue has served as the post office since 1935. The heavy cement posts and huge chain were once used to mark the boundary of Caesar Park and stand today as the border of the post office property. (Courtesy South Texas Archives, Texas A&M University-Kingsville.)

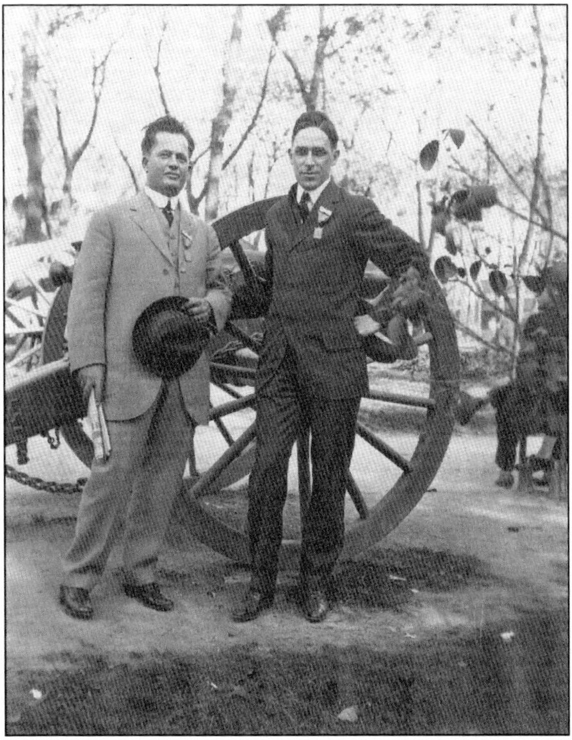

Charles Flato Jr. (left) was one of Kingsville's most effective boosters and took every opportunity to promote the new community. It was Flato Jr. who built the Opera House in an effort to bring culture to the town. (Courtesy South Texas Archives, Texas A&M University-Kingsville.)

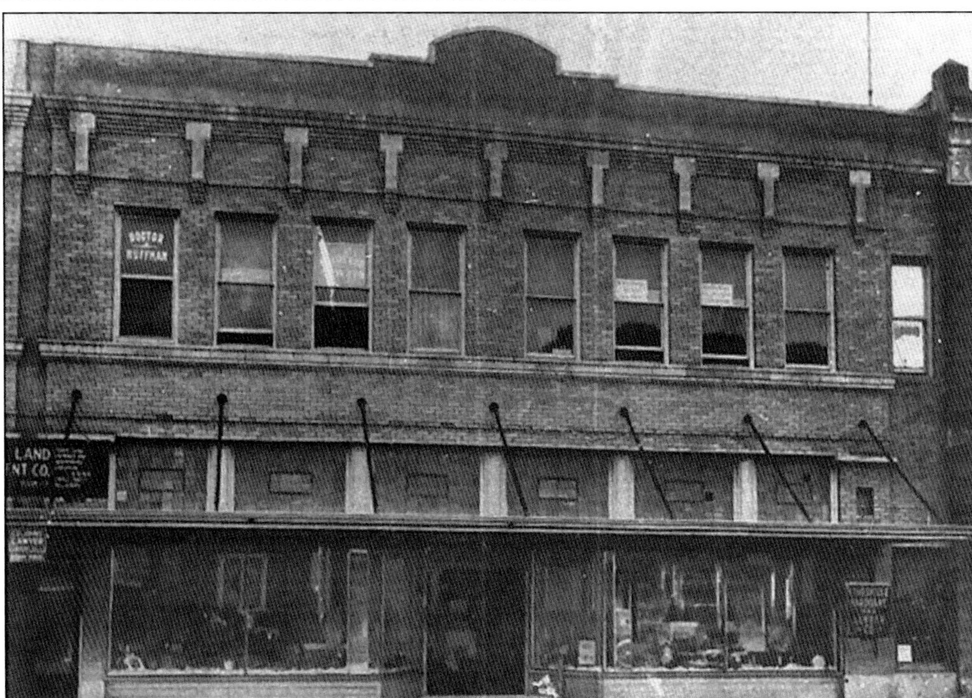

The views from some angles of the Charles Flato Jr. Building on Kleberg Avenue hid the fact that a whole theater was housed on the second floor. The theater could seat about 400 people. (Courtesy South Texas Archives, Texas A&M University-Kingsville.)

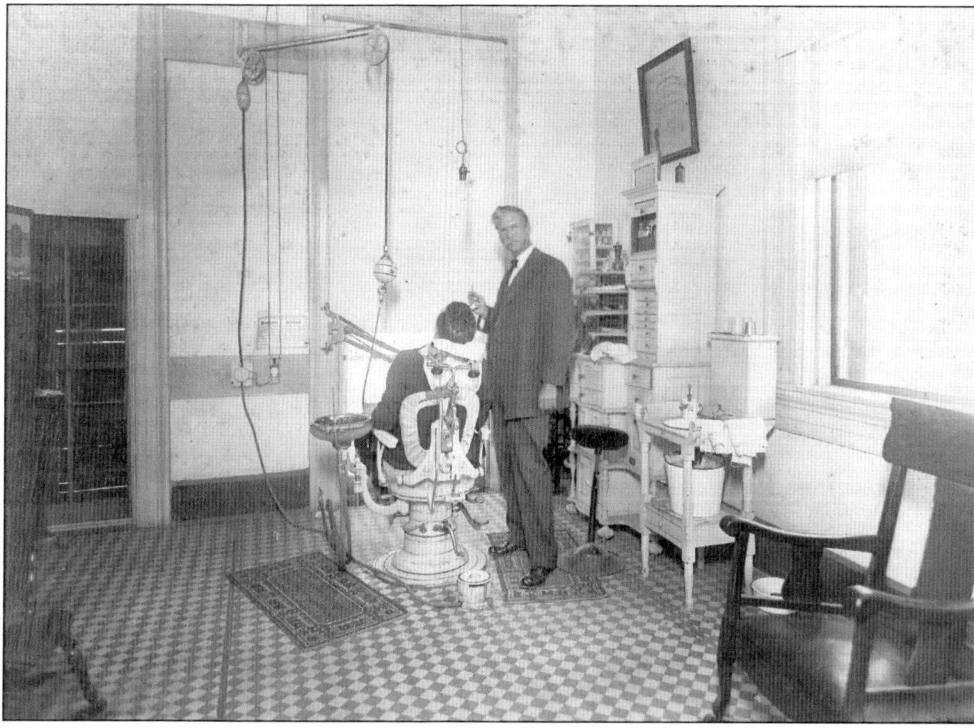

The second floor of the Flato Building, with windows looking down on bustling Kleberg Avenue, housed dentist's offices similar to the one pictured here in the 1940s, as well as doctors and lawyers. (Courtesy South Texas Archives, Texas A&M University-Kingsville.)

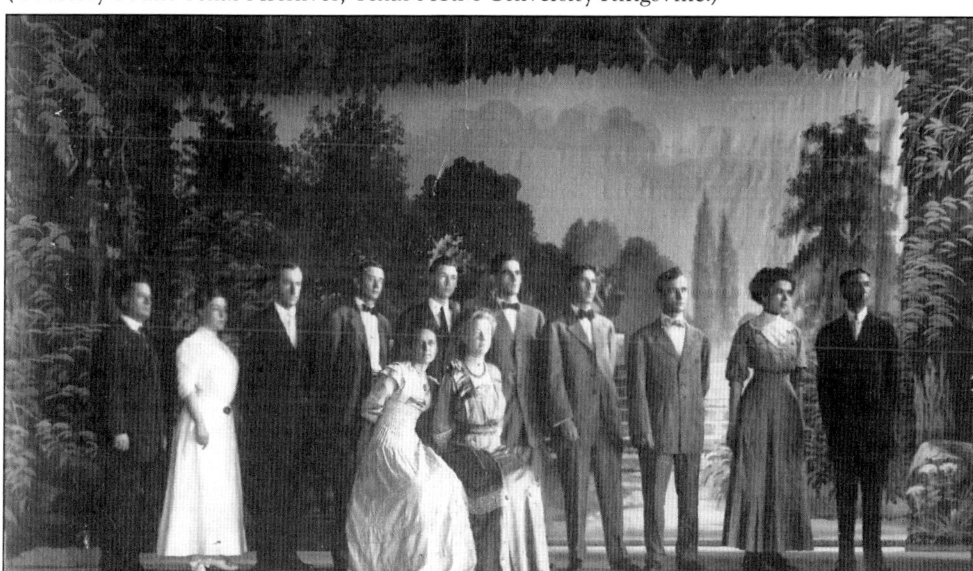

The cast of the play *Rio Grande* poses for a picture on the Opera House stage on May 3, 1911. Many plays, speakers, and community events used the Opera House, located above the Kingsville Lumber Company on Kleberg Avenue. Theater eventually faded away because of competition from the numerous motion picture establishments in Kingsville. (Courtesy South Texas Archives, Texas A&M University-Kingsville.)

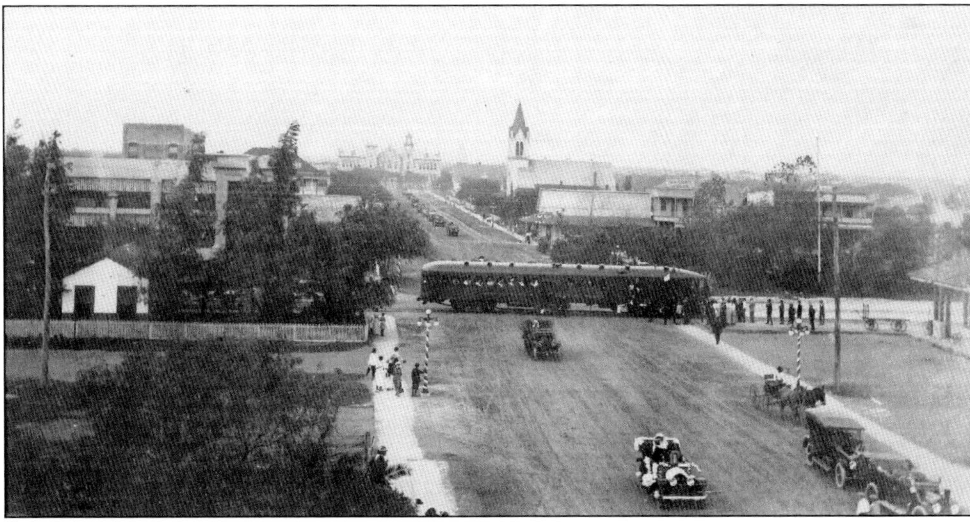

This image shows a parade heading east on Kleberg Avenue around 1915. The gas-powered commuter train in the center of the photograph made a couple of trips daily between Corpus Christi and Riviera. Just as in modern times, this parade has been blocked by a train; it would not be a true Kingsville parade if a train did not split things up. (Courtesy South Texas Archives, Texas A&M University-Kingsville.)

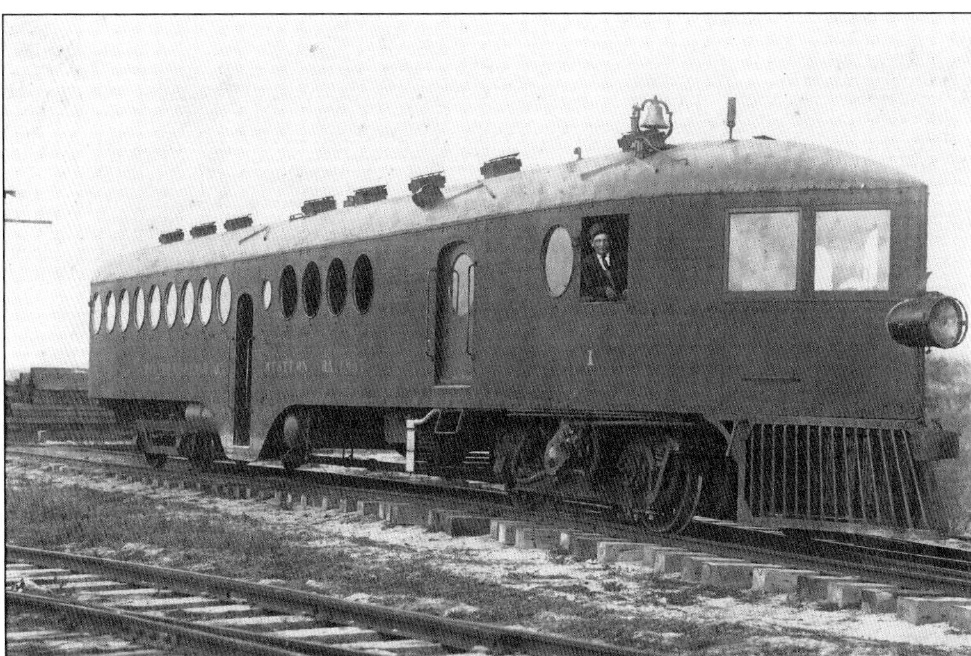

The Riviera Beach & Western Railway connected Riviera Beach with the main StLB&M line. It was not uncommon for the newspaper to announce a group picnic or day trip to Riviera Beach for Kingsvillians. (Courtesy South Texas Archives, Texas A&M University-Kingsville.)

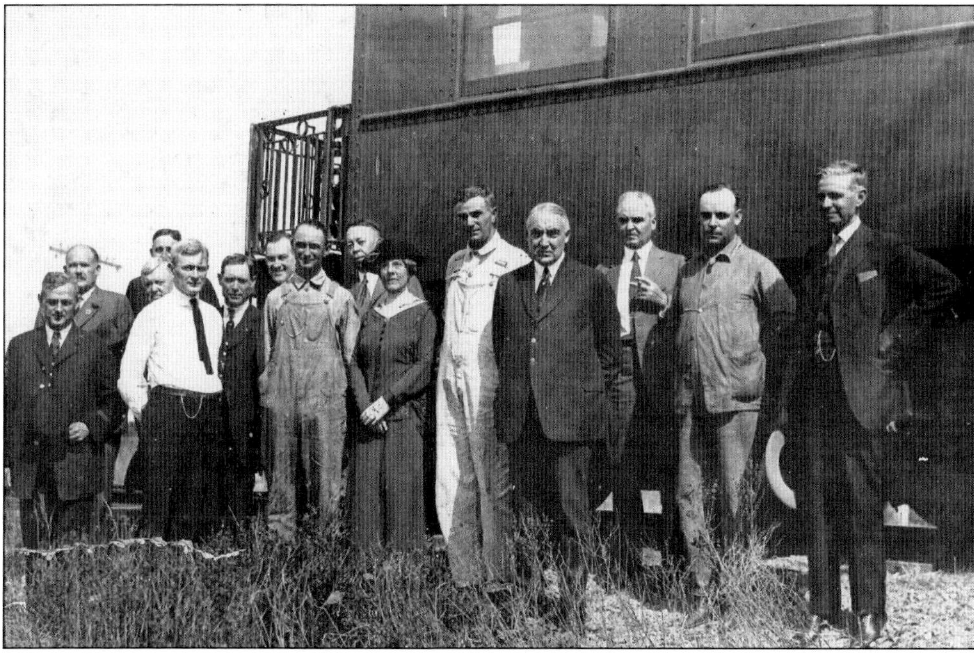

Kingsville hosted many important people over the years because of the power and prestige of King Ranch and Robert Kleberg. This picture, taken sometime after the 1920 election, shows President-elect Warren G. Harding (fourth from the right) and his wife, Florence (the only female in the picture). (Courtesy South Texas Archives, Texas A&M University-Kingsville.)

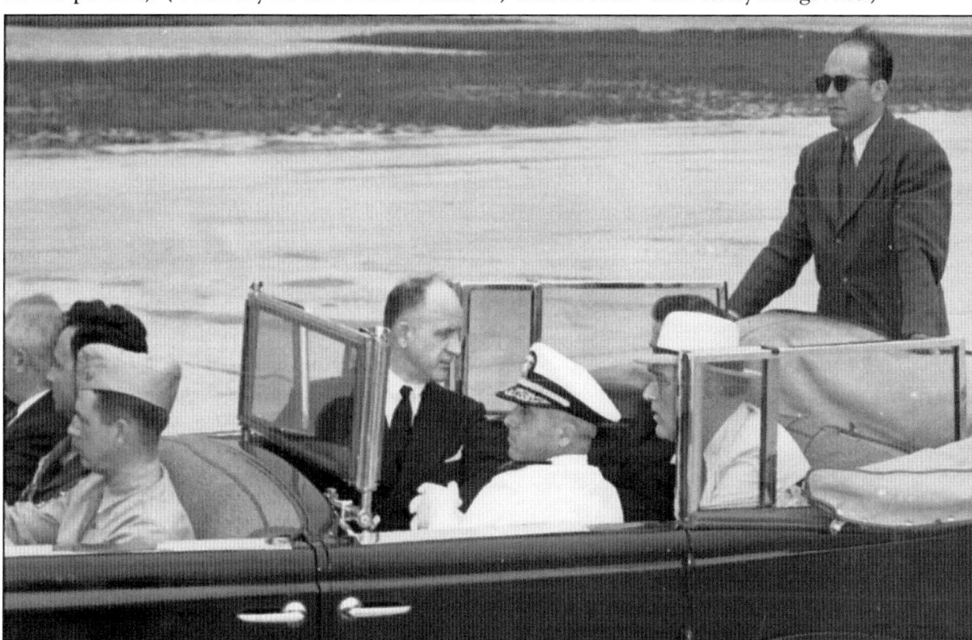

A presidential visit to NAS Kingsville on April 21, 1943, allowed for this picture of Franklin D. Roosevelt (backseat, in hat) making the rounds at the naval air station. Senators, congressmen, presidents, heads of state, film celebrities, and royalty visited King Ranch and Kingsville over the decades. (Courtesy South Texas Archives, Texas A&M University-Kingsville.)

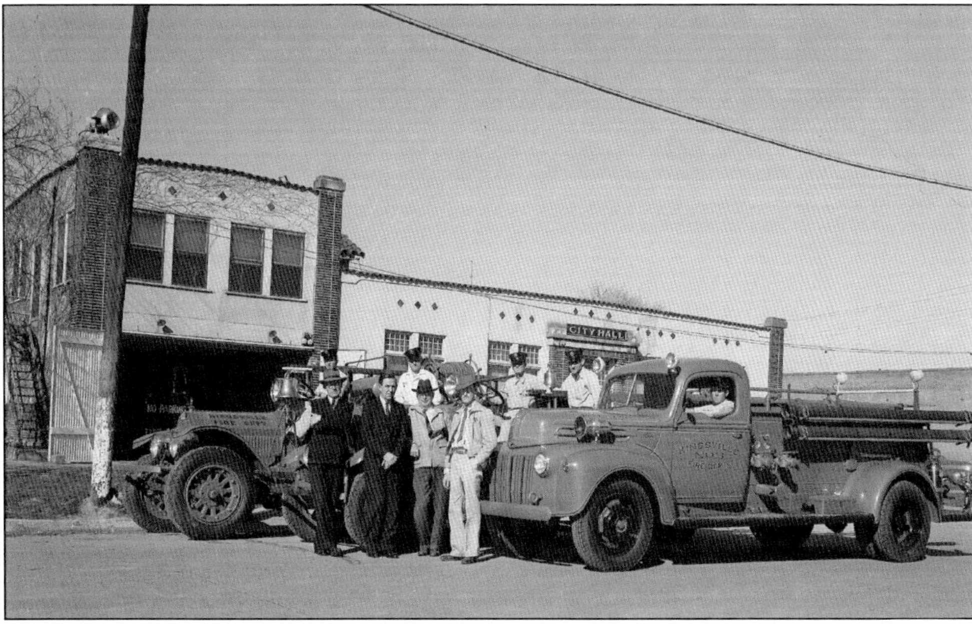

Kingsville City Hall was built in 1925 on Yoakum Avenue and Sixth Street. The city hall had four locations over the years. The pictured city hall housed not only the city government but also the fire department, police department, and, for a while, the public library. (Courtesy Dolph Briscoe Center for American History, The University of Texas at Austin, City Hall, Dodd (Jimmie) Photographic Collection, Creator: Dodd, Jimmie.)

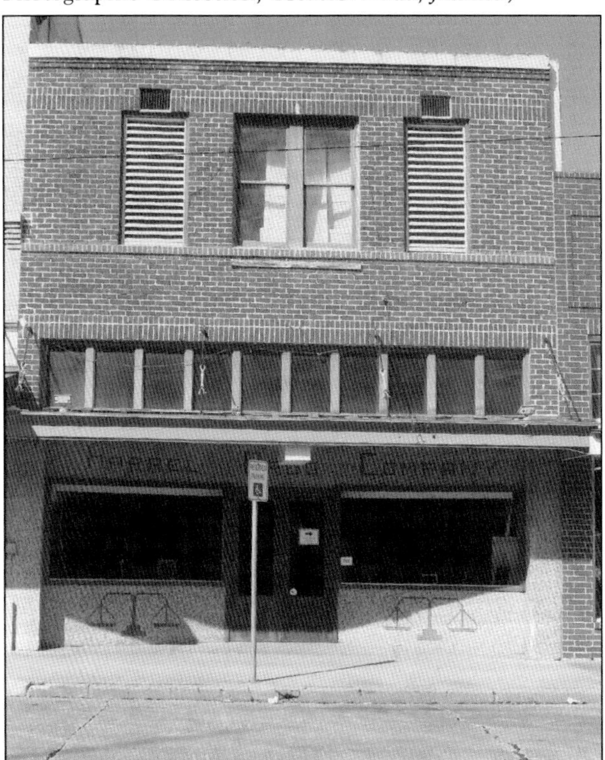

Nick Harrel Sr. established Harrel Drug Company in 1916. This structure is located east of the Municipal Building (the old Kleberg Bank building). It was built sometime between 1909 and 1915 and purchased by the drug company in 1916. The building was designed specifically for the hot climate, with louvered front windows and exhaust fans to draw out the hot air. (Photograph by the author.)

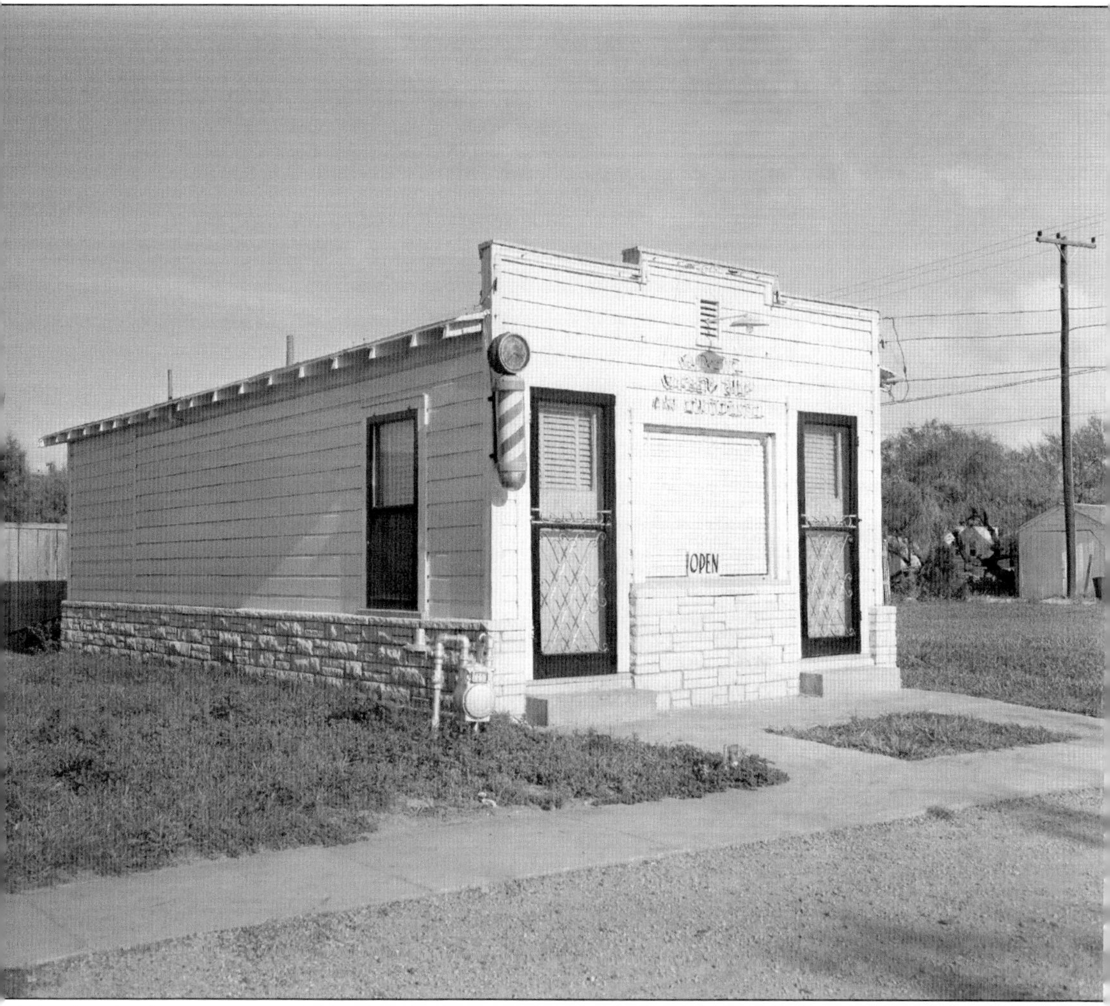

Charles Andrews was an African American civil rights advocate and community leader in Kingsville. Andrews moved to Kingsville in 1939 and, after serving in World War II, returned to open a barbershop and a cleaning business (located across the street from the barbershop). It was the first air-conditioned barbershop in Kingsville. Andrews, a member of Kingsville's Human Relations Committee, invited local restaurant owners to a meeting for the purpose of voluntarily desegregating their establishments. Only four of the 28 establishments failed to send representatives to the meeting. Andrews was well respected by all of Kingsville. He personally went to each of the restaurants that had missed the meeting and secured an agreement to desegregate. Andrews's barbershop is pictured here in 1951. (Courtesy Dolph Briscoe Center for American History, The University of Texas at Austin, Andrew's Barber Shop, 1951/08/21, Dodd (Jimmie) Photographic Collection, Creator: Dodd, Jimmie.)

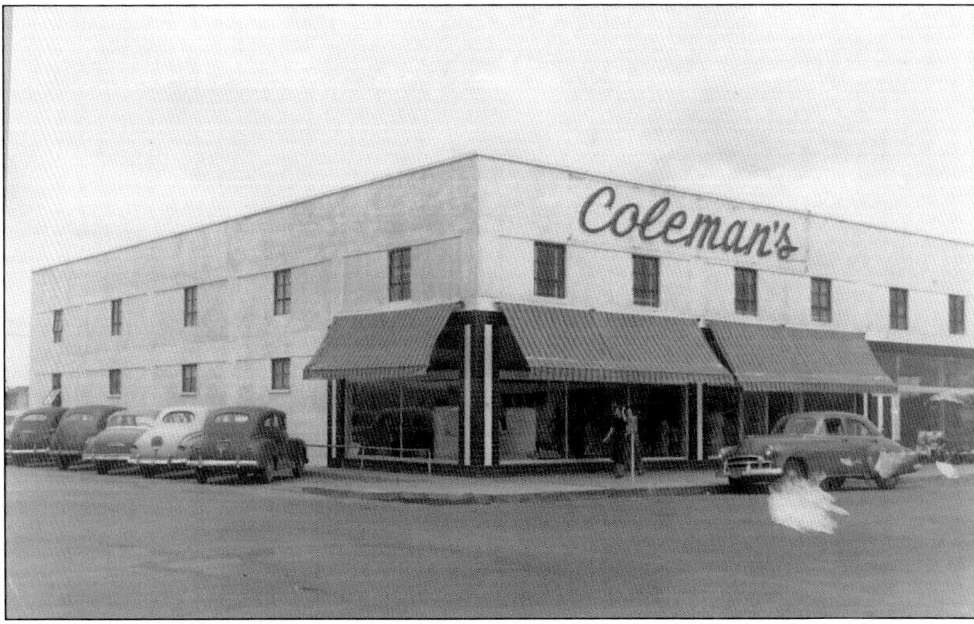

The advent of the automobile—and, subsequently, trucking—allowed for businesses to ease away from the railroad tracks between Fifth and Sixth Streets. Coleman's, an appliance store, sat on the corner of Eighth Street and Kleberg Avenue. The Highway 77 Bypass on Fourteenth Street routed most traffic away from the old Sixth Street downtown area in 1965, hurting some long-established Kleberg Avenue merchants. (Courtesy King Ranch, Inc., Kingsville, Texas.)

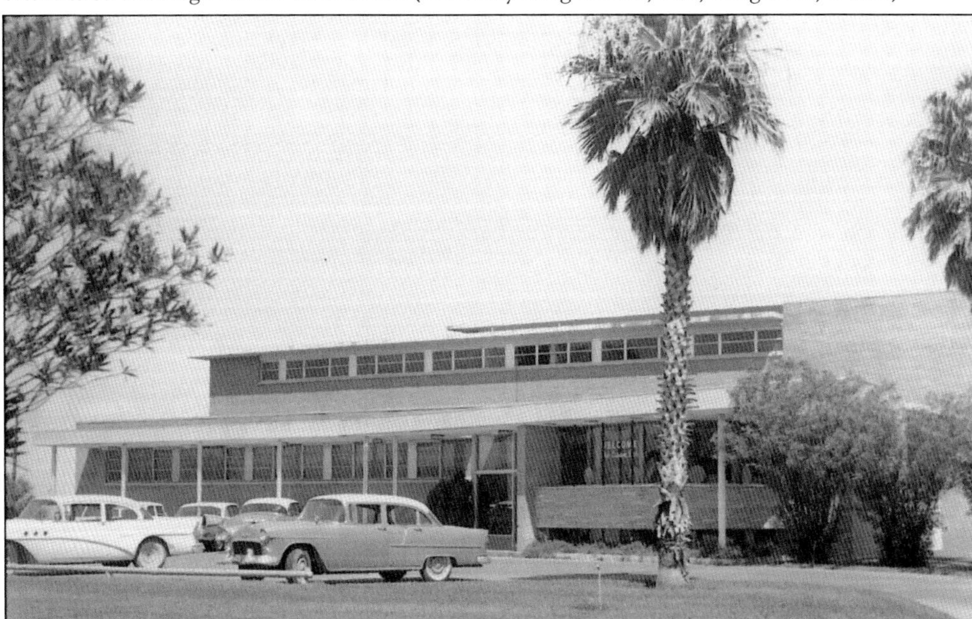

The Hygeia Dairy offered home deliveries of its milk in the 1950s. To accommodate and promote the dairy, the company had an ice-cream bar inside the building. On a hot summer day, families could take a drive out to the dairy and buy a scoop of ice cream or a Coke float to escape the heat of the Wild Horse Desert. (Courtesy King Ranch, Inc., Kingsville, Texas.)

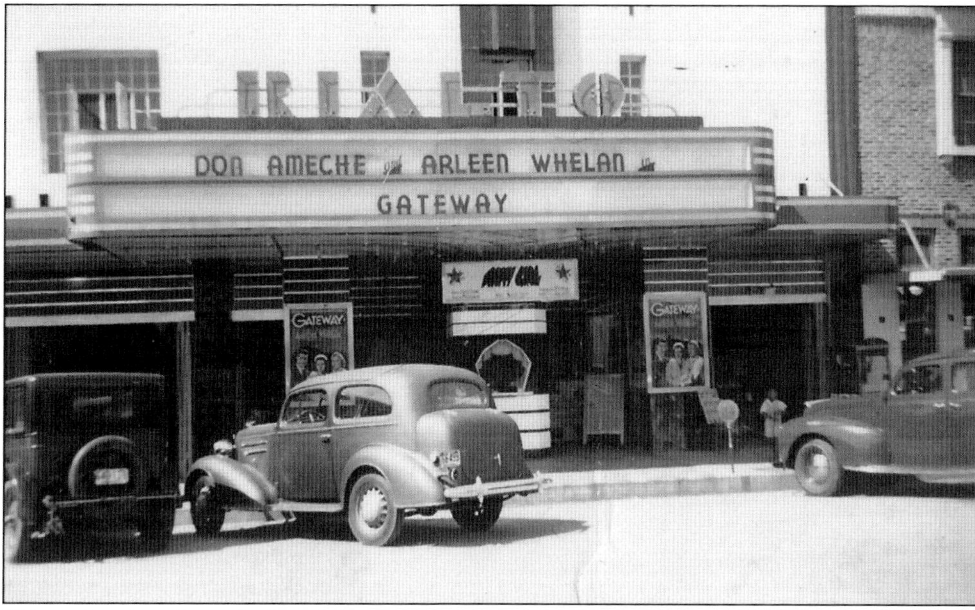

When the Casa Ricardo Hotel drew overnight visitors away, the King's Inn Hotel evolved to accommodate business offices and a movie theater. In 1915, the King's Inn Theater showed movies like *Idle Tongues* and *Twisted Trails*. King's Inn was purchased by Hall Industries and renamed Rialto in 1929; it was remodeled in 1937. The renovated theater seated 650 people. In this 1938 image of the Rialto Theater, the marquee heralds *Gateway*, starring Don Ameche. (Courtesy South Texas Archives, Texas A&M University-Kingsville.)

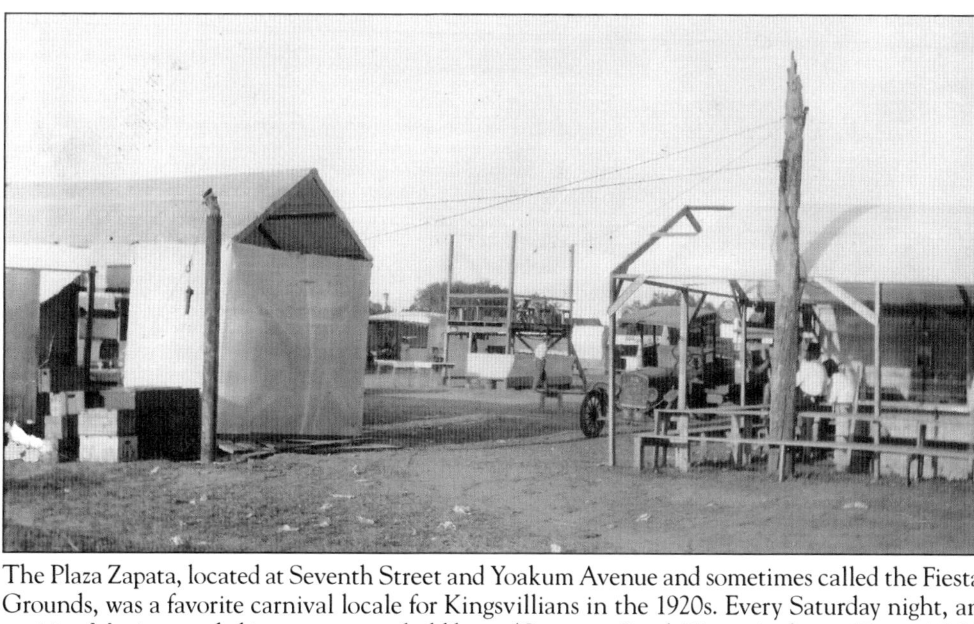

The Plaza Zapata, located at Seventh Street and Yoakum Avenue and sometimes called the Fiesta Grounds, was a favorite carnival locale for Kingsvillians in the 1920s. Every Saturday night, an exciting Mexican-style bingo game was held here. (Courtesy South Texas Archives, Texas A&M University-Kingsville.)

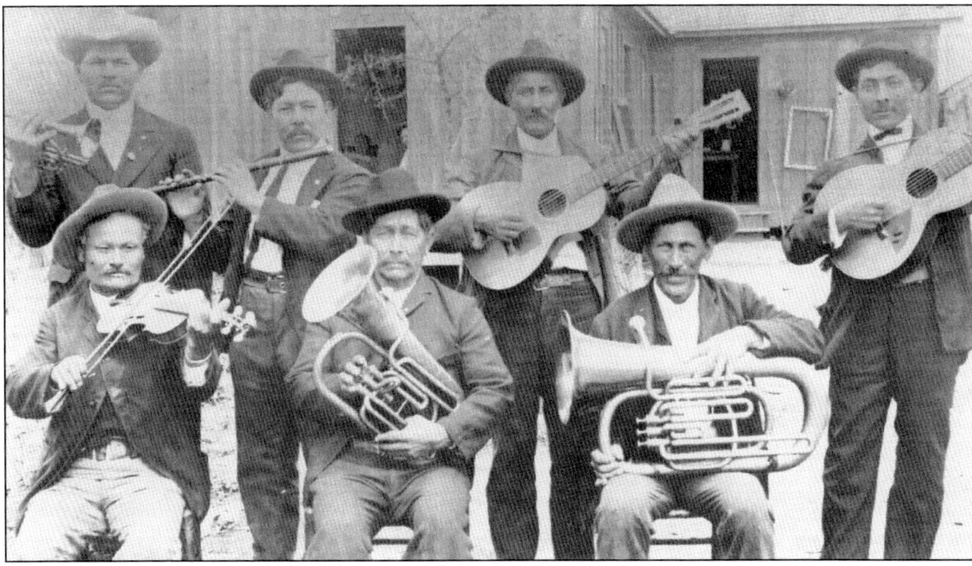

The Castulo Perez Orchestra was established around 1906, making this the first orchestra in Kingsville. The group was said to be an orchestra, rather than a band, because of the single violin. Castulo Perez was a blacksmith. (Courtesy South Texas Archives, Texas A&M University-Kingsville.)

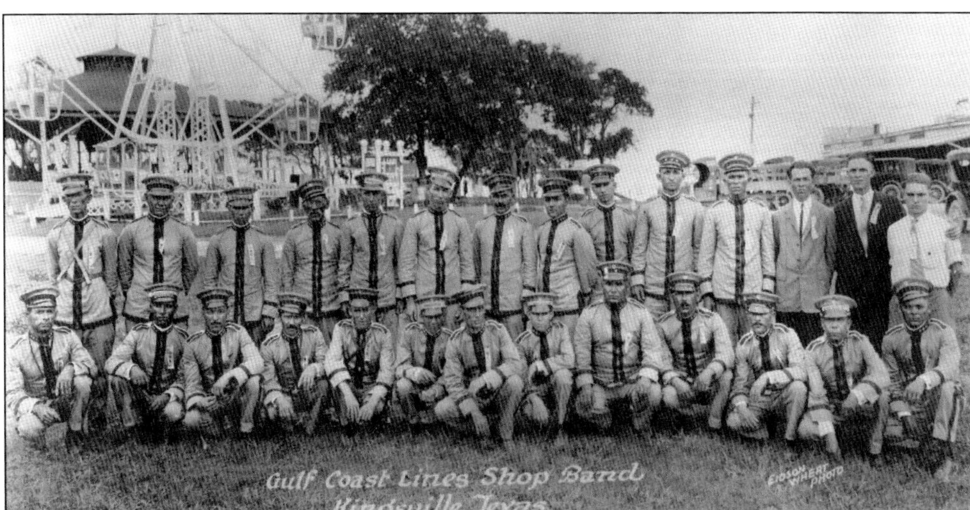

The Gulf Coast Lines Shop Band, composed of railroad workers, won awards throughout South Texas. Music and sporting events were important to the community. This was a time when people had to make their own entertainment. (Courtesy South Texas Archives, Texas A&M University-Kingsville.)

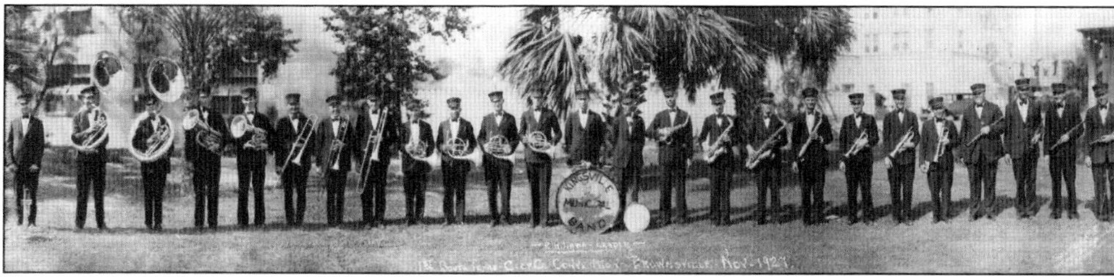

In 1927, a special tax was imposed by the town government to support the Kingsville Municipal Band. Before World War I, the Commercial Club paid to have the Band Boys, as the *Kingsville Record* referred to them, play weekly. After the war, people still wanted the pleasure of attending a frequent concert in the park. (Courtesy South Texas Archives, Texas A&M University-Kingsville.)

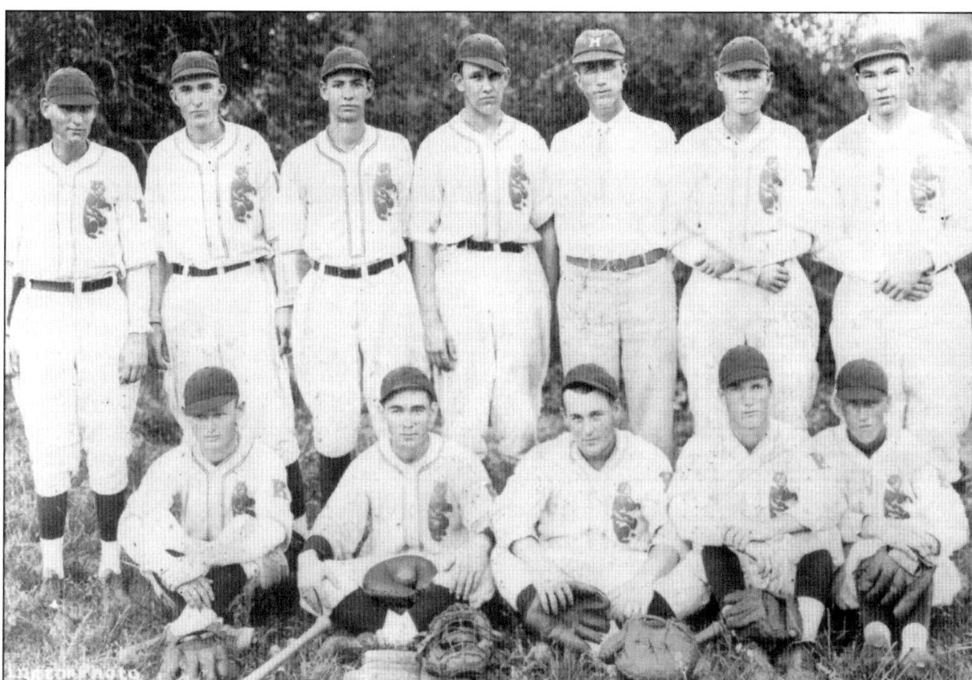

Baseball and football were important sports in Kingsville. Since Henrietta M. King High School did not yet have a team, this 1927 Kingsville Cubs baseball team played as an independent during the summer and was made up of both high school students and graduates. (Courtesy South Texas Archives, Texas A&M University-Kingsville.)

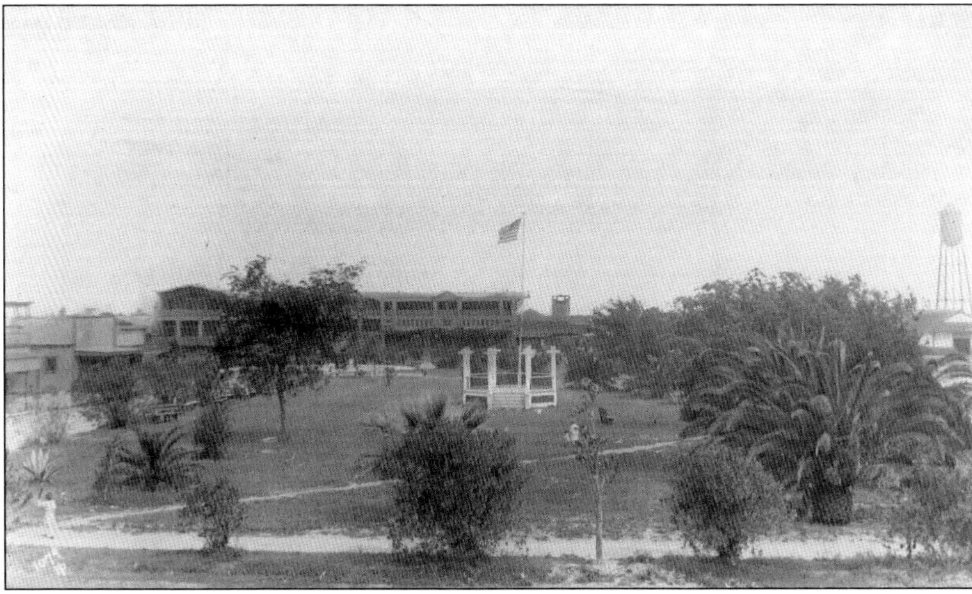

Miller Park was located one block west of the railroad tracks, with Casa Ricardo on the north side. The *Kingsville Record* reported in 1915 that when the band played in Miller Park, there were so many people in attendance it was standing room only. People strolled through the downtown area and enjoyed ice cream or dinner in local restaurants before the concerts. The Kingsville Concert Band was renamed Kingsville Municipal Band sometime in 1926 or 1927. (Courtesy King Ranch, Inc., Kingsville, Texas.)

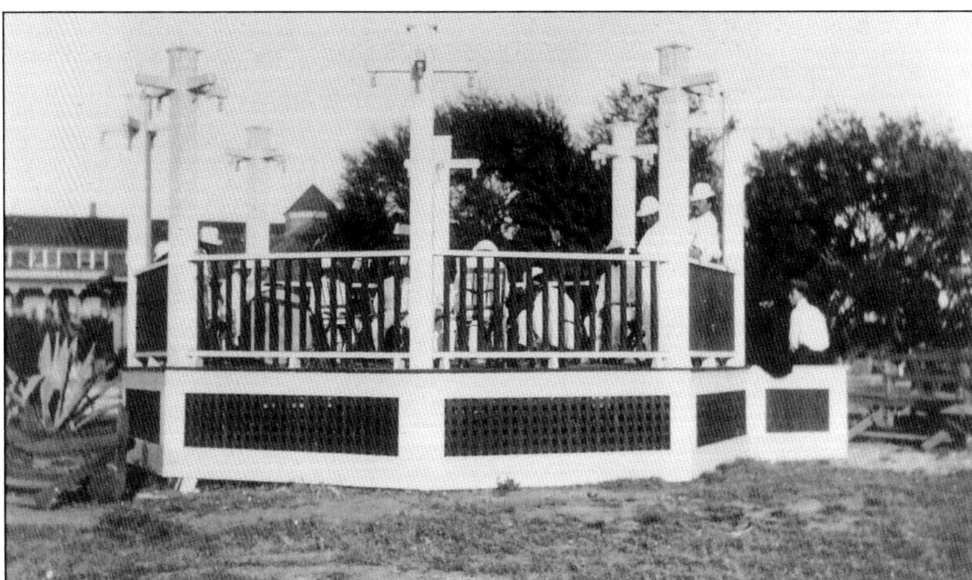

A storm blew the roof off of the bandstand in Miller Park, pictured here around 1915. The band members shown are assembling for their evening concert. King's Inn Hotel is in the background. (Courtesy South Texas Archives, Texas A&M University-Kingsville.)

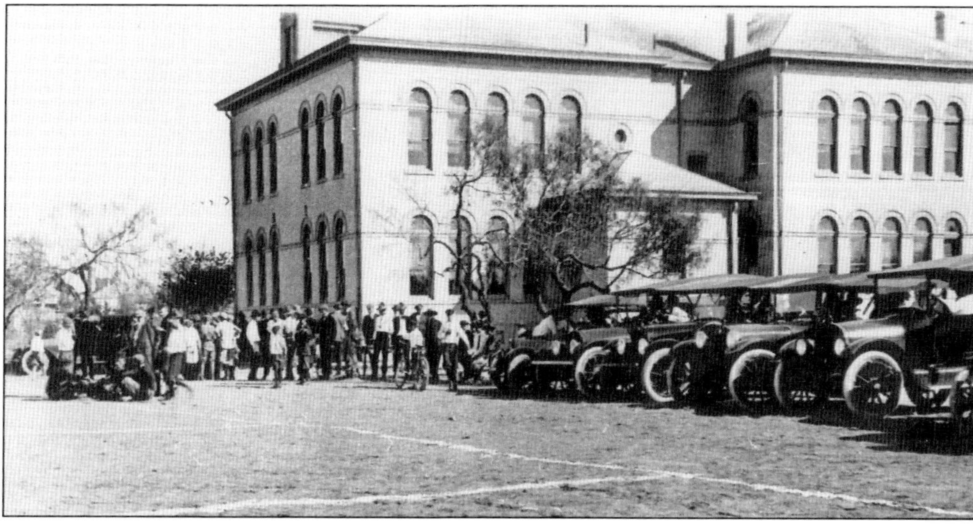

Students at H.M. King High School gather for an afternoon football game in 1915. Already, football was one of the passions of Kingsvillians. (Courtesy South Texas Archives, Texas A&M University-Kingsville.)

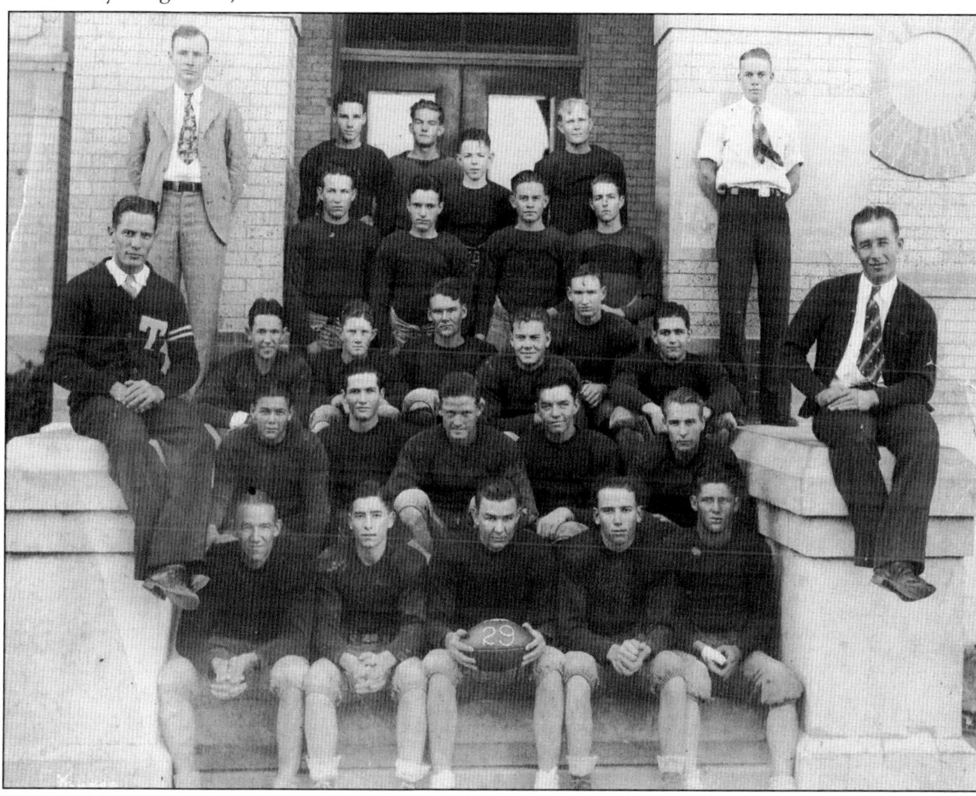

Pictured here is the 1929 district championship–winning H.M. King High School football team. This Kingsville Brahma squad was one of only two H.M. King football teams ever to win a district title; the other was in 1958. Football became the "king" of sports in Kingsville, and college football became an obsession for many. (Courtesy South Texas Archives, Texas A&M University-Kingsville.)

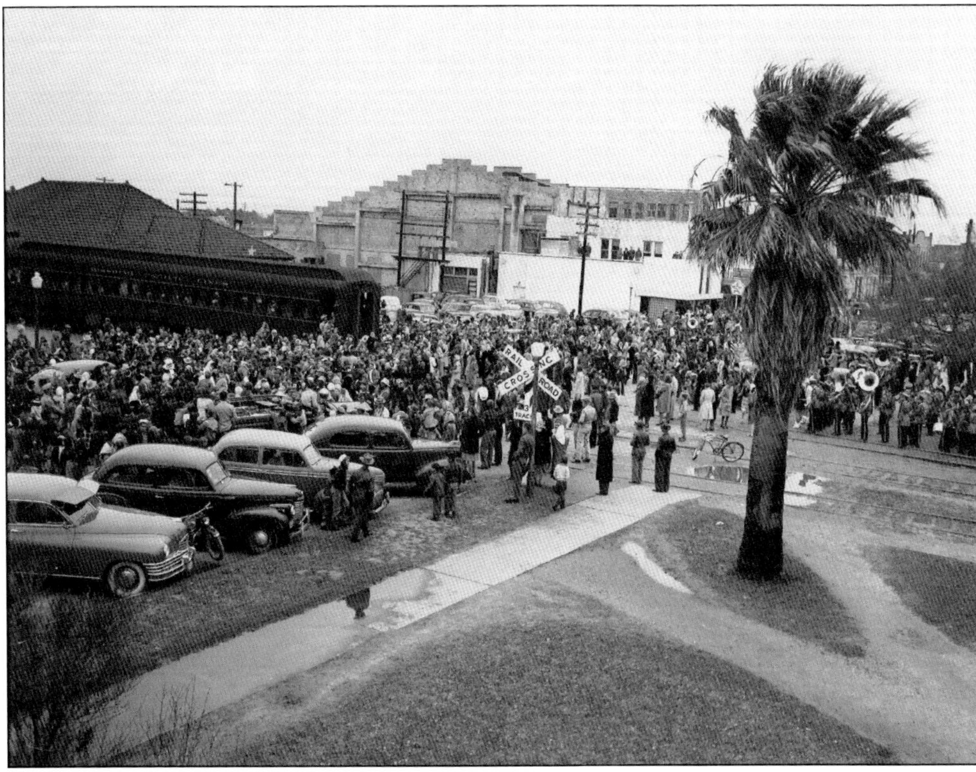

In this late-1940s photograph, Santa Claus has arrived by train at the passenger depot, and the whole town has gathered to greet him. Santa is visible in the crowd at left. The Rialto Theater, in the central background, stands where the King's Inn Hotel once was. (Courtesy Dolph Briscoe Center for American History, The University of Texas at Austin, Xman, Dodd (Jimmie) Photographic Collection, and Creator: Dodd, Jimmie.)

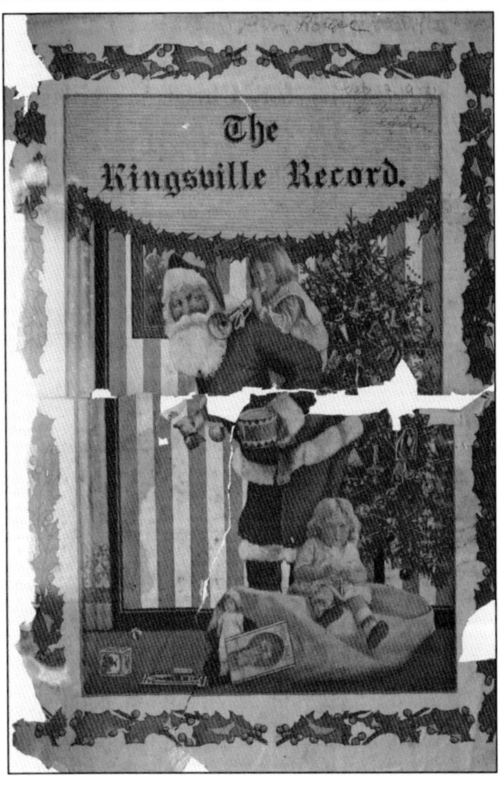

The Kingsville Record.

The early *Kingsville Record* always had a special Christmas insert with all of the local merchants advertising their holiday inventories. The front page of the insert was a full-page Christmas image. At a time when there were few color images in newspapers, the *Kingsville Record* went all out in 1912 with a four-color Santa Claus front page. (Courtesy *Kingsville Record and Bishop News.*)

Six

DIVERSIFICATION

Within just a couple of decades, Kingsville had already greatly changed. The years of the Great Depression deeply tested Kingsville's staying power. Many people were unemployed, including a lot of railroaders. The *Kingsville Record* printed numerous interesting stories of how the community pulled together to get through the hard times. King Ranch provided beef to the unemployed. Local clubs and organizations, such as the Lions Club of Kingsville, found ways to help schools provide lunches for students in need.

Probably the most touching story was from 1930, when Mrs. O.A. Smith provided Christmas dinner for 86 hobos camped south of the rail yards in "The Jungle." The meal, prepared in the basement of the Methodist church, consisted of soup, venison and vegetables, apples, oranges, real factory-made cigarettes, and coffee—and best of all, no speeches. Christmas postcards and postage were offered so the men could write home to their families. Also in 1930, the Knights of Columbus provided 100 turkey dinners to be distributed from St. Martin's School.

However, it was not all joy and sunshine. Kingsville, like most communities, discouraged transients. There were reports of violence in The Jungle. Later, Christmas holidays were not so welcoming. As the federal government developed welfare programs and the WPA, the transients were sent to camps, where they were supposed to get the help they needed. A WPA program built the US post office in Kingsville.

The Kingsville Division of the Missouri Pacific Lines held its own. However, MoPac went into receivership in 1933. The *Kingsville Record* reported that in 1931, Missouri Pacific total annual revenues had decreased from $2.2 million to $1.5 million.

The age of steam power waned as the dominance of diesel-electric locomotives began, and Kingsville was forced to look for other industries to fill the void left by the changing railroad.

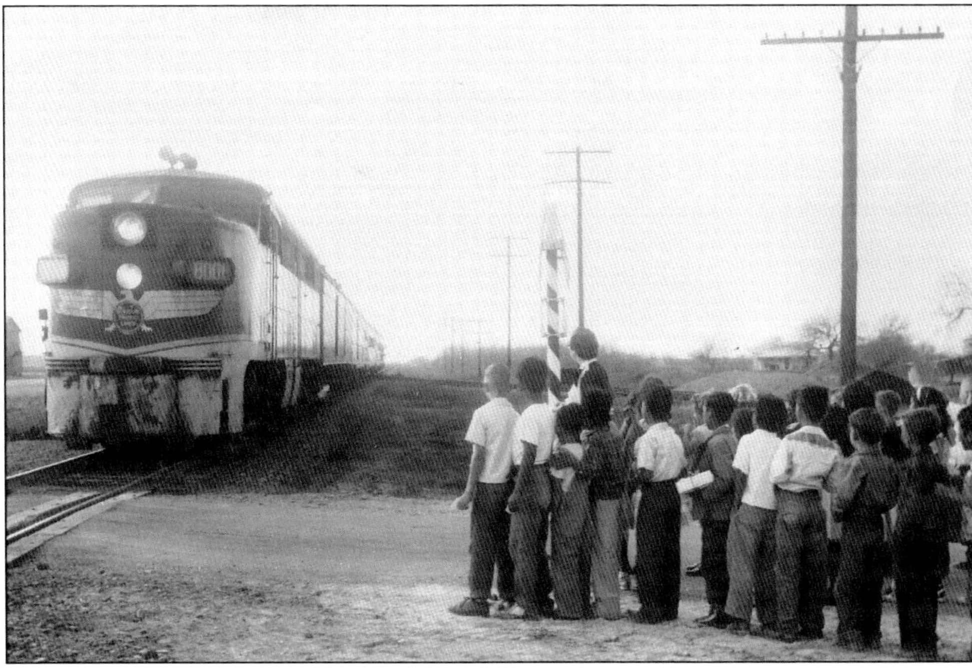

In January 1956, Missouri Pacific Lines employed 1,100 people in Kingsville who worked in the general office building, roundhouse, and shops. The battle over MoPac's proposed reorganization plan went all the way to the Supreme Court before being approved. Over a number of years, the Kingsville employees were all transferred to other cities or laid off. With the passenger service fading into history, a ride on the train became a popular school field trip. (Courtesy South Texas Archives, Texas A&M University-Kingsville.)

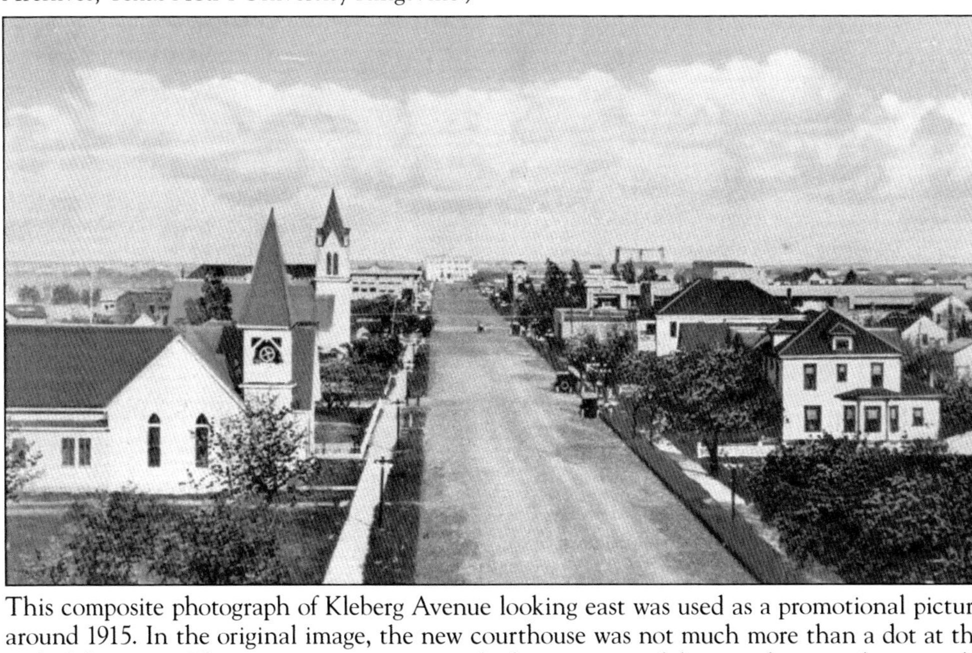

This composite photograph of Kleberg Avenue looking east was used as a promotional picture around 1915. In the original image, the new courthouse was not much more than a dot at the end of the street. The promoters superimposed a larger image of the courthouse to better make their sales pitch. (Courtesy South Texas Archives, Texas A&M University-Kingsville.)

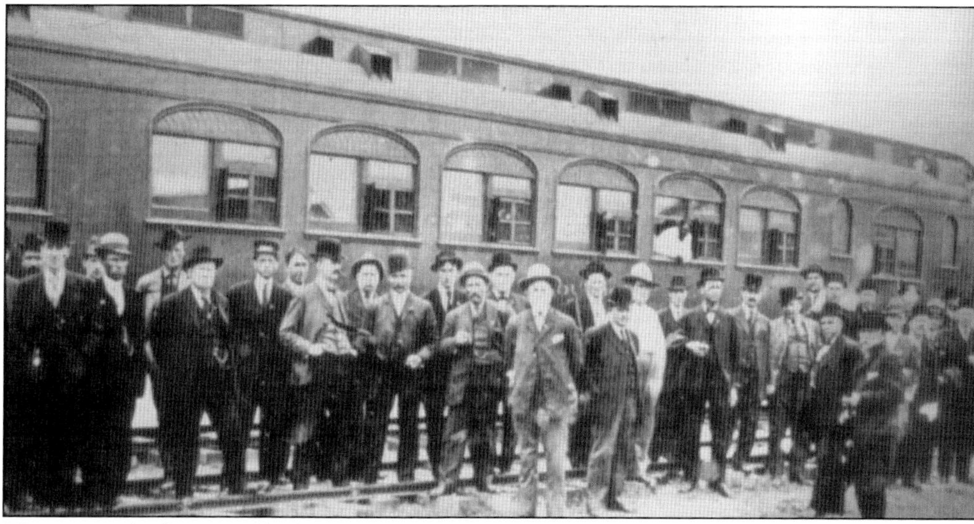

The survival of Kingsville depended on the ability to attract new people to the community. These potential homeseekers are pictured in Robstown. Theodore F. Koch would invite potential homeseekers to take a free ride to Riviera to view and hopefully purchase land in Riviera. Kingsville promoters would then invite Koch's visitors to have lunch in Kingsville and attempt to entice them to settle in Kingsville instead. (Courtesy King Ranch, Inc., Kingsville, Texas.)

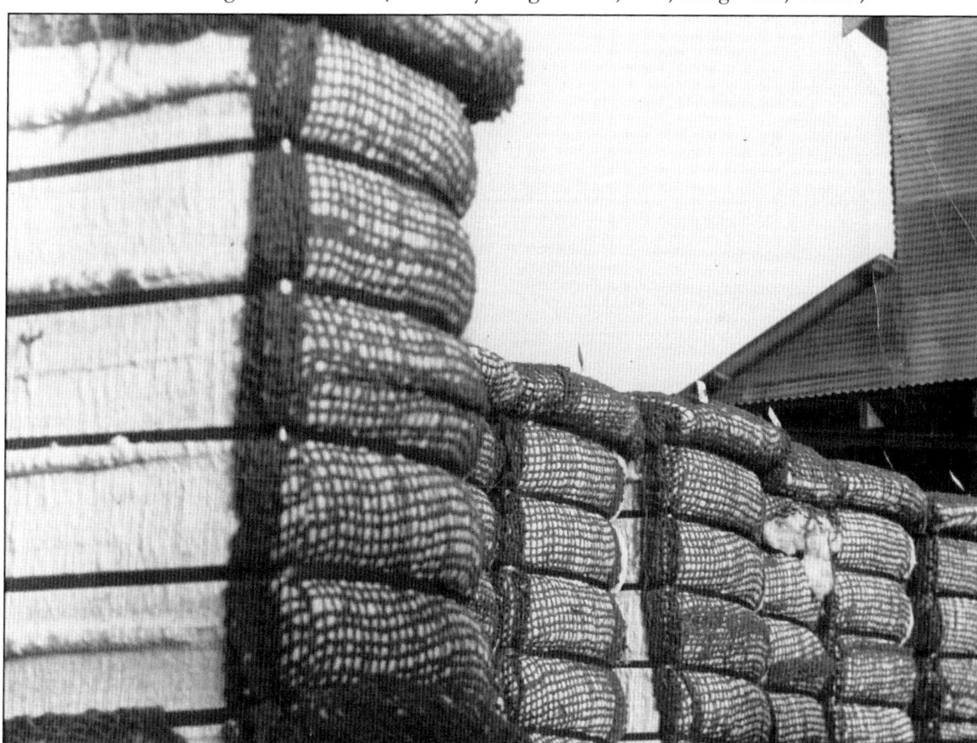

In this 1920s image, locally grown cotton, stacked in bales, is ready to be used by the Kingsville Cotton Mill to produce webbing; four-, eight-, and sixteen-ply twines; and Model T transmission and brake-band linings. The mill provided jobs for 250 local men and women working on day and night shifts. (Courtesy South Texas Archives, Texas A&M University-Kingsville.)

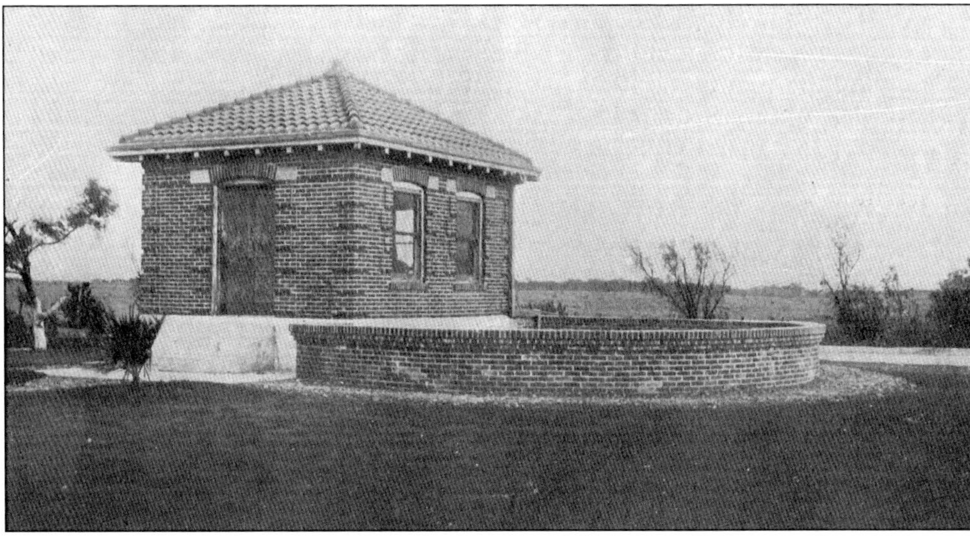

This photograph from 1919 is one of the few pictures of the Kingsville Sewage Plant. This image was used in a *Kingsville Merits Your Consideration* brochure to curry favor for getting a normal school located in the town. Sewage processing was a critical concern in 1915, and community leaders spared no expense to get the best and most modern facilities. (Courtesy South Texas Archives, Texas A&M University-Kingsville.)

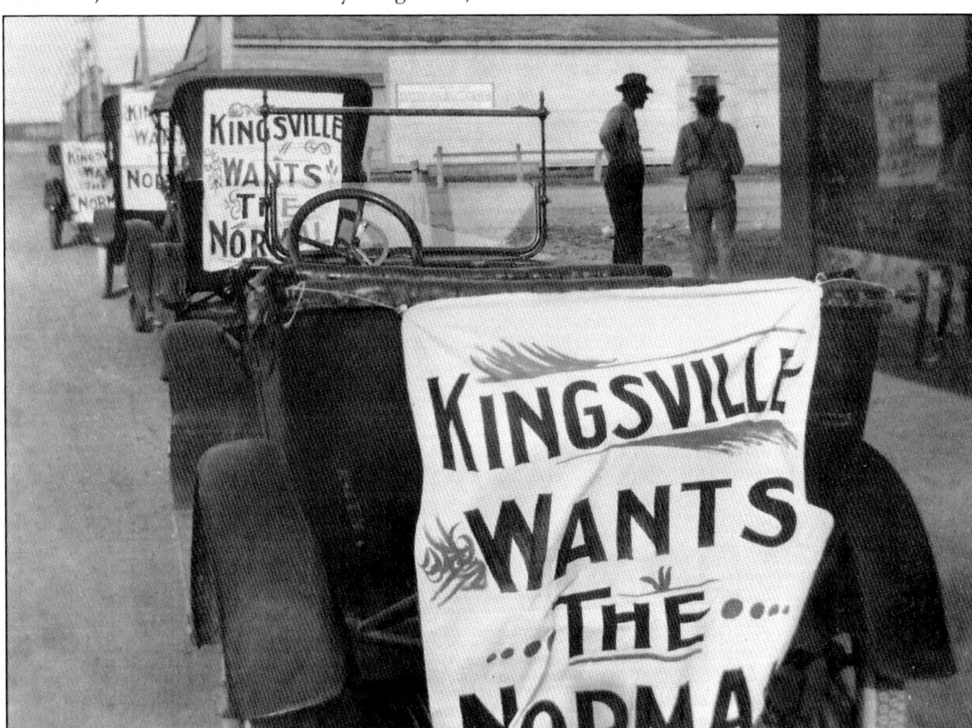

Citizens decorated their cars with signs and sought support from neighboring communities in an effort to get a normal school built in Kingsville. These promotional trips started as early as 1909 and were backed by the Commercial Club. (Courtesy South Texas Archives, Texas A&M University-Kingsville.)

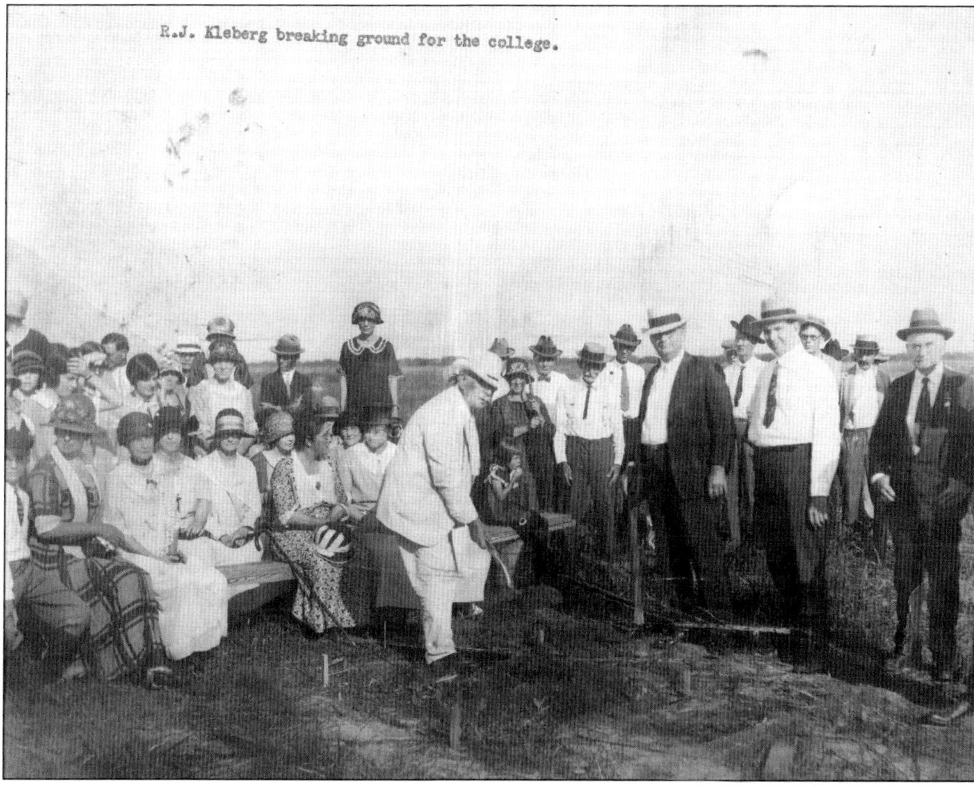

R.J. Kleberg is pictured breaking ground for the long anticipated South Texas State Teachers College in 1924. Following Kingsville tradition, the ladies are seated on benches quickly assembled from two-by-twelve boards resting on nail kegs. King Ranch provided the beef for a spectacular community barbecue to celebrate the town's success. (Courtesy South Texas Archives, Texas A&M University-Kingsville.)

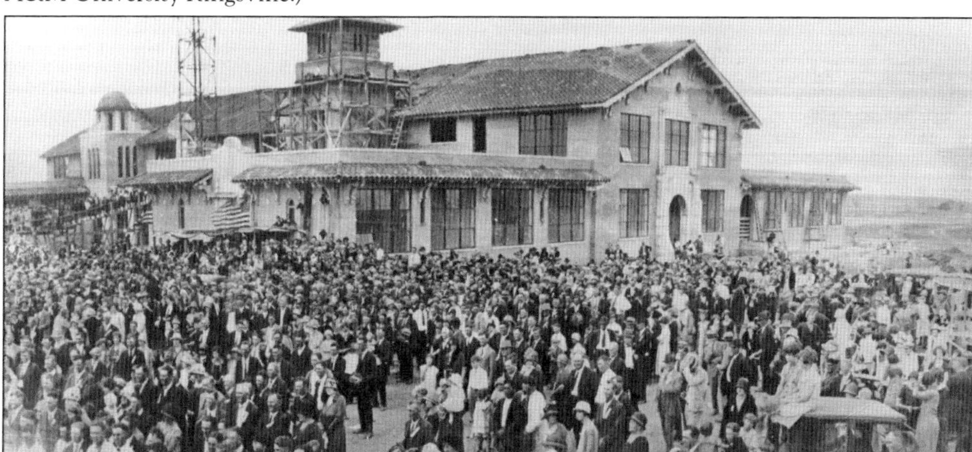

The scaffolding was still up at Manning Hall for the cornerstone celebration in 1925. The opening festivities for the South Texas State Teachers College were delayed until March due to bad weather in January. This particular picture is a testament to the total community involvement in the South Texas State Teachers College project. The very first building on campus was the president's residence. (Courtesy South Texas Archives, Texas A&M University-Kingsville.)

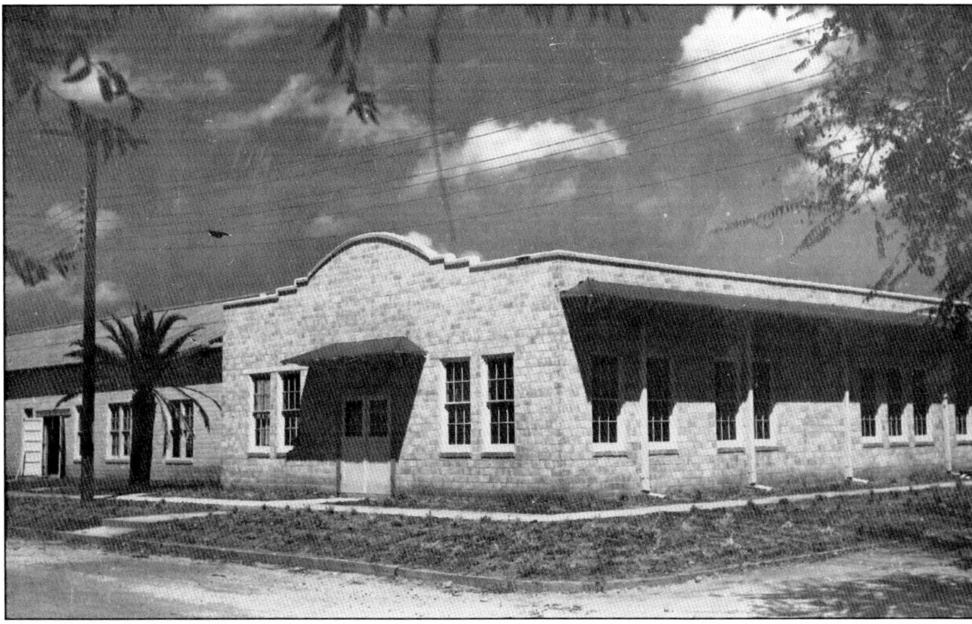

The South Texas State Teachers College evolved, grew, and changed names multiple times. The engineering building on the Texas College of Arts and Industries campus was built in 1941. Today, Texas A&M University-Kingsville is ranked as a National Role Model Institution by Minority Access Inc. and is a leader in graduating Hispanic engineering students. (Courtesy South Texas Archives, Texas A&M University-Kingsville.)

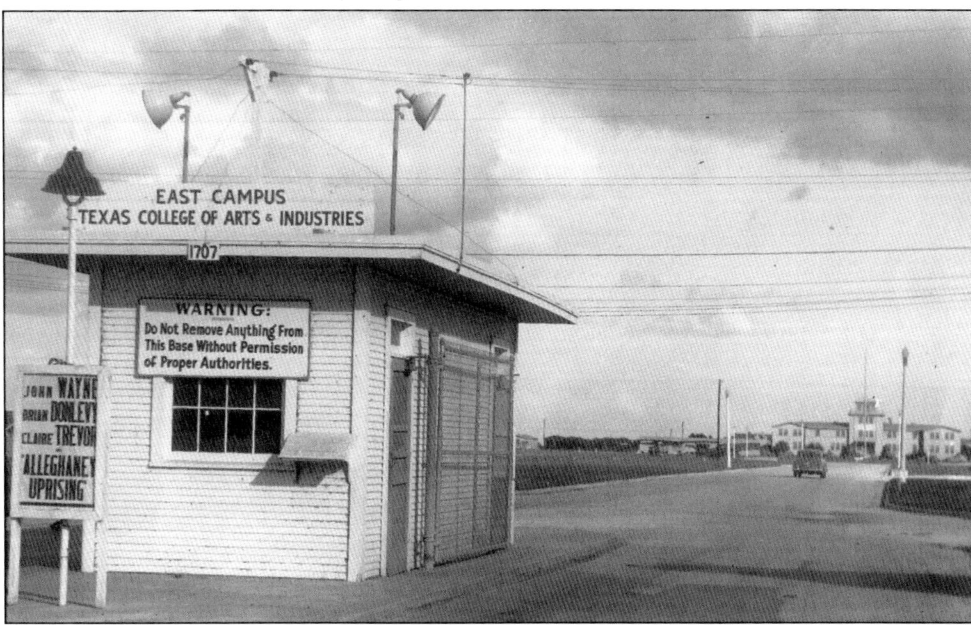

After World War II, the student population increased significantly at Texas A&I. In September 1945, the Naval Air Auxiliary Station-Kingsville was decommissioned. Kingsville and Kleberg County leased the NAAS facilities for $1 per year (plus maintenance costs) and allowed Texas A&I to use the property as housing for an additional 500 students in the 1946 fall semester. (Courtesy South Texas Archives, Texas A&M University-Kingsville.)

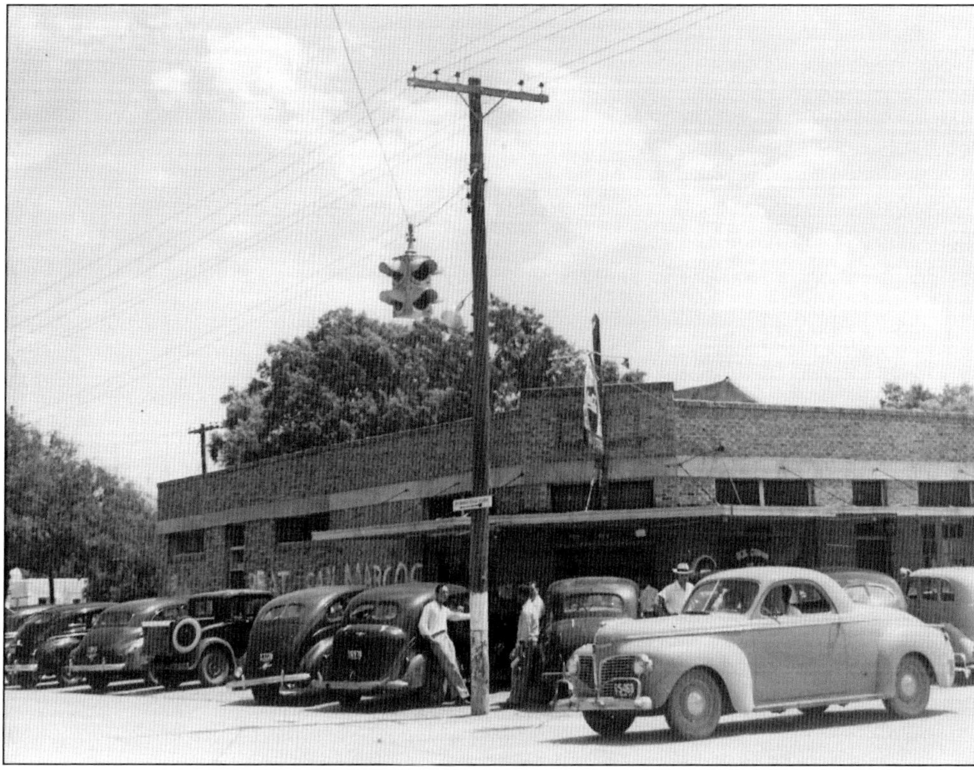

Tejac's, or T-Jacs, was a popular college hangout located at Armstrong Street and Santa Gertrudis Avenue. A&M-Kingsville student Fred Elmore opened the café and store, calling it the Javelina Sandwich Shop, in 1929. He later sold it to students E.J. Tegarden Jr. and R.J. "Jack" Sims. They renamed it Tejac's, which was a combination of their names. (Courtesy King Ranch, Inc., Kingsville, Texas.)

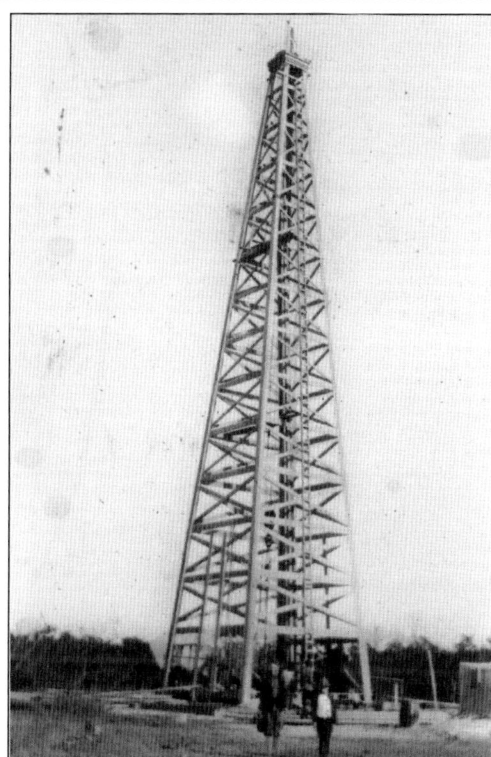

There were indications of gas and oil in Kleberg County in 1912, and the Kleberg County Oil and Gas Company was established in 1919. The company leased property, and the first gas well, drilled to 3,000 feet, was brought in. This image, taken on April 4, 1920, shows Kingsville's first oil derrick. (Courtesy South Texas Archives, Texas A&M University-Kingsville.)

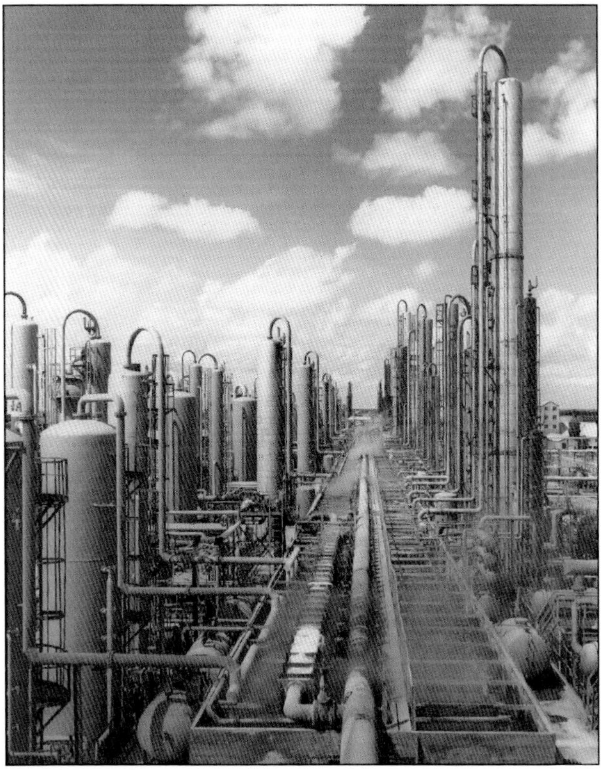

In late 1944, Celanese built a large chemical plant just a few miles north of Kingsville. The facility is actually in Nueces County, but it has provided employment for many citizens of Kingsville. With the railroad waning in importance, the arrival of the Celanese plant meant there would be new jobs available. (Courtesy Celanese International Corporation.)

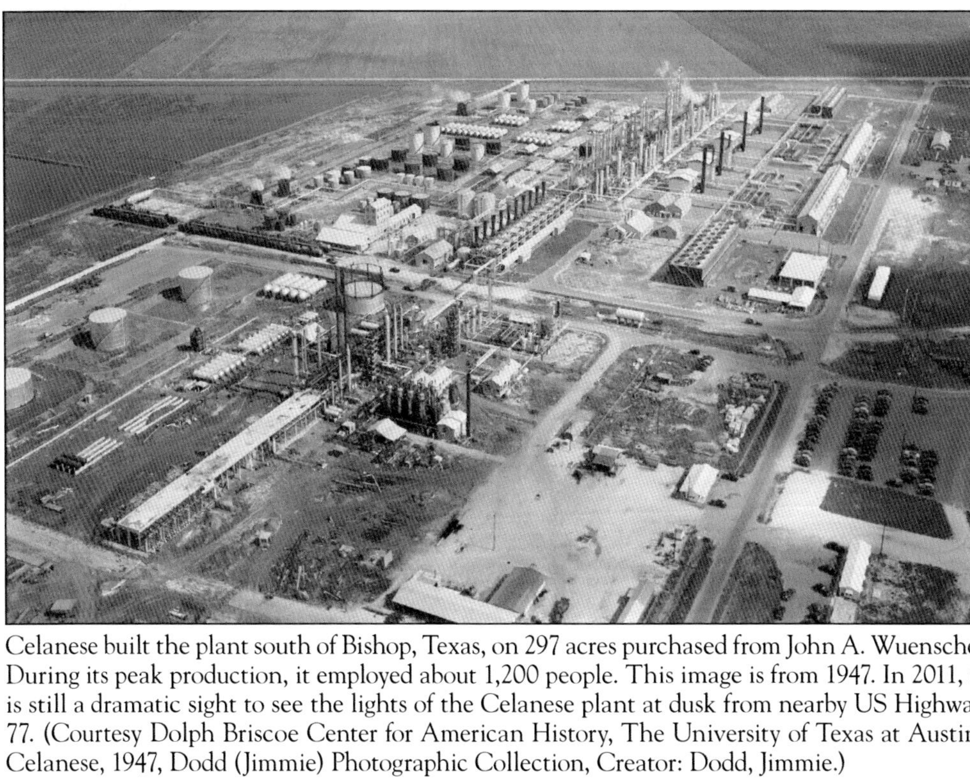

Celanese built the plant south of Bishop, Texas, on 297 acres purchased from John A. Wuensche. During its peak production, it employed about 1,200 people. This image is from 1947. In 2011, it is still a dramatic sight to see the lights of the Celanese plant at dusk from nearby US Highway 77. (Courtesy Dolph Briscoe Center for American History, The University of Texas at Austin, Celanese, 1947, Dodd (Jimmie) Photographic Collection, Creator: Dodd, Jimmie.)

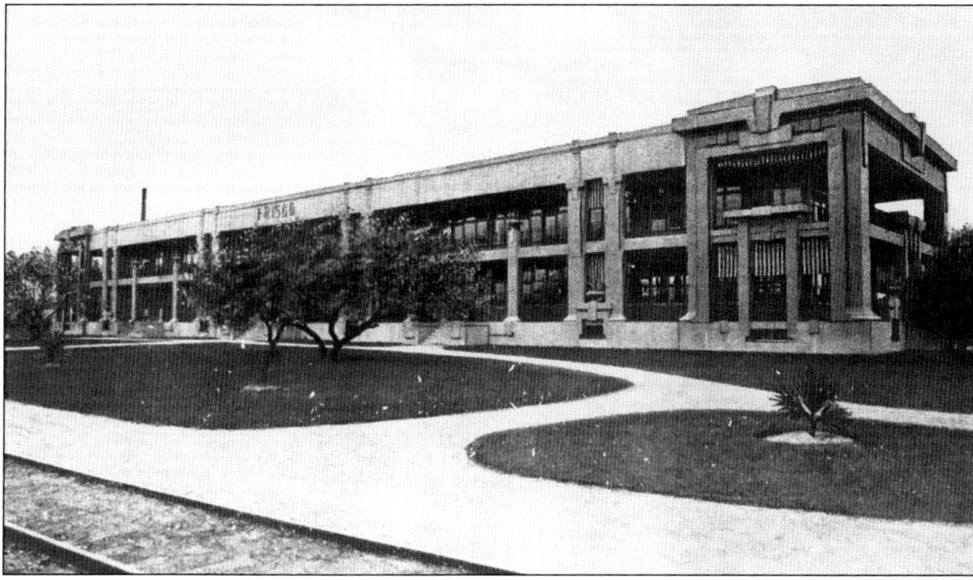

The Frisco Lines general office building, seen here in 1919, became the Kingsville Division of Missouri Pacific Lines, but as times changed, the staff gradually moved out. In 1964, the structure was empty and referred to by some as an eyesore. The building was demolished in June of that year. (Courtesy South Texas Archives, Texas A&M University-Kingsville.)

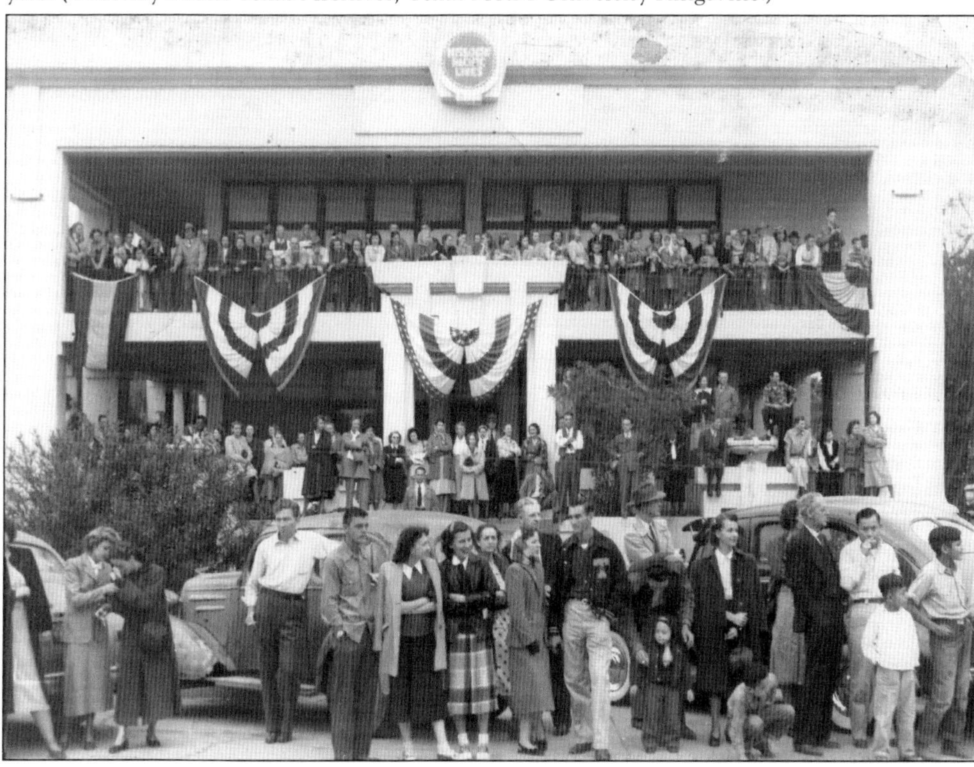

This picture of the MoPac general office building was taken on November 11, 1948. The structure is decorated for the South Texas State Fair. Railroad employees and other Kingsvillians await the start of the parade. (Courtesy South Texas Archives, Texas A&M University-Kingsville.)

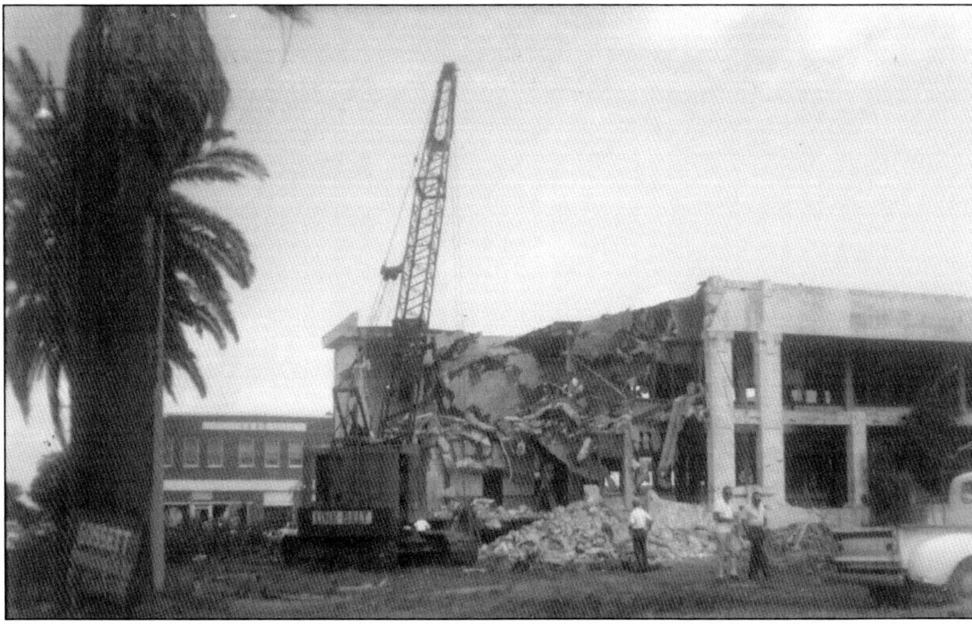

The demolition of the building that housed both the Frisco Lines and the MoPac general offices happened quickly in June 1964. The golden age of the railroad had come to a close because of cross-country trucking. Passenger service was about to end on the Kingsville line, and fewer local people were employed by the railroad. It was time to make room for a new industry—oil. (Courtesy Kathryn Evans Collection.)

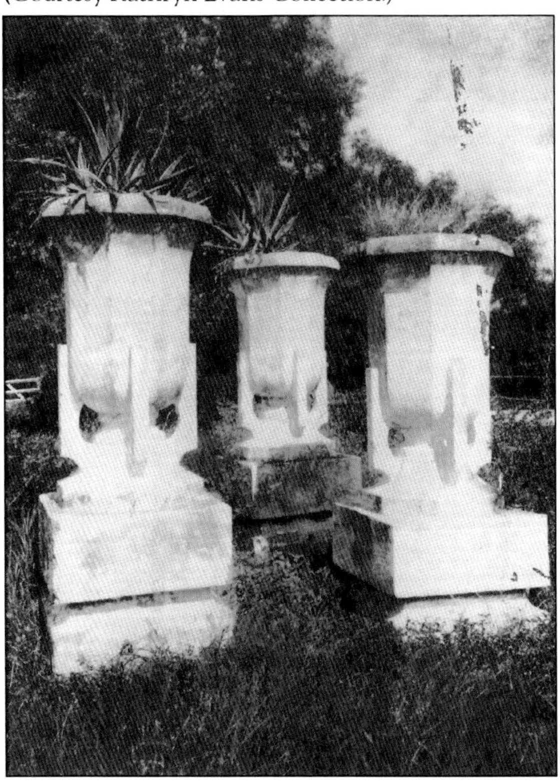

These large planters greeted people as they entered the Casa Ricardo Hotel. The elegant containers were saved after the razing of the building in 1969 and found a new home at the 1904 Kingsville Train Depot Museum, located in the old railroad passenger depot. (Courtesy South Texas Archives, Texas A&M University-Kingsville.)

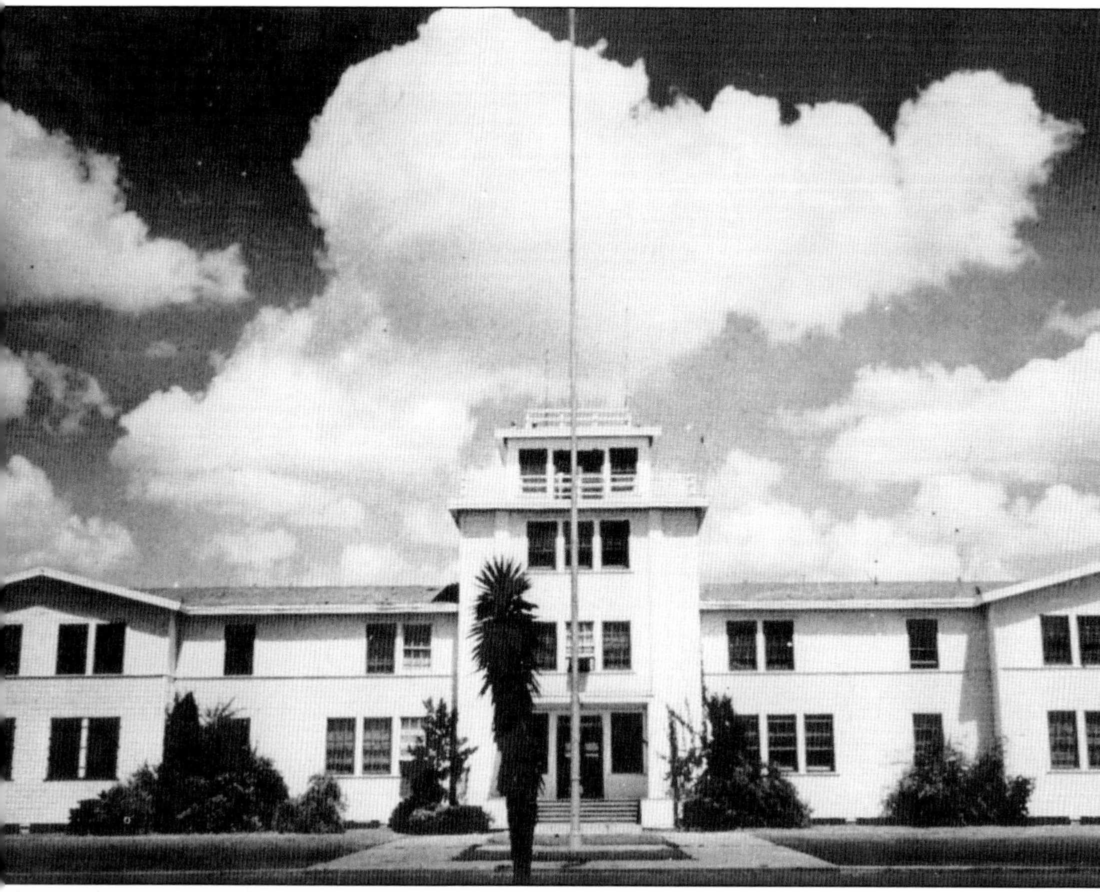

Before Pearl Harbor, the Army and Navy were preparing to train aviators. Corpus Christi had acquired an Army Air Corps station, but Kingsville was left out of the picture. Ed Erard, manager of the Kingsville Chamber of Commerce and sometimes remembered as Mr. Kingsville, was determined to secure some kind of military facility for the town. Erard visited with Capt. Alva D. Bernhard and showed him acreage on King Ranch. The final plot selection was 3,000 acres of the best farming land on the east side of Kingsville, and Naval Air Station Kingsville was built in a great hurry. After the war, the base property was used by Texas A&I as its east campus. In 1951, the property was reactivated in preparation for the Korean War. (Courtesy South Texas Archives, Texas A&M University-Kingsville.)

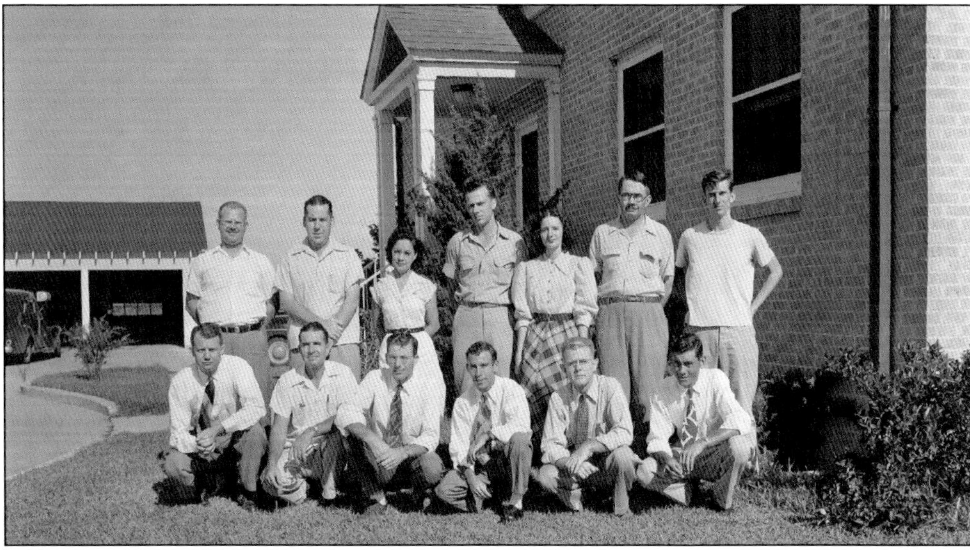

In February 1940, the Radio Intelligence Division of the Federal Communications Commission needed to set up a radio monitoring station, and land was selected south of Kingsville. The staff poses for this picture in 1948. The modern station is fully automated and operational. (Courtesy Dolph Briscoe Center for American History, The University of Texas at Austin, F. C. C. Monitoring Station, 1948, Dodd (Jimmie) Photographic Collection, Creator: Dodd, Jimmie.)

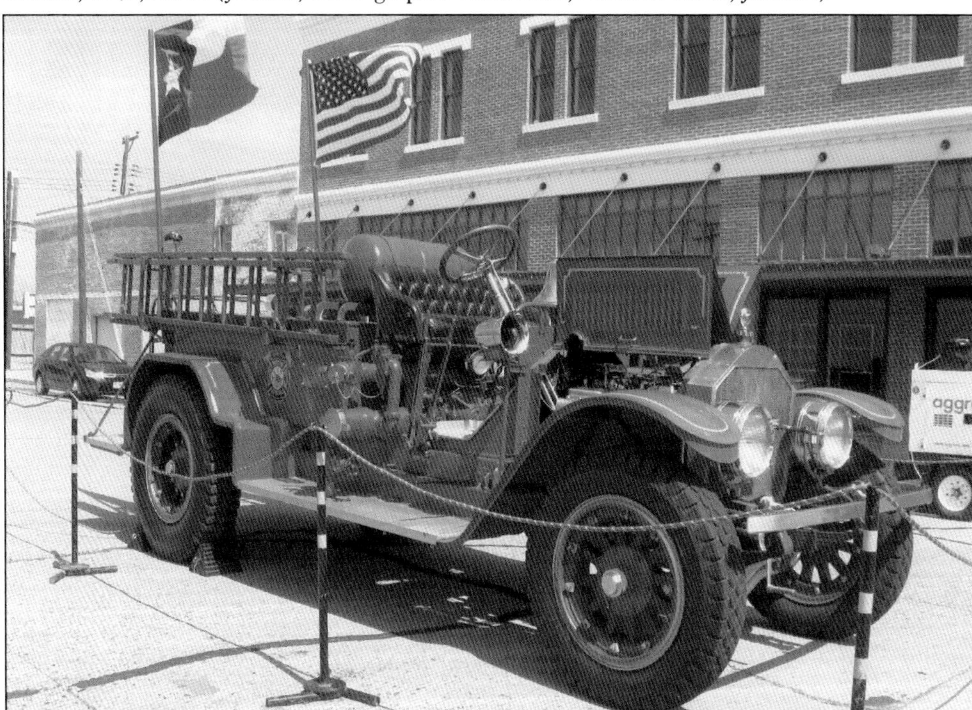

In March 2011, the old 1925 Kingsville Volunteer Fire Department engine was on display at the Kingsville Classic Car Show on Kleberg Avenue and Seventh Street. Along with numerous other restored cars, it made historic Kleberg Avenue look and feel like it had stepped back in time—at least for a day. (Photograph by the author.)

Bibliography

Alexander, Sheralyn Webber. "Ed Erard of the *Record*: 'Mr. Kingsville.' " Master of Journalism thesis, University of Texas, 1966.

Allhands, J.L. *Gringo Builders*. Joplin, MO: privately printed, 1931.

———. *Uriah Lott*. San Antonio, TX: Naylor, 1949.

Bass, Stirling Wesley. "History of Kleberg County." MA thesis, University of Texas, 1931.

Evans, Kathryn. *Come Aboard*. Kingsville, Texas: Kleberg County Historical Commission, 2004.

Graf, LeRoy P. "The Economic History of the Rio Grande Valley 1820–1875." PhD diss., Harvard University, 1942.

Hunter, Cecilia Aros and Leslie Gene, eds. *Historic Kingsville, Texas: Guide to the Original Townsites*. Kingsville, Texas: Kingsville Historical Development Board, 1994.

———. *Historic Kingsville, Texas: Guide to the Original Townsites, Volume II*. Kingsville, Texas: Kingsville Historical Development Board, 1997.

Journal of South Texas 2 no. 1 (1989), 4 no. 1 (1991), 6 no. 1 (1993), 9 no. 1 (1996), 11 no. 1 (1998), 13 no. 1 (2000).

Kleberg County Historical Commission. *Kleberg County Texas*. Kingsville, Texas: Kleberg County Historical Commission, 1979.

Lea, Tom. *The King Ranch*. Boston: Little, Brown, 1957.

Neely, Lisa Armitta Manheimer. "The Value of a Handshake: The controversy surrounding the location of the general offices of the St. Louis, Brownsville and Mexico Railway." MA thesis, Texas A&M University–Kingsville, 1994.

Rees, Floyd. "The History of the Railroad in Kingsville." Unpublished manuscript at South Texas Archives at Texas A&M University-Kingsville, n.d.

Wilson, Ben F. Jr. "The Economic History of Kleberg County." MS thesis, Texas College of Arts and Industry, 1939.

Consistent with our mission to preserve history on a local level, this book was printed in South Carolina on American-made paper and manufactured entirely in the United States. Products carrying the accredited Forest Stewardship Council (FSC) label are printed on 100 percent FSC-certified paper.

MADE IN THE USA